AF660853

VIŚVAKARMĀ'S CHILDREN

Stories of India's Craftspeople

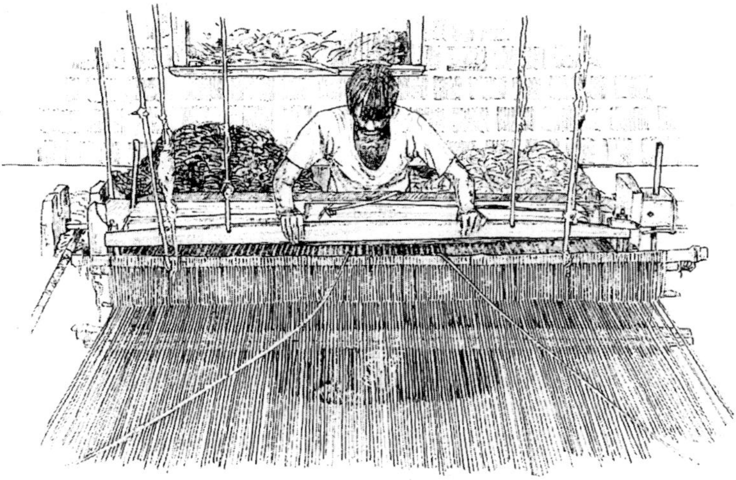

Viśvakarmā's Children

Stories of India's Craftspeople

Jaya Jaitly

Institute of Social Sciences
and
Concept Publishing Company

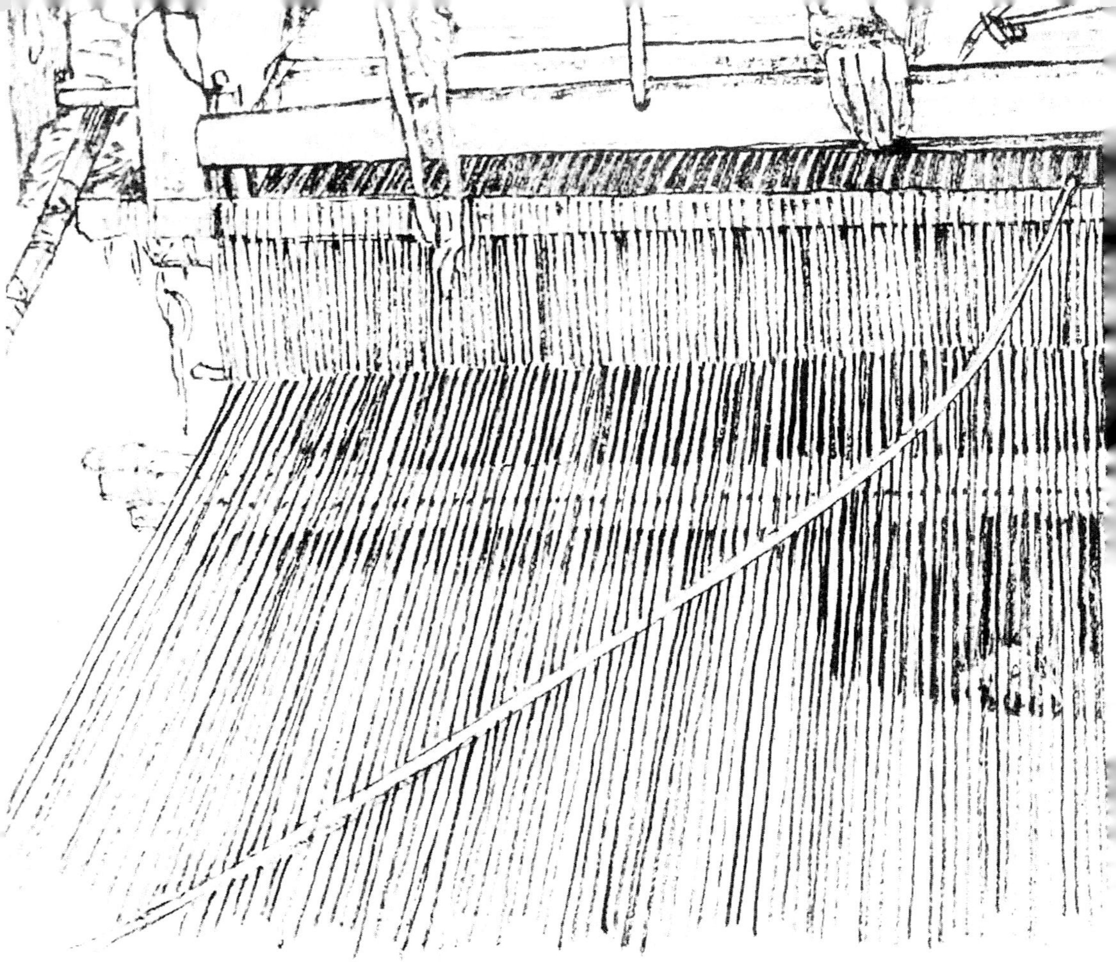

Fine, finely woven is this spread
Tell of which warp, and tell what fills,
Of which thread woven, is this spread?
With nerve threads of the sun and moon,
with the Pure-Thread that seeks its end.
Eight maidens spin and this wheel swings
With the five elements the warp is laid
Ten months to ready it, the Maker takes,
Close, closely woven is this spread.
This, men, the gods and sages wear.
And in the wearing, some they soil
Kabir, Truth-Server, wore from birth
This spread; now homing, leaves it as it is;
Fine, finely woven is this spread.

Kabir

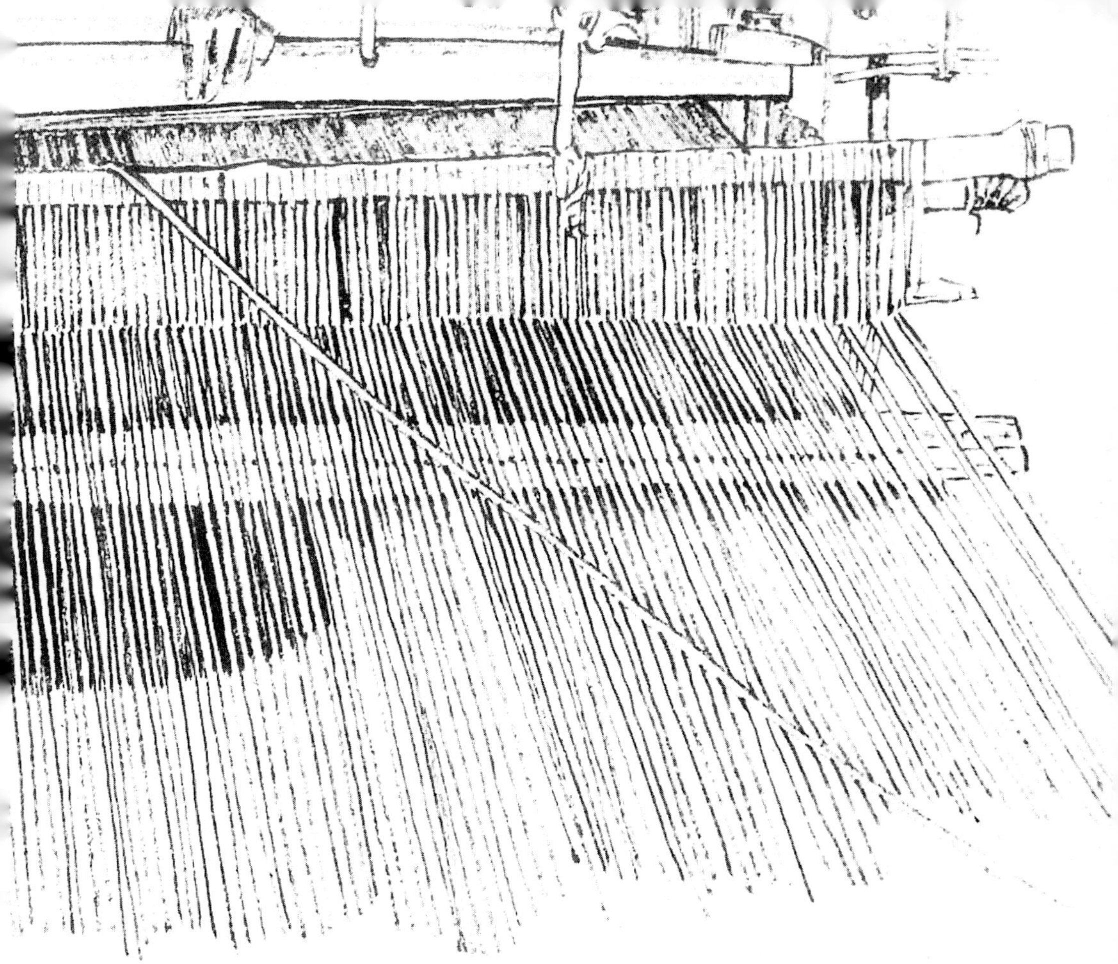

The Indian craftsman conceives of his art, not as the accumulated skill of ages, but as originating in the divine skill of Viśvakarmā, and revealed by him. Beauty, rhythm, proportion, idea have an absolute existence on an ideal plane, where all who seek may find. The reality of things exists in the mind, not in the detail of their appearance to the eye. Their inward inspiration upon which the Indian artist is taught to rely, appearing like the still small voice of a god, that god was conceived of as Viśvakarmā. He may be thought of as that part of divinity which is conditioned by a special relation to artistic expression: or in another way, as the sum total of consciousness, the group soul of the individual craftsmen of all times and places.

Ananda K. Coomaraswamy

The research study on Craftspeople of India and the publication of this book were made possible by a grant from MISEREOR, Germany.

First Published 2001
Reprint 2019
© Institute of Social Sciences.
8 Nelson Mandela Road
New Delhi 110070, India
Email: iss@nda.vsnl.net.in

Printed and published by
Ashok Kumar Mittal
Concept Publishing Company
A/15-16, Commercial Block,
Mohan Garden
New Delhi 110059, India
Email: publishing@conceptpub.com

All rights reserved. No part of this book may be reproduced, or transmitted in any form or by any means, electronic or mechanical, photocopying, recording or otherwise, without the prior written permission of the Institute of Social Sciences.

ISBN: 81-7022-895-6

Illustrations by Sitt Nyein Aye
Computer typesetting by Jaswinder Singh

Acknowledgements

It is difficult to get anyone interested in anything beyond coffee-table books on handicrafts and handmade textiles, so the support given by MISEREOR to study the lives of some of India's craftspeople is something for which I shall be ever grateful.

All the craftspeople who gave of their time, experiences and wisdom are central to this work. It is their book, for them, and in a sense by them.

Dr. George Mathew, Director of the Institute of Social Sciences, kept everyone going with his unflagging enthusiasm. My friend Krishen Kak raised many useful questions at the manuscript stage and helped with his unerring eye for flaws. Joya Roy assisted by Rekha Natarajan edited with great care and became, I hope, converts to the cause of craftspeople.

The team of researchers who gathered the supplementary data performed their task with dedication and more than the required amount of involvement. Mr. H. N. Singh of Jawaharlal Nehru University analysed the data of this section of the work.

P.N. Kuttappan, P. Nandakumar, and Joshy Jose have my grateful thanks for entering many drafts of the manuscript into the computer.

My friend Sitt Nyein Aye, a well-known Burmese artist, converted my very ordinary photographs into the evocative pen and ink sketches which illustrate this work.

A special thanks must go to Vinay Jain for designing the book, including the cover, as a labour of love.

Professor U.R. Ananthamurthy is a democratic socialist, a Gandhian and an outstanding writer in Kannada and English. That he should honour this work by writing the Foreword is a matter of great pride. That he is also currently Chairman of the Governing Body of the Institute of Social Sciences is a matter of serendipity.

Jaya Jaitly

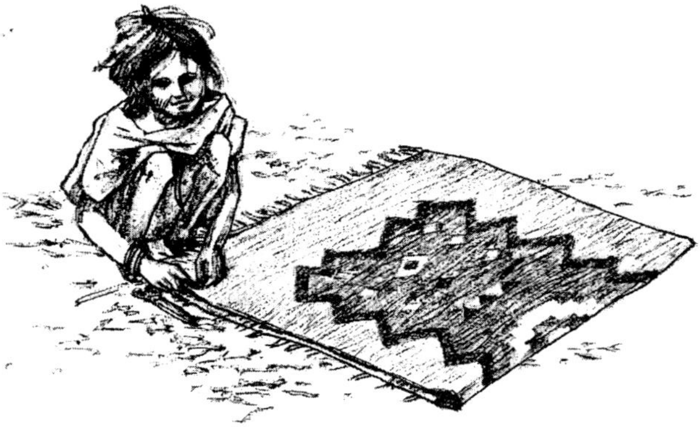

Contents

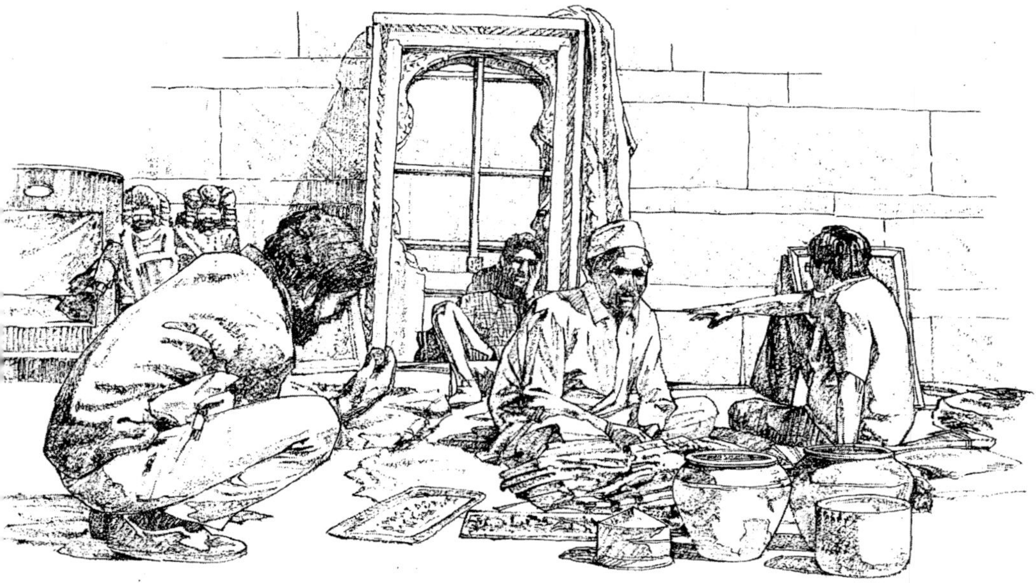

Foreword

What is important about this significantly titled, beautifully conceived book on Indian craftspeople is both its range and depth, made possible by the descriptive-analytical approach Jaya Jaitly employs to achieve them. In ten chapters we get to know about craftspeople living in different parts of India as persons, as well as representative figures of their craft. Jaya Jaitly not only speaks for them but gets them to speak for themselves, and the conclusion she draws from her study doesn't seem imposed, but emerges unobtrusively from the range and depth of her observations.

I have said intentionally that we get to know these craftspeople 'personally'; they come through to the reader like vivid characters in a realistic novel. They are not bloodless, generalized, notional beings of a clinically analyzed sociological tract. Here is an example; Jaya Jaitly is writing about the Karnataka sandalwood carvers:

> Vimalamma (the mother of the sandalwood carver) came in and sat on the floor nearby as the evening drew on and our discussions were coming to an end. Silently, she sharpened a flat metal spatula under her feet and oiled it against her hair. With it she peeled a strip of shola pith and cut it into small rectangles. These were piled together in layers. She cut around them to make them oval shaped, and rolled some to form a stem which she wrapped with thread. Into the stem she layered the oval pieces in steps to form a perfect imitation of mogra flower buds. With some more oval pieces she made rose petal shapes and tied them to the stem. Their edges curled like real petals. She dipped this flower in a glass of water to soften it and gently tied it in my hair...

While they remain real people with their own specific problems, Jaya Jaitly's approach also makes it possible for us to read beyond individual life-histories (interesting in themselves), to understand the general social, economic and cultural ethos in which they struggle with dignity to make a living. The author is a sensitive listener. She has an eye for significant details and, at the same time, a capacity for empathizing with the thought-processes of the craftspeople themselves. Therefore her generalizations do not seem to emanate from an opinionated mind. She is able to bring home to us the excitement with which a group of craftspeople discuss among themselves their situation, as, for instance, in the chapter on 'The Dhokra Metal Worker of Jhigdi'.

The central preoccupation of the book is this: These celebrated children of Viśvakarmā are pursuing an endangered traditional occupation. After we listen to Jaya Jaitly's moving description of their gradual impoverishment, we can no longer speak complacently of 'modernizing' India and at the same time preserve our unique cultural identity; the contradictions are hard to resolve and we need to be politically committed as a nation to resolve them. Mahatma Gandhi had no hesitation in saying that we will have to reject western civilization, although, paradoxically, it has fast been disappearing after our independence. We have neither the vision nor the will to accept Gandhiji's radical alternative, nor a liberal humanist concern to honestly do whatever we can to promote the crafts in the competitive capitalist economy.

We must at least be honest to acknowledge that there is no so-called 'perennial' Indian culture, which our nostalgic revivalists talk about, without the contributions made through the ages by our craftspeople. And we must remember they belong not to the upper castes of India, who are fast getting anglicized and westernized, but to the backward and lower castes and the minority communities. What these people pursue is 'crystallized tradition', unlike western art, fashionable with the elitist ruling classes of our country, which is individualistic.

I must now touch upon an important philosophical perspective from which the book is written. I am reminded here of the poet W.B. Yeats, who wrote the great poem Sailing to Byzantium. He wrote in A Vision:

> "I think that in early Byzantium...religious, aesthetic, and practical life were one, that architect and artificers...spoke to the multitude and the few alike. The painter, mosaic worker, the worker in gold and silver, the illuminator of sacred books, were almost impersonal, almost perhaps without the consciousness of individual design, absorbed in their subject-matter and that the vision of a whole people."

Jaya Jaitly makes us see that even the palm leaf basket makers of Pulicat, the Dhokra metal workers of Jhigdi, the potters of Vishnupur and the sandalwood carvers of Karnataka share the ethos of ancient Byzantium in modern India. This is how she describes them:

Torchbearers of India's crafts traditions, inheritors of ancient technologies and cultural systems, artists and creators living within a binding community ethos, producers in an agro based economy, and philosophers who accept the link between the spiritual and material – these are the many roles that craftspeople serve.

Jaya Jaitly goes on from here to make another important point. The fortunate elites of the country understand by handicrafts only the decorative, ornamental ethnic part. They forget that in ancient India, as in Yeats's Byzantium, there is no division between the decorative, artistic object and the objects made for everyday use. Therefore, in order to save craftspeople from penury, Jaya Jaitly suggests we should call utility items Indian handmade crafts rather than ethnic goodies. This would save them from the vagaries of fickle export markets. Jaya Jaitly makes a practical suggestion for our policy makers:

> ... while some handmade goods received development inputs at the decorative, higher-income bracket level, village industries became a separate entity, starved and at times obliterated, although they were the feeder industries for the more elevated, decorative skills of the handicrafts industry. So while a few thousand craftsmen and women are acknowledged and honoured, hundreds of thousands have been divorced from their skills through loss of access to raw material, credit, and most importantly, markets amongst the masses. The incongruity of having khadi and village industries in the Ministry of Industry and handlooms and handicrafts in the Ministry of Textiles, when they are all part of village industry needs to be rectified.

As Jaya Jaitly puts it forcibly, no craft was ever purely decorative. Our craftsmen and women are capable of making our everyday life beautiful. They are still there, impoverished but struggling to keep alive whatever is healthy and wholesome in our ancient tradition. How can we save them from destruction? Can we force (or at least persuade) the evil, illusory, but tempting modern world system to make enough space for their survival? But it is not only their survival we are speaking of, Jaya Jaitly makes us see that their survival and growth are essential for a new democratic Indian civilization which is not imitative of the West.

U.R. Ananthamurthy

Mysore
November 2000

Introduction

In India, traditional artisans and craftspeople have been employed for centuries in producing handmade goods for the use of their communities or for trade and export. In an economy based on agriculture, artisans form the second largest number of self-employed workers in the country. At present there are over twenty million artisans who include weavers, potters, cobblers, cane and bamboo workers, metal workers, wood carvers, silver and goldsmiths, rope, basket and mat makers, and many more.

Artisans and craftspeople are today divided into many categories – the skilled master craftsman, the wage worker, the fully self- employed artisan, the village artisan producing wares for local use, the part-time artisan whose craft activities supplement his meagre earnings from the land, and the landless artisan. Markets for many of the crafts produced by them are dwindling rapidly because of the lack of infrastructural support and competition from industrially manufactured goods.

In all these categories, the support or patronage received so far has been superficial and counteracted by policies and market forces dominated by the organized industrial lobby and technological advances that leave them out of consideration. In a country where employment is one of the most important priorities, today, artisans and craftspersons possessing traditional skills need improved technology, credit facilities, access to raw materials at reasonable prices, basic supportive infrastructure, and quality and design improvements or adaptations of traditional product lines to reach new markets in order to sustain their livelihoods. In India only ten percent of the entire workforce is organized, and artisans largely belong to the unorganized sector. They must be viewed as a skilled and productive workforce who need a clear and effective support system to survive. This is inextricably linked with the need for a positive government policy to uphold the interests of artisans and craftspeople.

Three serious problems have arisen over the years after independence which have affected the approach and consequently development policies relating to Indian crafts and their producers. First, the unorganized and diverse nature of craft activities has prevented politicians, policy makers, scientists, intellectuals, technologists, economists and desk-bound professionals in both developed and developing countries from understanding or formulating effective policies or strategies by which this segment of the population can be part of a general advancement. New technologies, macro-level planning, industrial policies, marketing systems, all pass them by. Both through design or through neglect the majority of artisans are left to fend for themselves. In some areas this has become a struggle against hopelessness and extinction particularly when new employment in other sectors does not match the numbers of those whose products are displaced by machine-made goods or whose skills are found redundant.

Secondly, the accepted government description of handicrafts as objects of artistic value which may also be utilitarian is very narrow and almost elitist in approach. It fails to recognize that the artisan/ craftsperson anywhere has always turned out articles of utility. The decorative aspect is purely incidental and stems from cultural trends, creative sensibilities and individual or group inputs in product or design variations. No craft was ever purely decorative. Yet, gradually, only decorative or embellished hand-made products have been considered as 'handicrafts' worthy of recognition or development through government intervention, and in all cases they are converted into goods fit only for the more affluent fashion-oriented rung of society or for export.

Thirdly, resulting from this narrow attitude towards crafts, millions of artisans who make utility objects by hand from natural materials are neglected. Since their products are generally low value and required by the less affluent segment of the population they have not been the object of anyone's effective concern. Ironically, at the same time, their problems are tackled by a plethora of departments, boards and corporations with no deep knowledge of the sector or even a coherent common viewpoint with interlinking strategies.

Craftspeople belong to a caste or tribe, religious community or professional group, and yet each worker is an individual with his or her own past and particular hopes for the future. While collecting information from craftspeople by using a structured questionnaire it is possible to obtain details that would provide an objective picture of the condition of their lives and their situation in the marketplace. Often, however, the data is obtained, but the human face is absent. The constant work, the daily routine, their humour, sorrows and joys remain invisible. The questionnaire-based survey serves as a normative framework in which the fairly rigid methods do not allow much discussion and debate. Craftspeople are often unsure of the nature of the question, and therefore prefer to give a restricted answer. Qualitative material that may emerge in a supplementary description is put down in words that cannot be statistically analysed. These constraints indicated the nature and methodology of this research study. I wished to focus on the human beings behind each craft activity so that the flesh and blood and essence of their lives could be recognized. Case studies of each major craft in a selected geographic area formed the main component of the study, with supplementary data collected from groups or persons practising the same craft in different regions of the country. These surveys and case studies were conducted between 1995 and 1998.

The choice of area was made after considering the importance of the craft in a state, the concentration of craftspeople therein, and to effect a contrast between north and south, east and west so that the vast span of the country could be represented and a wide canvas of crafts and craftspeople could be portrayed. A minimum of five and maximum of twenty craftspersons in each craft were interviewed in twelve Indian states for the supplementary study which I have preferred to call 'explorations.'

The selection of crafts was based on: (a) the proportion of population engaged in each craft; (b) the number of problems faced by craftspeople, such as availability of raw material and lack of access to markets; and (c) increased competition from industrial and other substitutes. The craftsperson recognized as the most representative of the community was identified for an indepth case study. The criteria adopted for selection were: (a) the person should be a traditional practitioner of the craft; (b) the person should, through his or her lifestyle, reflect the condition of his/her community; and (c) the person would allow detailed personal discussions and interviews to be conducted. While there was strict adherence to the questionnaire for supplementary data, several rounds of informal conversations were also held with the respondents for the indepth individual profiles. Informal conversations aimed at collecting information about their local problems, social and cultural life, efforts at seeking alternative employment and plans for the future. Although the conversations strayed from the questionnaire format, all its points were discussed. These conversations were spread over many hours and days, interspersed with numerous cups of tea or coffee, a meal or a plate of small bananas. In the poorer households even a glass of potable water would not be available and we would have to go away for refreshments, returning later to resume the conversation. It was necessary to engage the potter in a discussion where he could consider why he did not become a full-fledged ceramicist producing modern glazed tableware. Available statistics do not reveal the fact that he is losing hold of his access to raw materials and has no finances to spend on fuel and kilns for improved technological operations. Why did the weaver not find place in a textile mill? What happens to the *chappal* makers when plastic footwear floods the market? Can a shoemaker produce as fast as a machine? Where should the craftsperson go with his problems in order to improve his skill or widen his market? Through the long hours of discussion, depending on their various preoccupations, we talked about what artisans and craftspersons need to do to produce more and better products, of how much they had to rely on their own initiatives and also about the nature of the role of women in the production process. As a response to the last issue, it was often revealed that the women not only managed the housework but also participated in important craft-related activities.

The most crucial part of a craft producer's life is the marketplace. It could be either at his doorstep or in far-off countries. Are these markets accessible without intermediaries who exploit them? Can they sell their goods or are they prisoners of greater market forces? Many of the answers to these questions emerged only obliquely. A smile, a story, an experience, would subtly contain within it answers to our queries. They could only talk about their own world and found it too overwhelming to comment on international markets, export potential or globalization and the associated concept of market driven development. Still, within the confines of their world and their own understanding of it lay answers to a wider range of questions.

Chapter One of this book gives the broad historical backdrop against which today's craftsperson needs to be placed, followed by seven profiles of craftspeople in different parts of the country, presented in Chapters Two to Eight. Further explorations into their lives, economies and markets, conducted through a more formal questionnaire approach, are analysed in Chapter Nine. There can be no foresight into the future, nor any definitive answers as to what will bring a new dawn into craftspeople's lives, but Chapter Ten attempts to define new attitudes and approaches that might help to take them to a better tomorrow.

India's craftspeople are inextricably linked with its history, culture and social systems spanning many millenia. A brief account of this vast epic, touching upon some important milestones and influences in their collective lives brings us to view them today as unknown people in uncertain numbers.

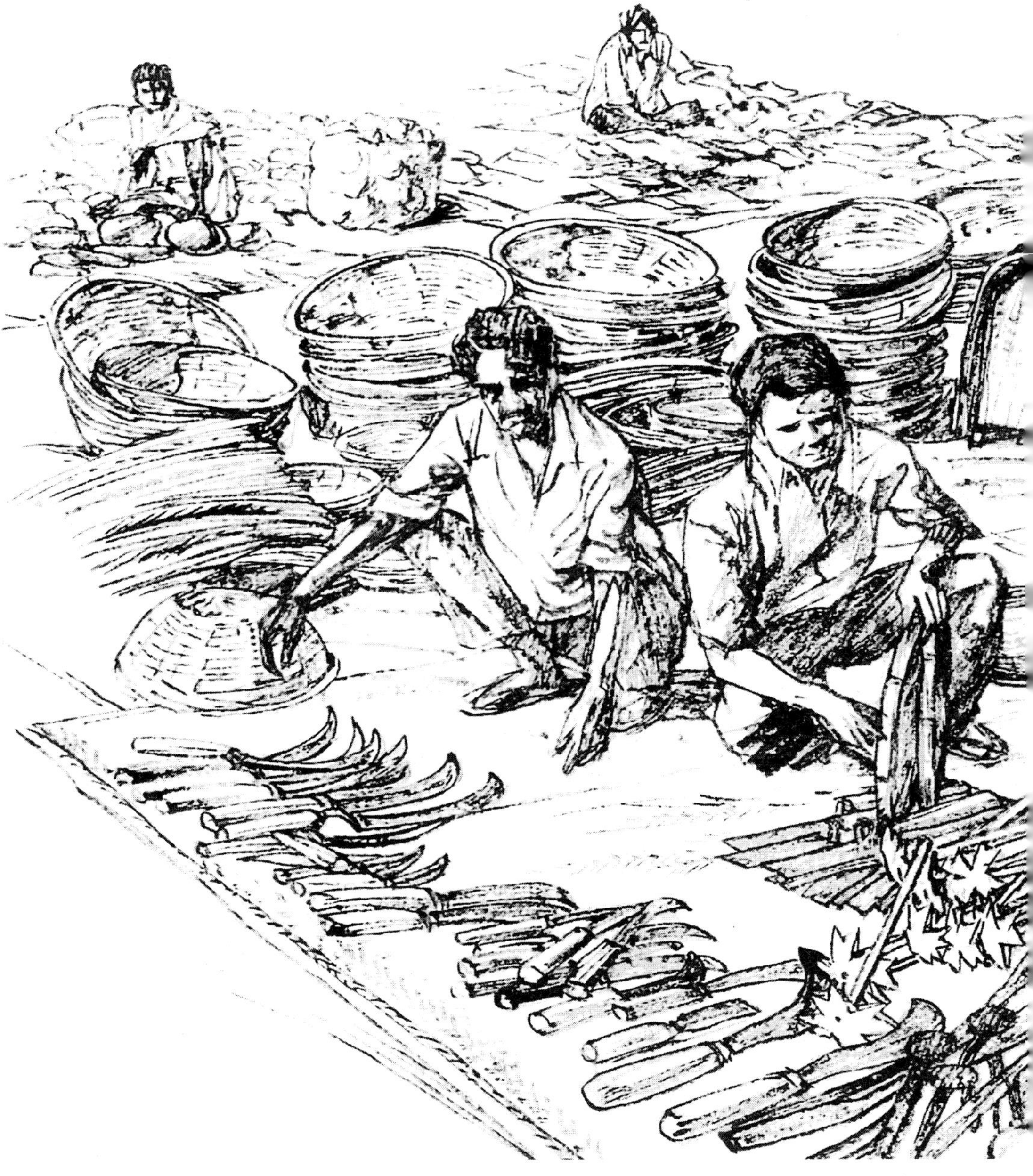

CHAPTER ONE

The Story So Far

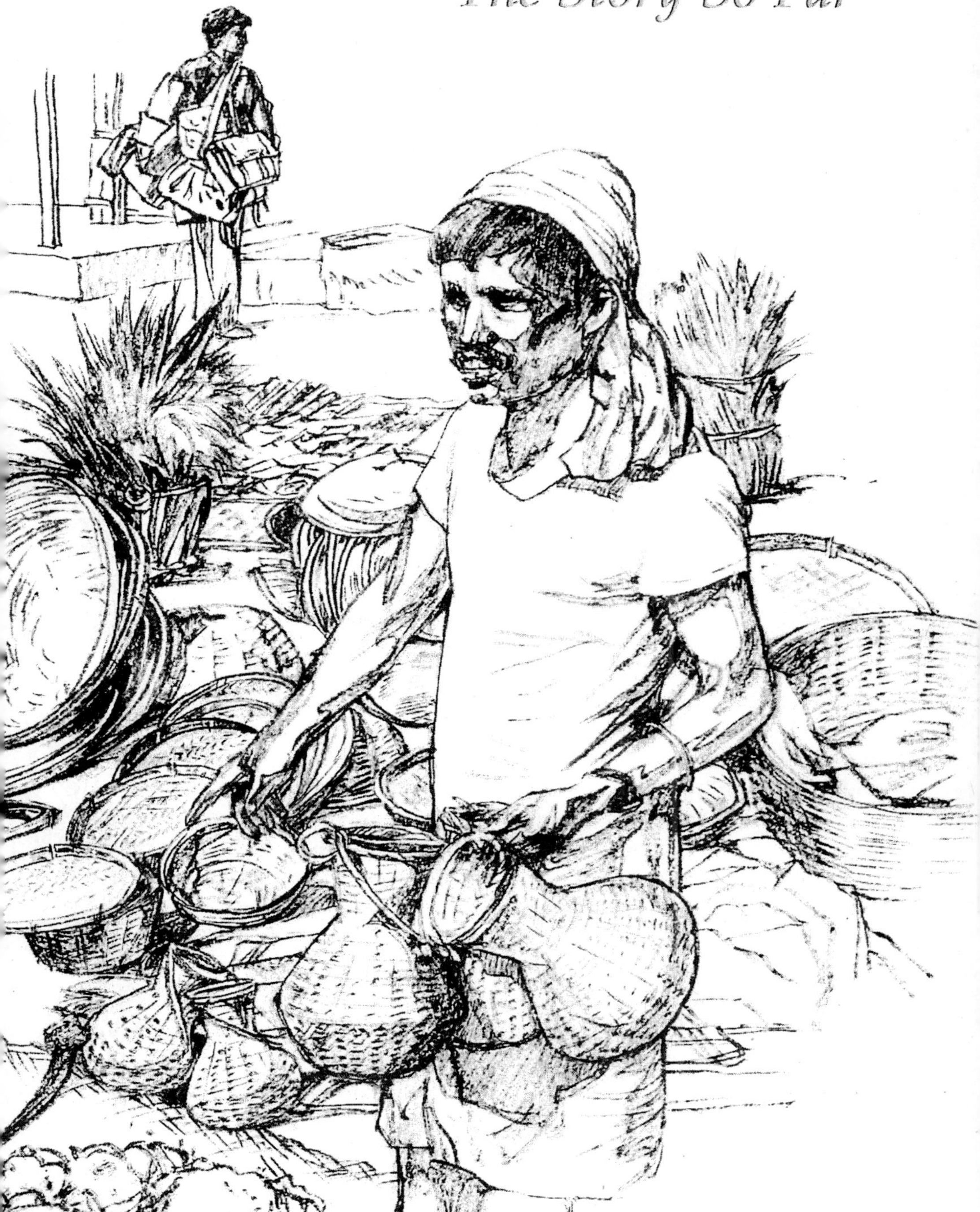

Viśvakarmā is the god of India's arts and crafts. He is said to have had five sons: Manu, who worked in iron, Maya in wood, Tvaṣṭā in brass, copper and alloys, Śilpī in stone, and finally Viśvajña, who was a gold and silversmith and jeweller.[1] In South India, a group of artisans known as the Kammalars claim descent from the five divine artisans. Well-versed in the *shilpa shastras*, the technical works on art in Sanskrit, they follow a strict regimen combining religious and technical prescriptions in all craft processes. Viśvakarmā was worshipped as the guide of all artisans and it is still common practice for artisans, craftspersons, even motor mechanics and factory workers, to worship their tools and implements on a day designated in honour of Viśvakarmā every year. His blessings are invoked irrespective of the religion or nature of work of the artisan or craftsperson.

The crafts and craftspeople of India are a deeply integrated part of such folk and classical traditions and historical assimilations which together span many millennia. As articles made purely by hand for the daily use of both the common people in an agrarian economy and the urban elite, crafts reflect the cultural ethos of India. While the craftspeople have been cradled by the caste system, their skills were fostered by cultural and religious needs and the impetus provided by local, national and international trade.

The cultural aesthetic can be located in prehistoric Indian art which has been part of a living tradition dating back thousands of years. Clear proof of organized production emanating out of an ordered society is seen in the objects that were retrieved from the Indus valley sites of the third millennium B.C.[2]

While the tradition of making articles of daily use by hand is termed as craft and craftsmanship, the fact that each article is created individually through the creative hands and spirit of an artisan accords the article a place in the range of decorative arts. However, unlike Western art which is individualistic in its approach, Indian art and craft are part of what George C.M. Birdwood, writing in 1880, referred to as "crystallized tradition" which prevents the artist from "acting on his own spontaneous inspiration" and indulging in true creation.[3] This crystallized tradition has kept the forms and skills alive, well away from "the taint and degradation of foreign fashions," because of "the caste system of the Code of Manu", which Birdwood saw as their best defence.

Caste divisions were seen as trade and occupational guilds. They are described in the *Ayodhya-Kanda* of the *Ramayana* epic in which the inhabitants of the city go out in a procession with Bharata to search for Rama in the order of their trade guilds: "jewellers, potters, ivory-workers, perfumers, goldsmiths, weavers, carpenters, braziers, painters, musical instrument-makers, armourers, curriers, blacksmiths, coppersmiths, makers of figures, cutters of crystals, glassmakers, inlayers and others; with the chief of the guild bringing up the rear."[4] In his *Arts of India*, Birdwood compares this list with the schedule of artisan groups in contemporary Bengal and finds them almost identical. These and many others were the artisans of village and urban communities who engaged in the production of craft both for the needs of an agricultural society and for temple or courtly needs.

The tribal communities inhabiting the length and breadth of India have been closely linked to the economic network of weekly village markets and built links with the Hindu or "Hinduized" artisan castes. Whether nomadic or settled, artisans working almost exclusively for tribes who maintained a distinctly different culture and identity from the settled and cultivating sections of the population, outside the caste society, very often adopted the cultural practices and design aesthetic of the tribes, and derived their sustenance from the sale or barter of their goods at weekly markets. These were the earliest organized marketing efforts of artisans.

Early craft traditions

Cotton was cultivated in India in the third millenium B.C., and signs of artisanal production are evident in the Indus valley sites of the same period. The pottery made at that time, with its deep red and black tones, is still being made in some areas in western India. While this demonstrates what has been termed 'the static nature of India's rural culture' it also displays the timelessness of the design aesthetic and its acceptability even today.[5] The continuity of cultural traits over five millennia has ensured the survival of such craft traditions. Pottery has metamorphosed when production has shifted to urban localities and followed urban tastes, but these have largely ended up as unaesthetic copies of Western designs, or an amalgam of styles and techniques drawn from different cultural streams. The development of ceramics has almost entirely remained in the hands of the elite, with high technology manufacturing units substituting the village kiln-fired pots with local glazes.

To the ancient world India was known primarily

as a producer of fine textiles and high quality iron. *The Periplus of the Erythraean Sea*, an anonymous seaman's account of the 1st century A.D., mentions iron and steel as objects of commerce in the trade between India and the Middle East.[6] Early iron foundry remains are found in association with finely made microliths, the first tools of Indian leather workers and basket makers. Indigenous iron-smelters produced a high quality wrought iron, an example of which is seen in the superbly crafted iron pillar of Chandra erected near the Qutab Minar in Delhi in the 4th century A.D.[7] The Romans called India's fine muslins "woven winds" which commanded a high price as far back as the 2nd century B.C. The textiles of Bengal became important items of trade for the Arabs, the Portuguese and then the British. Cloth printing and dyeing was so developed by the 12th century that it facilitated brisk internal and external trade. The 15th century poet Srinatha speaks of men ploughing fields while women engaged in spinning.[8] This indicates the pattern that continues in many areas today, where farmers are also part-time weavers, Kashmir being an example.

During the Chola dynasty in medieval South India the kings had lent considerable patronage through the state and the temples to the artisan classes. After a period of decline, there was a revival of artisan fortunes during the Vijayanagar and Brahmani kingdoms when economic and administrative expansions created a market for woven goods.[9] Writing in the 17th century, a foreign traveller remarked that "everyone from the Cape of Good Hope to China, man and woman, is clothed from head to foot in the products of Indian looms."[10] Indeed, Indian textiles went to Sumatra, Java, Thailand and Cambodia while Mausilipatnam muslins were the rage in England. The *kani* shawls of Kashmir adorned the ladies of the court of Napoleon Bonaparte. Aden, Arabia and Africa, were also buyers of Golconda muslins, Gujarat's embroidered satin textiles and Bengal's fine muslins.

From the 14th to the 16th century, trade was largely in the hands of merchant guilds but weavers also produced coarse cloth for local consumption and sold it at weekly fairs. This system is prevalent even at the present time with the famed Mangal Haat (Tuesday fair) in Calcutta's Howrah district setting up over two thousand stalls selling cotton saris, towels and sheets woven in the villages of rural Bengal. Through local sales, inter-regional trade and temple patronage the livelihoods of handloom weavers were adequately sustained.

Craftspeople in the social hierarchy

In his study of Indian culture and society, *The Speaking Tree*, Richard Lannoy describes the role of the craftsman in Vedic society: "According to ancient Hindu tradition, the artist, or *śilpin* is the intermediary who transmits the revelation of Viśvakarma, the divine artificer, to society. Art, or *śilpa*, includes the full spectrum of creative activity: ritual, skill, craft, the formative imagination. The act of creation is itself a rite, surrounded by esoteric lore and invested with the aura of magical powers. Until modern times the *śilpin* was assigned an organic role within society through membership in a *group*; that is to say he was a member of an artisan caste, a guild, or a court, and these groups were a part of the larger social order."[11]

In those early times "each artist was endowed with individual land holdings which were cultivated by each *śilpin* family. There were no such persons as individual, self-sufficient artists in the Western sense."[12] Lannoy describes the relations between the artist/craftsman, his patron, and society as "sacrificial", centred on the construction of the Vedic sacrificial altar. "The building of the altar was a symbolic reconstitution of the dismembered Cosmic Man, from whose limbs the divisions of society sprang.

"Like the sacrificial offering (e.g. an animal or harvest produce), the work of art was invested with magical potency and merit by its makers and this was transferred to the patron as the society's elected representative, thereby leading to the acquisition of a spiritual value by the community. In this sense the artist's role was one of fundamental solidarity, ensuring the restoration to the society of its lost unity."[13]

Most importantly, it was believed that art in all its forms counterbalanced the tensions created by an uneven society. It was because of this that in spite of a social hierarchy and division of labour, tribal pockets also survived in the midst of caste and urban societies. Each had a sound link with the other, becoming very active during the time of seasonal festivals.[14]

In many parts of India, artisans and craftspersons have retained the high status accorded them in Vedic times. The master craftsmen among groups like the Kammalars are called 'acharya,' a title shared by Brahmanical teachers. India's remarkable ethos also nurtured a Kabir, a poor Muslim weaver who lived in Varanasi from 1440 to 1518 and became a great religious leader. Kabir preached against caste and idol worship, and attempted a deeper integration between Hindu and Muslim communities, while remaining all along wedded to his simple profession of weaving.

Within the caste structure that evolved in the post-Vedic period, the status of most artisans was that of the Shudra caste, the lowest of the four main caste divisions in Hindu society — Brahmana, Kshatriya, Vaishya and Shudra. Weavers, potters, metalsmiths, jewellers, stoneworkers and carpenters were considered 'clean' Shudras and allowed to associate with temple related activities. Artisans associated with 'unclean' occupations such as the curing of hides and leather work were considered polluting and were made to live on the peripheries of the city and village. The status of such castes in the social hierarchy has remained ambiguous; they were called both 'outcaste' and 'untouchable' and yet were part of the Hindu social order.[15] They are the precursors of the 'Scheduled Castes' of modern India. Prominent among them are the Chamars, an ancient caste of leather-workers, and the Doms who make baskets and practice a number of other crafts.[16]

On the social position of the artisan castes, M.K. Pal writes: "the profession of the artisan may have been considered as an honoured one in different ages, but their social status has almost remained unchanged in the traditional caste hierarchy of the Hindu society."[17] Perhaps it was this adverse social status coupled with low economic strength that prevented artisan groups from becoming a significant political force in Indian society.

Craftspeople's organisations

Craft guilds are known to have existed in post-Vedic times during pre-Mauryan, Mauryan, Shunga, Kushana and Gupta periods (600 B.C. to 550 A.D.) and they played a prominent part in the socio-economic life of the people. They developed as urban centres grew in the Indo-Gangetic plains and along the important trade routes.[18]

The Buddhist *Jatakas* mention eighteen types of guilds including several of artisans. The earliest Sanskrit dictionary, the *Amarakosha*, describes the *shilpi* and their associations, the *shreni*.[19] Export of artisanal produce, spices and minerals brought in imported bullion which served as coinage in many kingdoms, and merchant guilds must have controlled much of this wealth.[20] Some guilds even functioned as banks and had their own laws of governance. They financed the war efforts of kings, built and maintained temples, and supported a majority of urban craftsman. They were close to civil authority and were allowed to migrate according to their wishes by the king. The 5th century A.D. inscription of Mandasor records the munificence of a guild of silk weavers who repaired the Sun Temple which they had built and endowed three decades earlier.[21] By the time of the *Arthashastra*, the text on polity ascribed to Kautilya, the wealth and power of the merchant and artisan guilds were perceived as a threat by the princes and priestly class.[22]

Throughout the history of the artisan class it was the weavers alone who were able to organize themselves effectively, and that too largely in southern India, although with varying results depending on the social and historical factors of each period. In her study on the textile industry of medieval South India, Vijaya Ramaswamy has documented the work of weavers' organizations or "guilds called *samaya*, *sreni*, or *mata*."[23] "Guild" is more a word of convenience in the South Indian context since, according to epigraphic evidence, although it was a corporate body it did not perform the functions usually performed by medieval guilds in Europe such as maintenance of uniform standards in products and prices. In India, heredity and caste formed an essential part of the professional guild.[24]

From accounts of the few remaining artisan guilds of his time, Birdwood correctly assesses the role of caste in the preservation of crafts when he notes that apart from the fact that usually the head of the caste also acted as the head of the guild: "the guilds by the stubborn resistance, further stimulated by caste prejudice which they oppose to all innovations, still continue, in this forlorn way, to serve a beneficial end, in maintaining, for probably another generation, the traditional excellence of the sumptuary arts of India, against the fierce and merciless competition of the English manufacturers." [25] During the medieval period, weavers in South India made concerted efforts through their guilds to enhance their economic and social status, demanding economic, ritual and social privileges. Some ascribed to themselves mythological origins, and thus supra-brahminical status, while others participated in caste-related conflicts through the Vira Shaiva movement which organized social protests against Brahminism.[26] According to Ramaswamy, the prosperity of the weavers was at its height during the Vijayanagar empire when they were vested with significant social and ritual privileges in recognition of their economic importance. In the 17th century they even participated in the administration but by the 18th century the 'cotton revolution' of England led the weavers of India into steady decline and negligible social recognition. The guilds lapsed into a stagnant grouping of mere occupational sub-castes following professions as a matter of heredity. The artisan's son was always an apprentice to the trade.

Also a part of indigenous tradition was the *jajmani* system of patronage "where there exists an exchange of services and gifts between patron and client and payment in kind is the general practice".[27] Craftspeople made objects to barter in exchange for grain and special services, and achieved for themselves some form of protection through this system after the guilds weakened.

The closest to an organizational structure that replaced the guilds was the cooperative society which enabled artisans to form a group in order to further their economic interests. Post-Independence cooperatives were either multi-skill or multi-product societies, or mono-skill and single material, multi-product societies. Separate societies for marketing also formed part of these groupings. Being purely industrial in nature and empowered only to access raw material, obtain credit from banks and other lending institutions, obtain orders for production, and distribute the profits equitably, these have been unable to serve a more political or social purpose unlike those in agriculture and dairying. They have largely become victims of maladministration, corruption and politicization, with considerable loss of autonomy to the bureaucracy at one level, and are weakened by the inability to function cohesively at another level. Many other types of federations and associations also exist but have not evolved into significant instruments of socio-economic change in the artisans' interest, largely because they lack funds to sustain their activities and also because artisans cannot afford to sacrifice precious production time to pursue such goals.

Cross-cultural influences

Those crafts which were exposed to international trade or came under courtly partronage were the most susceptible to change in pattern or design. Craftsmen had experimented with and adapted forms and techniques from contemporary cultures, from Sumer, Persia and the Hellenic world. Elements of Sumerian, Achamenean,

Macedonian, and later Sassanian, Turanian and Graeco-Roman art forms found their way into the art and architecture of pre-Mauryan India, culminating in a synthesis of indigenous and exotic elements in the age of the imperial Mauryas in 4th century B.C.[28] About this time certain internal trends led to the development of characteristically Indian traditions in architecture and the plastic arts. Indian architecture, for instance, became more adept in stone than in brick or ceramic – the terracotta temples at Vishnupur in West Bengal being an exception. The polished Mauryan columns with their bell capitals surmounted by animal forms are an early example of this trend. In the Deccan, the rock-cut shrines of the 2nd and 1st centuries B.C. and early temple forms demonstrate highly skilled carving. The early stone-cutters rendered the forms of wood and bamboo construction faithfully into sandstone and granite, preserving every detail of the carpenter's joints in the new material. Art historians have noted that the Ellora temples, hewn out of solid rock, are more sculpture than architecture, a characteristic of many other Hindu temples.[29] Much later, the mosques, palaces and tombs of Mughal India also demonstrate great skill in stone carving while the Taj Mahal is often considered closer to jewellery than architecture, with its fine stone inlay upon marble.

Under Mughal patronage the best craftsmen followed the courts from Delhi to Fatehpur Sikri, Agra and Aurangabad. Under courtly influence artisans decorated swords and wove carpets and brocades with motifs influenced by Persian exemplars.[30] They carved artefacts in jade and hardstone, inlaid with precious gems, copying designs invented by Renaissance goldsmiths.

In his study of the arts and crafts of Mughal India, Shanti Swarup finds that fine handicrafts were the most sought after requirements of high Mughal society. The emperor, his family and the nobility were its principal patrons and it was the indigenous artisan working in the Mughal workshops who contributed substantially to the aesthetic character of the designs, bringing to his art a tradition of ideas and attitudes and "the philosophy which viewed life as a spiritual progression wherein all activities of life were essentially designed to lead one to the awakening of the soul."[31] The belief that art was integral to life thereby created a mindset wherein the artisan ceased to question too radically his social and economic status.

The Mughals found on arrival in India that indigenous Indian art was as decorative as the arts of China, Iran and Central Asia. Since the number of foreign craftspeople coming to India was small, they depended largely on the skills of local people and the products that emerged from their work were neither imitations of foreign forms nor a mere continuation of Indian ideals. The Indian factor, however, became fairly strong in Mughal art and Emperor Akbar was a particularly keen patron. The *Ain-i-Akbari* or Institutes of Emperor Akbar (A.D. 1556-1605) written by his minister Abu'l Fazl, tells us that the Emperor maintained skilled craftsmen from all over India. Akbar personally inspected the work of his men and honoured the best with bonuses and increased salaries.[32] Special types of armour, gilded and decorated weapons, royal insignia, and a vast range of woven and embroidered textiles were commissioned for the royal household as well as for gifts. The shawls of Kashmir received a new lease of life, while the artisans of Rajasthan and Delhi made the finest courtly jewellery.

Persia had also come into contact with China in the early 13th century and by the end of the century, when the Mongols embraced Islam, the rulers extended patronage to Chinese artists, importing textiles and porcelain into Iran. Apart from Chinese influence through the Mughals, India had its own long association with China. According to Shanti Swarup, "The Tun-huang and Yun-Kung grottos contain superb relics of Buddhist sculptures which reflect direct influence from India. Tibet, the land stretching across the northern border of India was also a meeting ground of Indian travellers and missionaries and Chinese artists who were continuously in employment in Tibet since the 7th Century."[33] It is interesting to note that Indian versions of European *chinoiseries* influenced by Chinese design were in due course exported to China where Indian cottons sometimes served as the inspiration for these embroideries on silk with Chinese motifs which were exported to Europe.[34]

At the beginning of the 16th century Mughal India and western Europe were in close contact. The Portuguese had established themselves as a major trading power in the west coast of India and in 1573 Emperor Akbar came in contact with them when he conquered Surat. He established diplomatic relations with European rulers and exchanged treasures of common artistic interest. Growing Muslim influence on Indian costumes led to a demand for specific types of cloth and a move from draped to tailored garments in the 16th and 17th centuries. It was during this period that a mixed culture of Indian, Iranian, Chinese and Western elements were evolved and defined, but despite the expanded horizons the framework of tradition and skill remained unbroken and basically Indian. A highly evolved fusion always elevated the art. At another level, cheap imitation for the sake of commercialization as in the case of the Kashmir shawls that adopted the "improved" shawl patterns which French agents of the Paris import houses provided ruined the skill and designs that had previously been developed.[35]

Crafts under colonialism

Between courtly patronage, trade, the *jajmani* system and the demand for everyday utility crafts by the rural population, until the second half of the 17th century Indian crafts enjoyed a steady home market and a worldwide reputation. This situation began to disintegrate with the advent of the British in India. D.R. Gadgil's major work on the evolution of Indian industry outlines the causes working towards the decline both in artistic excellence and in the economic importance of India's traditional industries. The disappearance of native courts, the establishment of alien rule and, subsequently, the competition of a more highly developed form of industry led to radical changes in the economic structure of colonized lands, while the onset of the Industrial Revolution marked an economic transition in world history.[36]

As the Mughal empire declined and princely states gave way to the extended control of the East India Company from the mid-17th century onwards, the initial years saw high value goods from India exported to Britain which included elaborate handmade textiles. However, indebtedness to masterweavers, money lenders and merchants was already endemic among weavers since the beginning of the 17th century because rival European companies had already established themselves and the weavers had turned from temples and courts to their factories. The Battle of Plassey in 1757 finally ended the era of court patronage for Indian crafts. The East India Company created a new method of dealing with the textile industry. Edward Lucie-Smith in *The Story of Craft* describes how the Company worked through brokers: "Its factors advanced the bulk of the finished price through these brokers, and they, in turn, made advances to the weavers. An independent valuer assessed the finished product and the balance was then paid. Since the advance often covered the work of more than a year the

Company was able to create a monopoly of the Bengali weaving industry."[37] This process led to the weavers losing their independence and bargaining power as well as their creativity since their work consisted of copying mechanically for an alien market.

While the weavers strength declined, export of Indian textiles rose, and led to consequences that affected the world. Lucie-Smith refers to Sir Dudley North's *Considerations upon the East India Trade,* published in England in 1701, which points out that "the competition of cheap East India goods would in the end force Europeans to make machines for making things. It was in fact precisely the competition of Indian textiles which sparked off the industrialization of the European cloth making industry ... which spearheaded the European Industrial Revolution." This had direct repercussions in India by the end of the 18th century, when "the great Indian enterprises were virtually defunct." Protectionist acts which imposed heavy duties on Indian goods reaching Britain and an iniquitous system of transit duties, customs and tariffs choked the marketing of Indian crafts and textiles.[38] The ultimate blow came in periods of famine when paddy was cornered by the East India Company or by grain merchants who had contracts with the Company. Prices soared, and since the weavers' incomes were fixed as part of the tight organizational structure created by the East India Company, it lead to destitution and death for the weavers.[39] Large-scale migration took place from primarily weaving towns like Dacca in Bengal, where the population dwindled from 200,000 to 68,000.

Gadgil has described the impact of road and railway networks on the opening up of Indian markets and raw materials to the West in the 19th century. The failure of the cotton crop in Britain's American colonies in 1846 and disruption of trade during the Civil War led to a "cotton famine" in England. Indian cotton was soon adopted as a substitute for the textile mills in Lancashire. By the mid-19th century many textile producing areas in western and eastern India saw a reversal of trade. India became a net importer of cotton cloth from English mills.[40] However, "finely woven handkerchiefs for the memsahibs rather than saris for the princesses continued," just as did coarse cloth for peasant society.[41]

While it is indisputable that employment in hand spinning and weaving declined as a result of trade between India and an industrializing Britain, Tirthankar Roy in *Artisans and Industrialization* discusses the more complex effects caused by the integration of markets, mobility of labour and hastening urbanization which created conditions for mass production and capital accumulation. These were the equally important factors arising out of industrialization.[42] Some weavers did adapt to new textile-related industries even while "English yarn and powerloom cloth since the mid-nineteenth century induced a long crisis for weavers in Asia." The result was not so much a reduction of handloom cloth but "a general widening of inequality and a heightening contrast between progressive and backward segments" of weavers.[43]

Crafts, including handlooms, that managed to survive colonial rule, did so not by making the same product cheaper but by making different or luxury products, or by subtly adapting to structural changes such as turning from selling at weekly *haat*s to entering into contracts with large traders and producers.[44] Another change during this period was the gradual acceptance of stitched garments by larger sections of society, suiting the producers of mill cloth rather than handloom weavers who provided finished pieces of cloth like the sari or dhoti which were ready for draping. The first powerlooms and the shift from rural to urban centres contributed to the decline of handmade textiles.

As cheap machine-made cloth and other mass-produced industrial goods from Britain began to flood village and urban markets, many other products of local village industry were displaced. Gadgil enumerates the general decline of craft production in the first part of the 20th century. To the extent that new machinery was introduced in agricultural production, the economic position of the village carpenter deteriorated. With the diminishing demand for the services of the village blacksmith, a section of them migrated to urban centres to seek employment in modern engineering works. The village dyer and his repertoire of natural dyes found his services and skills redundant, following the import of cheap aniline dyes. The increased use of imported enamelled ware reduced the demand for the village potter's wares, but since the rural poor of the village continued to use earthenware vessels and, in some areas, roof tiles, he was not quite ruined. According to Gadgil, tanners and leather workers were most affected by these changes due to the profitable sale of hides and skins by cattle owners to the new tanning industries.[45] Another aspect of these changes was that the artisans and craftsmen increasingly became dependent on the merchants or *sahukar* for the sale of their products in local or distant markets.

By the late 19th century the British government had become somewhat responsive to public opinion. According to Tirthankar Roy, there was a new interest in craft-related questions. This interest devived partly from a revival, or perhaps one should say survival, of the two-million strong handloom industry itself, and partly from "growing doubts about the inevitability of India's march into the machine age."[46] It was in this milieu that George Birdwood catalogued the crafts of India in his sympathetic two-volume classic *Industrial Arts of India.* Between 1895 and the mid-1930s a series of studies and reports were commissioned, covering technologies in the first stage and pricing and fiscal policy in the second. In the '30s independent scholars also published studies on crafts, particularly weaving, focussing on change rather than on what actually existed at that point of time. The colonial administration appointed a Fact Finding Committee on textiles to look into the plight of handloom weavers.[47] However, the British government's concern was mainly for its own commercial and trade interests and certainly did not take into account the sufferings of the artisans, weavers or women spinners.

In the early 20th century, Mohandas Karamchand Gandhi had begun his Swaraj movement for self-rule. He saw industrialization as a curse for mankind, and mounted a campaign linking the spinning wheel and handspun khadi cloth with the economic strength of the Indian village and every Indian who sought freedom. In the book *Khadi,* we find Gandhi's writing on the beginnings of the struggle: "It was in London in 1908 that I discovered the wheel ... I saw as in a flash that without the spinning wheel there was no Swaraj."[48] He wore Indian clothing for the first time in 1913. The first Khadi vow was taken in 1919 and the spinning wheel found a place in the Congress programme in 1921. By the end of the 1930s he had set up the All India Spinners Association and the All India Village Industries Association to carry the campaign forward and establish centres for production and marketing. Although spinning and khadi became the non-violent instruments of struggle against British rule and stirred the nation's emotions, they had no significant or lasting impact on the rural economy and village crafts which went along with their own strengths and weaknesses, surviving because of the resilience inbuilt over centuries and dying when the inexorable onslaught of industrialization provided no escape.

In the decades after Independence

While the British period could be characterized as one of indifference or destruction, wherein craftsmen were left to the mercy of market forces and colonial interests, after Independence the Government of India attempted to identify the roots of the problems afflicting village industries and the handloom sector and provided some form of rectification. The revival, development and promotion of handicrafts came to be pursued as a national policy. Recognizing the importance of the contribution that traditional crafts could make to the development of the economy, the Five Year Plans and the Industrial Policy Resolutions not only allocated resources but also emphasized the need to protect cottage and small scale sector from competition.

The early years

The decade spanning the period 1950-1960 saw the establishment of institutions that dealt with policy and its implementation. The purpose was to provide support that would not only sustain but develop the handicraft and handloom sector. The legacy of Mahatma Gandhi, J.C. Kumarappa's work, and the writings of Ananda K. Coomaraswamy had highlighted the importance of this sector which is both integral to India's cultural identity and to its economic development. The sensitive and constructive approach of women like Kamaladevi Chattopadhyay helped to keep the interests of this sector prominent in the eyes of the government, even while India's first Prime Minister, Jawaharlal Nehru, gave emphasis to the development of heavy industries. "Small" and "cottage" industry did find a respectable, though not prominent enough place. Budgetary allocations in the first and second Five Year Plans were reflections of this.[49]

The first plan also proposed reservation of spheres of production for cottage and village industries, control of the expansion of large scale industry, and fiscal devices such as a handloom cess on mill cloth. The objectives were not merely to keep India's heritage and culture alive but to provide employment. The fact that the basic human need of employment, i.e., the sustenance of livelihoods, was the primary objective rather than the dictates of markets, demonstrated a commitment that rested on firm foundations.

During this period the All India Handicrafts Board and All India Handloom Board were set up with prominent and committed social workers among their members in order to guide the policies of the Ministry of Industry. Handicraft Design Centres and Weaver's Service Centres were set up to provide creative innovations to artisan communities. The Central Cottage Industries Emporium became the main showcase of the government's commitment towards marketing of crafts, and Handloom Houses across the country provided an array of India's textiles ranging from simple towels to elaborately woven silk saris. Similarly, the seeds of what later became major regional efforts were sown at state level. In the early sixties, Kamaladevi Chattopadhyay, Pupul Jayakar, L. C. Jain and others contributed towards shaping the institutions set up by the government. Jain and Chattopadhyay built the co-operative movement and co-operative societies which could organize production and marketing more effectively. This included significant work among the refugees after India's partition. Some of these stalwarts disagreed with each other on priorities but their basic commitment could not be questioned. The importance of aesthetics and the appeal to the elite were natural results of the contribution of those from the upper echelons of society. Artisans were like romanticized beneficiaries of an aristocratic establishment. While the Gandhians and socialists among the patrons kept their links with ground realities and the common artisan, others concentrated on standards of quality of production. Some pursued academic work, exploring the crafts of India, and others approached it as a form of social work of an aesthetic nature. The government itself, while bureaucratic in its ways of functioning, allowed itself to be guided by those outside it who had a genuine commitment to craftspeople whatever their perspective, whether social, artistic, academic or economic.

A number of important studies of specific craft traditions also appeared in this period, sponsored by the Office of the Registrar General and Census Commissioner, the Anthropological Survey of India, and the All India Handicrafts and Handloom Board.[50]

Institutions for marketing and export

In the early seventies, state governments geared up their own organizations, and linked them to individual artisans or groups and co-operative apex bodies formed by them. The handloom co-operatives became well-organized institutions. APCO in Andhra Pradesh,

Co-optex in Tamil Nadu and Haryana Handlooms established their own marketing outlets across the country, providing reasonably priced handloom fabrics for all sections of society. Their strength lay in firm government support. State governments also set up showrooms as extensions of their state handicrafts or handloom development corporations. Some, like Uttar Pradesh, incorporated local marketing of handicrafts with their general export corporations. Efficiency, attitudes and progress varied from state to state depending on the political will of the leadership and the commitment and efficiency of the bureaucracy. The central government had only general guidelines and funds for various schemes to offer. A new industrial policy formulated in 1977 laid special emphasis on the support and protection of cottage and small scale industry which infused great hope in this sector, but this was gradually whittled away by successive governments who were dominated by the interests of heavy industries and large business houses.

The Handicraft and Handloom Export Corporation (HHEC) was set up for centralized channelling of exports. This did not prevent state organisations from looking after their own business orders. These were often multiple in nature with considerable duplication of work, resulting in a lack of focus and coordination. The HHEC set up shops abroad and incurred considerable expense trying to tailor production to foreign demand and sell large quantities of carpets under the rupee-payment scheme to the USSR. Unfortunately, a plethora of carpet training programmes failed to garner western markets because of their poor quality, resulting in large stocks languishing in Germany's godowns. While the intentions behind such efforts were good, quite often such mishaps proved detrimental as blame went to the sector rather than to the planners. The HHEC made an effort to bring both technology and design to the craft and garment sector but it worked as long as there were no better efforts from the private sector. By the '80s and '90s private export establishments linked themselves to the fashion industry abroad, rendering HHEC's role more or less redundant. Financial mismanagement and political interference over the years destroyed its primacy in defining the thrust of India's handicraft exports. Considering the vast treasury of crafts that are still available in India, our exports are nowhere near the desired quantity. In 1999 exports of textiles reached US$ 9582 million, out of which handlooms contributed US$ 322.5 million and handicrafts (carpets and other floor coverings) earned US$ 377.1 million. The export of handicrafts achieved 71 per cent of the target, but handlooms could achieve only 64 per cent.[51]

The 1980s

In the eighties the marketing efforts of state governments brought the crafts and textiles of each region on to the urban map. Showrooms were opened in major state capitals, and rich design inputs which brought contemporary relevance to traditional products and skills allowed a wider clientele a choice of crafts for their homes and wardrobes. In the early eighties international expositions such as the Festivals of India, and exhibitions like Viśvakarmā and Aditi, designed and displayed a highly aesthetic and popular range of crafts and textiles. Unfortunately, they were show windows without production lines to back them. They were not linked to genuine marketing and employment generating efforts and therefore led nowhere. Tamil Nadu, Maharashtra, Gujarat, Rajasthan were among the states that understood the fact that if government involved itself in marketing, it had to define and incorporate a social purpose and also show a profit. The north-eastern states grouped together and set up a combined organization which largely concentrated on woven textiles and cane and bamboo crafts.

The Gujarat State Handicrafts Corporation showrooms, named Gurjari, brought fabrics and crafts that provided an alternative to western imitations and the lifeless array of stagnant artefacts from Moradabad, Agra, and similar craft clusters. The word "ethnic" was adopted to describe these very Indian crafts and fashions, unfortunately displaying the mindset of the English-speaking elite who confused indigenous with ethnic, little realising that "ethnic" was a word used by foreigners for anything "native," and could at best be used only in the context of races or cultures. Private entrepreneurs bought these fabrics and converted them into ready-to-wear outfits, thus starting the honeymoon between the private urban entrepreneurs, many of them women, and crafts. Export houses formed associations and councils. Trade fairs began to be held in the nineties to display wares developed and marketed abroad by private business houses.

During this period, many social-work oriented organizations came up as a result of the repercussions of the rise and fall of the political movement that took place between 1970 and 1977, led by Jayaprakash Narayan, who followed an ideology strongly influenced by Mahatma

Gandhi. In the following decade, development work in rural areas became an important agenda for educated urban youth, resulting in the establishment of many small registered societies. They worked with artisans who lived within their area of work, which generally included education, health, water-conservation projects, and income generation activities. These latter categories linked themselves to marketing societies based in urban areas and to the DWCRA programmes set up by the government for the benefit of women and children in rural areas.

All these efforts resulted in increasing awareness of the need for marketing. After all, women can be taught to weave *durries*, fashion ornamental cane baskets, or stitch handloom and khadi fabric into garments, but there was no income gained out of this unless they were marketable. The offices of the Development Commissioner (Handlooms) and Development Commissioner (Handicrafts) had, during these years, moved from the Ministry of Commerce to the Ministry of Industry and then to the Ministry of Textiles. The Khadi and Village Industries Commission and its emporia, the Gramodyog Bhandars, stayed with the Ministry of Industry. The Council for the Advancement of People's Action and Rural Technology (CAPART) was set up in the mid-eighties to fund voluntary organisations variously termed as NGOs, societies, *samitis*, and *sansthans*, that were involved in rural development work. Between all these central government institutions, a series of national fairs and expositions were held or sponsored in order to provide opportunities to exhibit and market craft products.

The late eighties unfortunately also saw a tragic downward trend for handloom weavers, particularly in Andhra Pradesh. A sudden rise in prices of cotton yarn combined with the runaway growth of powerlooms that encroached upon handloom markets led to widespread destitution among handloom weavers, with many committing suicide. In 1999, a revised industrial policy that followed the dictates of liberalization, economic reforms and the new gospel of globalization further weakened subsidy-related development schemes for this sector.

The last decade of the 20th century

By the late nineties, the horizon was replete with central and state emporia, private showrooms and boutiques, "craft villages" belonging to cultural wings of the Ministry of Human Resource Development, and prestigious annual craft fairs. These were all at the level of government and NGO activity. Quite apart, thousands of traditional rural artisans continued to be untouched by these developments. They worked at home, waiting for some local trader to buy their wares at rock bottom prices, or trudged to weekly shanty markets to sell their wares. Many continued to sit by the roadside, making fans, baskets, earthenware pots, iron implements, floor mats, and different kinds of items for local use.

Around the mid-nineties, the idea of creating an urban *haat*, modelled on the temporary village marketplace, took shape in the capital, Delhi. Its success has been gauged by the high level of acceptance by both artisan and customer alike, resulting in the central government incorporating the concept into the Ninth Five Year Plan for the marketing of crafts. By the year 2005, there should be twenty more *haat*s, providing a comfortable and informal marketing infrastructure for craftspersons to sell their products directly to customers with very low overheads. Crafts items and artefacts which are India-specific in colour and design and traditional fabrics used by domestic customers do not fare well when sent to foreign markets, but private enterprise took up the challenge of developing glass, metal, wood, and handloom and jute furnishings for exports with a fair amount of success. The last years of the nineties also saw the appearance of trade fairs providing a wide range of products attempting to match contemporary foreign demands.

The pace of effective intervention to sustain craftspeople and crafts has been mired in the red tape surrounding various welfare, revival, training or marketing schemes. These are with the Ministry of Textiles. Market Development Assistance for exports is with the Ministry of Commerce and Industry, and, on the whole, it is only the smart urban entrepreneur or NGO who manage to access these funds. Despite their manifold skills the artisans still seem to lack the ability to handle all the ropes needed to rise above their present condition.

Uncertain numbers, unknown people

In 1995-96, the National Council of Applied Economic Research (NCAER) was commissioned by the Ministry of Textiles to conduct censuses of artisans in the handloom and handicraft sectors, with the collaboration of state governments. The figures in the handloom census, that was admittedly not exhaustive in methodology or reach, revealed that there are 65.5 lakh (6.5 million) persons in the handloom sector, including weavers who operate the loom as well as those who are involved in pre- and post-loom processes, and that the 2.5 million weaver households have a total population of about 13 million people, a majority of whom are entirely dependent on this sector for their survival.[52] In the crafts sector the assessment was even more difficult because of dispersed locations, the part-time nature of some craft activities and various other reasons. The figure given in the NCAER document is 48.2 lakhs or 4.8 million craftspersons, but officials prefer to qualify this informally by actually doubling the number.[53] The Ninth Five Year Plan documents of the Government of India present the large numbers working in the Khadi and Village Industries sector in the year 1999-2000. Employment in the production of khadi yarn and fabric is 16.7 lakhs (1.7 million). In mineral, forest, agro-based and food industries, polymers and chemicals, and engineering and non-conventional energy, the numbers add up to a total of 66.8 lakhs (6.7 million), of which those who are exclusively engaged in craft and artisanal activities are 37.3 lakhs (3.7 million).[54] Multiplied by an average family size of 5.6, this adds up to over 25 million people dependent on such activities.

The fact is that large numbers of craftspeople, along with an unknown number of many more people who are involved in ancillary activities, do not enter the databases compiled by the government, and therefore there is no firm statistical basis to prove their existence, let alone assess their condition and economic status, their successes, failures or needs.

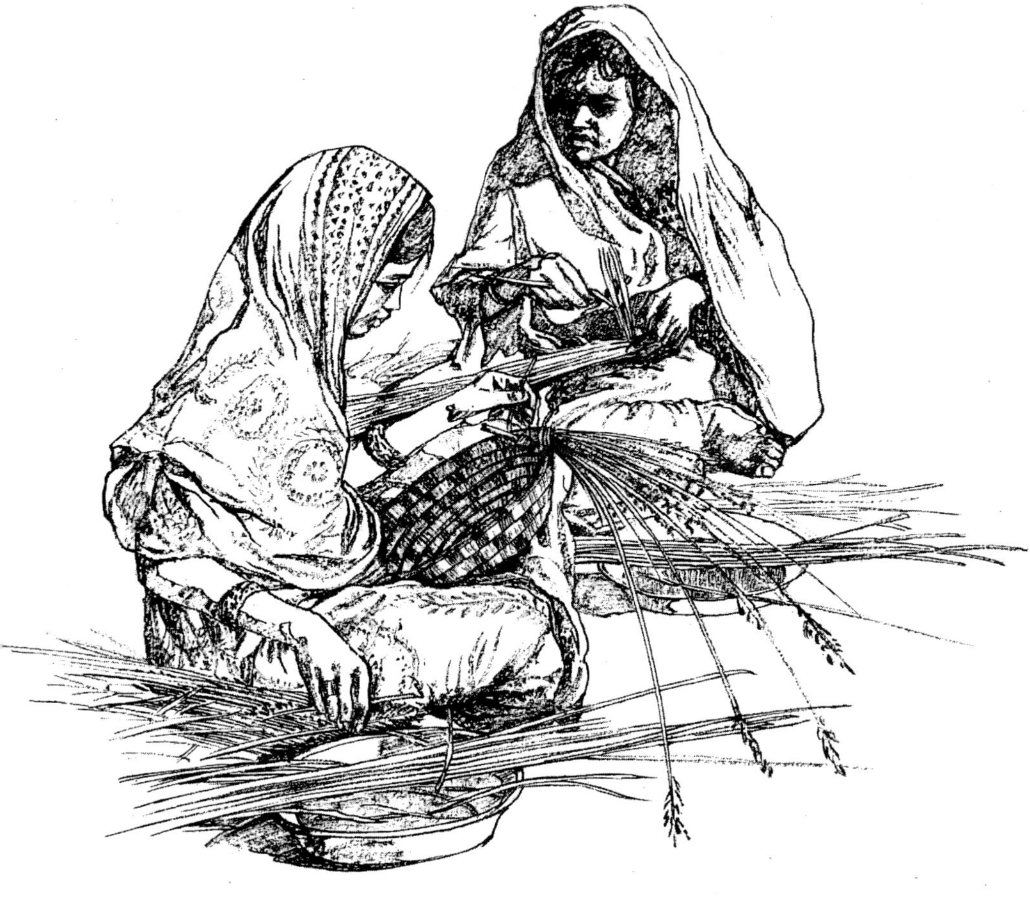

References

1. Ananda K. Coomaraswamy, *The Indian Craftsman*, p. 35. See also Max Weber, *The Religions of India*, p. 97
2. Raymond and Bridget Allchin, *The Birth of Indian Civilization*, p. 268
3. George C.M. Birdwood, *The Arts of India*, p. 137
4. Ibid., p. 138
5. Edward Lucie-Smith, *The Story of Craft*, p. 61
6. *The Periplus of the Erythraean Sea*, tr. by W.H. Schoff, pp. 24-39
7. D.D. Kosambi, *Introduction to the Study of Indian History*, p. 334
8. Vijaya Ramaswamy, *Textiles and Weavers in Medieval South India*, p. 69
9. Ibid., p. 4
10. Ibid., p. 70
11. Richard Lannoy, *The Speaking Tree*, p. 17
12. Ibid.
13. Ibid.
14. Ibid. p. 19
15. Oliver Mendelsohn and Marika Vicziany, *The Untouchables*, pp. 5-8; and K.S. Singh, *The Scheduled Castes*, pp. 5-11
16. K.S. Singh, *The People of India*, Vol.VII.
17. M.K. Pal, *Crafts and Craftsmen in Traditional India*, p. 119
18. Weber, op. cit. p. 33
19. T.W. Rhys Davids, *Buddhist India;* Kosambi, op. cit. p. 277, and the *Amarakosha*, ed. N.G. Sardesai and D.G. Padhye
20. Weber, op. cit. p. 86
21. Kosambi, op. cit. pp. 334-5
22. Weber, op. cit. p. 38
23. Ramaswamy, op. cit. p. 38
24. Ibid.
25. Birdwood, op. cit. pp. 139-40
26. Ramaswamy, op. cit. p. 52, pp. 169-70
27. Lannoy, op. cit. p. 157
28. K.A. Nilkanta Sastri, *Age of the Nandas and Mauryas*, pp. 362-70
29. Lucie-Smith, op. cit. pp. 61-62
30. Ibid., pp. 67-68
31. Shanti Swarup, *Mughal Art: A Study in Handicrafts*
32. *Ain-i-Akbari*, tr. by H. Blochmann
33. Shanti Swarup, op. cit.
34. Lucie-Smith. p. 66
35. Birdwood, op. cit. p. 134
36. D.R. Gadgil, *The Industrial Evolution of India in Recent Times*, pp. 38-42
37. Lucie-Smith, p. 65
38. A.R. Desai, *Social Background of Indian Nationalism*, pp. 83-85
39. Ramaswamy, op. cit. p. 170
40. SRUTI, *India's Artisans*, p. 14
41. Lucie-Smith, p. 66
42. Tirthankar Roy, *Artisans and Industrialization*, p.ix.
43. Ibid., p. 2
44. Ibid., p. 5
45. Gadgil, op. cit. p. 175
46. Roy, op. cit. p. 21
47. Ibid., pp. 21-23
48. M.K. Gandhi, *Khadi*, p. 1
49. B.B. Bhasin and K. Kak, *Towards an Objective for the Handicrafts Sector*
50. SRUTI's status report *India's Artisans* lists over 200 such publications in its bibliography
51. Ministry of Textiles' *Annual Report 1999-2000*, pp. 73-74
52. NCAER, *Joint Census of Handlooms & Powerlooms 1995-96: Handloom Sector.* The Handloom Census does not include data from Meghalaya, Sikkim, Mizoram, and Dadra & Nagar Haveli
53. NCAER, *Census of Handicraft Artisans, Phase I*, p. 4, and the project's state reports
54. Khadi & Village Industries Commission, Mumbai, from a summary of projections of Ninth Plan (1997-2000) employment targets

Most weavers in the southern state of Andhra Pradesh are men, so the selection of a woman weaver for our profile may appear unusual. However, the terms and conditions of her work are not very different from those of male weavers. A vast majority of the weavers in Andhra Pradesh are totally dependent on the masterweavers, who are generally looked upon as middlemen who provide the workspace, loom, and raw material. Both production and marketing endeavours are therefore dependent on him. The strong link between the two necessitated inclusion of the masterweaver in the profile.

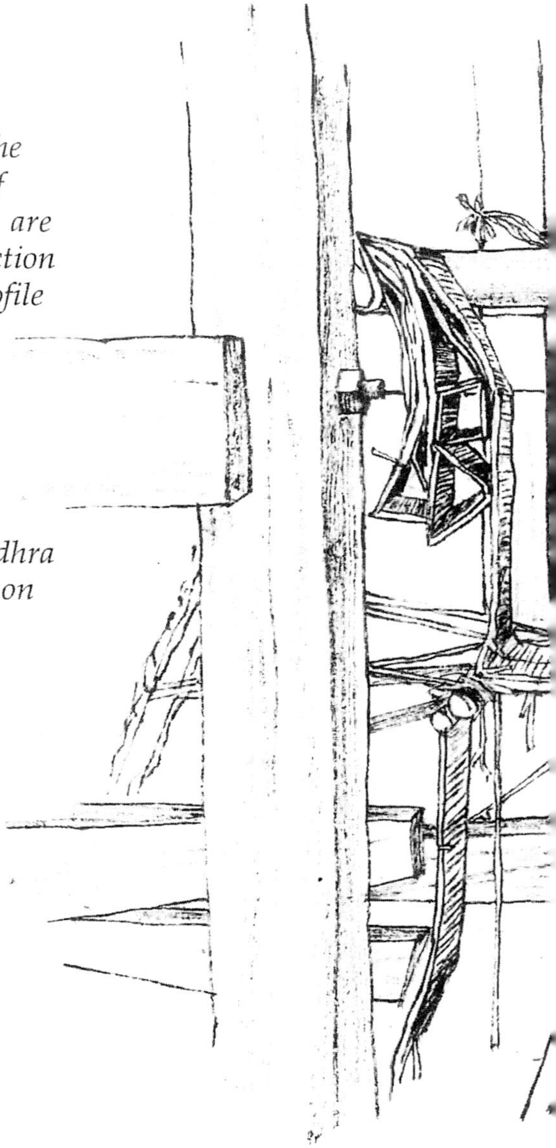

CHAPTER TWO

The Handloom Weavers of Mangalagiri

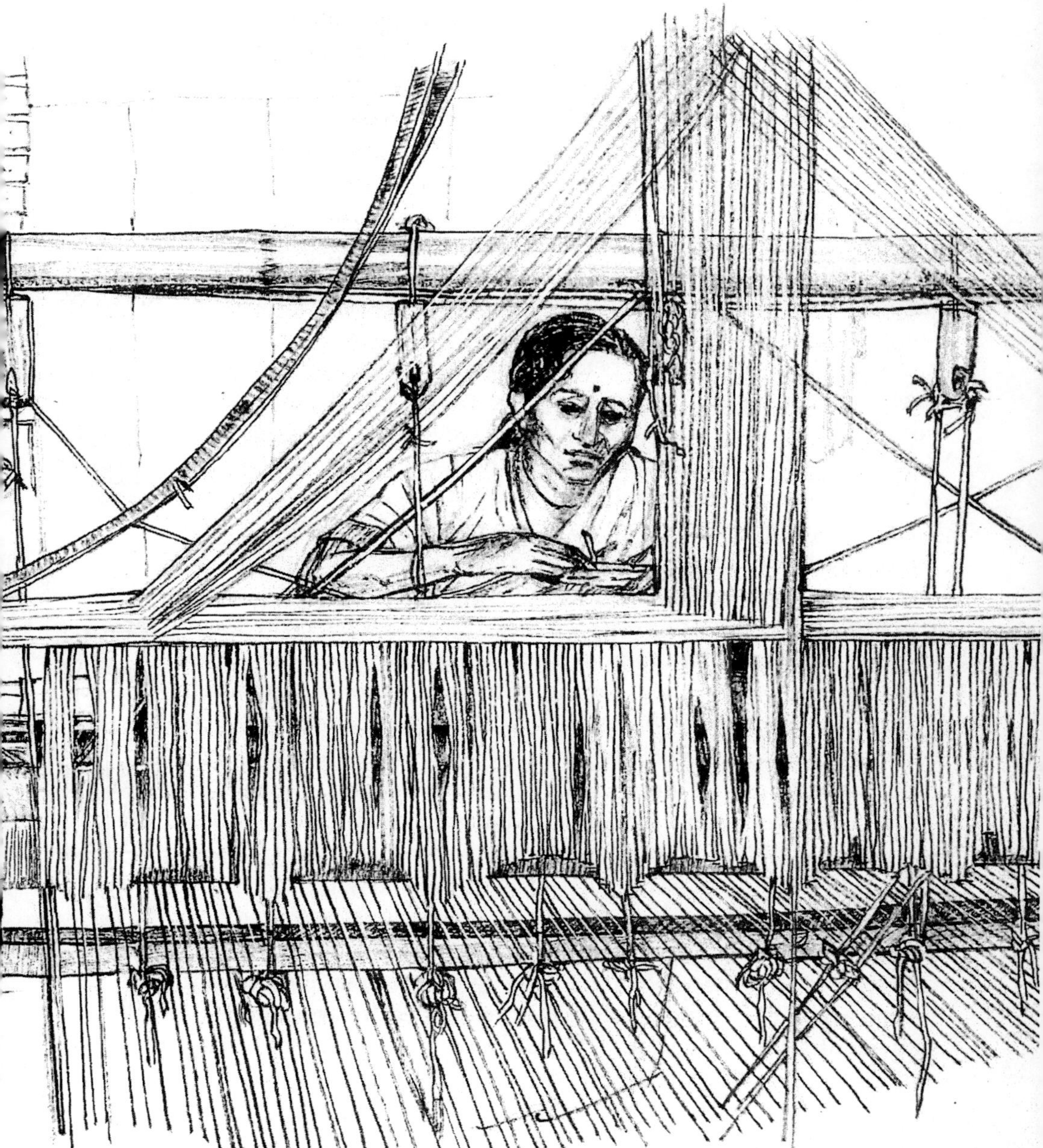

Venkataramanamma, aged 30, thin and slightly built, finds herself working at the loom for twelve hours a day every day of the year, facing almost the same conditions as did her forefathers. She is a member of the backward Padmasali caste of weavers of Mangalagiri village in Andhra Pradesh.

Along with the Padmasalis, there are other traditional weaving groups such as the Devanga, Thogati and Tharinibatlu in the village. Individual members of these traditional occupational groups largely work for masterweavers who set up weaving sheds, each employing 10 to 15 weavers. These weavers have neither the financial support nor the knowledge or enterprise to move to other occupations. Only the knowledge of their traditional skills has ensured their survival.

Venkataramanamma's husband Narasimha Rao used to be a weaver but, being the sole breadwinner, he could not provide the family with more than Rs 900 per month, so he switched over to vending cloth and saris from house to house in nearby villages, and taught his wife how to weave. With a small amount of cash which he had saved and some small personal loans he set up an alternative livelihood for himself, earning approximately Rs 800 per month, while his wife brought in an additional Rs 800-900 by working as a daily wage weaver for a masterweaver in the village. Narasimha Rao's loan was obtained under the traditional *rozhwari* system which entails a daily repayment. If a loan of Rs 900 is taken it is counted as Rs 1000 and Rs 10 has to be returned daily for one hundred days. All such financial transactions are carried out through the masterweaver.

They had begun life in Atmapur, a village not far away from their present home, and had migrated to Mangalagiri after the cyclone of 1977, leaving behind their parents who are in their sixties, along with Narasimha Rao's three brothers and two sisters. His brothers had been educated only up to the primary level. Venkataramanamma has never been to school and is illiterate. Their daughter Nagalakshmi, aged 12, studied up to the 3rd standard but dropped out to look after the younger siblings when her mother went out to work. Their son Nageshwar Rao, is 7 years old and is in the 2nd standard and the youngest, Nagamani, aged 4, stays at home.

Mangalagiri has a small but impressive temple built for the weavers' special deity Bhavana Rishi whose festival falls around the second week of February when it is celebrated in two temples in the settlement. They quote the *Atreya Purana*, which describes Bhavana as the originator of cotton thread. He is said to have climbed the "cotton tree," plucked the cotton flower, found a way of making it into thread and weaving the threads into cloth. They believe that before this all men wore the bark of trees to cover their bodies. All over Andhra Pradesh, weavers place the statue of Bhavana Rishi in a prime place at marriages and on other special occasions. According to Narasimha Rao this trend of worship has increased in the past sixty years. Visiting the temple is their only cultural activity apart from occasional visits to the local cinema hall.

Mangalagiri has always been a weaving centre and boasts of a community hall built with the donations of the masterweavers. It is maintained by renting out a portion of the building to a post office and a chemist's shop and is also rented out for meetings and marriages. The weavers use the hall to discuss their problems and the masterweavers join in to discuss wage parities and increments. The leadership naturally goes to the articulate weavers, while Venkataramanamma, like most of the other silent workers, says: "We go on strike occasionally, but we feel disheartened when our demands are not fulfilled and we get only minor benefits." For instance, in last year's struggle they managed to get a wage increase of Rs 50 per *patsam* (a unit of four saris). Some of them have even been to the offices of the communist parties to discuss their problems, but to no avail.

Mangalagiri is equipped with a 20-bed government hospital. Luckily, Venkataramanamma said, her family had no health problems. Their son was studying satisfactorily, but, she said, "I have to believe whatever he tells me about his studies since I am not educated. I sometimes scold him and tell him to study harder, but I don't know the result of my efforts. My husband looks at his books, but the truth is that neither of us have time to look after the children.

"If we earned more our children's future would be more secure. Even though we do not discriminate between boys and girls, we have no elders to look after the home and children. Although I do not like the fact that my daughter is being denied an education, I have no option. If our children are properly educated, they can expand their father's business.

"We are not teaching our children the craft of weaving. We want the tradition to come to an end with us. There is no scope in the weaving sector. We have to carry on because we have no other alternative, but we will not bequeath this knowledge to our children."

Venkataramanamma's home in Mangalagiri village in Guntur district of Andhra Pradesh is no different from that of other weavers of the state. A tiny shack within a small, open compound shares space with another shack belonging to a manual labourer. It is made of mud and lime plaster with a thatched roof of dried palm leaves. The dwelling unit would be packed tightly if seven people were to sit close together on the floor. Clothes hang on pegs on the walls, and narrow wooden shelves at one end of the room hold the aluminium cooking utensils and a brass water container. One wall is covered with a transparent plastic sheet to prevent rainwater from coming in. A wooden plank hung with red yarn serves as a platform for a small transistor radio. A toothbrush and a tube of toothpaste are stuck between the bamboo splats that hold up the roof of leaves. Outside, a small enclosure has been constructed out of long stalks of dried scrub tied together. This is where Venkataramanamma's family members bathe in privacy. In the open courtyard lie a couple of cots made with left over yarn from the looms, forming a beautiful multicoloured weave of light pink, green and grey hues. A grinding stone, a couple of tin buckets and heaps of mud and plastic pots lie scattered around in the open. The sum total of their possessions are there for everyone to see. A small cement grill window brings in a few rays of daylight and a kerosene lamp provides light at night. Water has to be fetched from the public tap and the nearby fields provide toilet space.

Venkataramanamma works all days of the week, stopping only for a special festival or in case of sickness. She sets off for her workplace at 6 am and returns by 6 pm, earning between Rs 30 to 40 per twelve-hour day, depending on the pattern and style of cloth she is weaving. Remuneration is according to the capacity of each weaver, who weaves on an average three to four metres a day. Yarn is provided for four saris at a time and payments are made in advance. It works out to Rs 300 for each unit of four saris, which takes 10 to 12 days to complete. Venkataramanamma pointed out simply but without regret, that she was losing her weaving time and earnings while she was talking to us. As landless weavers with no other source of income, the couple's combined earnings barely touched Rs 2000. This was all they had to cover the cost of their domestic needs, and it left them little or nothing for slack days, illness or leisure.

The family rises at 5 am A tiffin of tea and *idli* is brought from a nearby hotel where you get two *idli*s for one rupee. The family spends five rupees on this breakfast, and by 6 am Venkataramanamma leaves for work, to return only at noon for a lunch of rice, *dal,* pickle and buttermilk prepared by her daughter. She goes back to work till 4 pm, when she comes home again for a cup of tea, not provided at the workshed. The weavers who live farther away and cannot go home for meals spend up to Rs 10 a day eating at hotels. At night, Venkataramanamma helps her daughter prepare the evening meal. The rest of her housework consists of washing clothes, fetching water, and sweeping and cleaning the house and yard. She does not expect her husband to do any housework as he is out at work from 6 am to 8 pm every day.

The Sankranti festival in mid-January is a special time for weavers. The entire workshed remains closed at that time. They do not celebrate or stop work on national holidays like Independence Day or Republic Day, and in fact Venkataramanamma only comes to know about them when the children announce that their school is closed. On Diwali, the festival of lights, and Mukoti, a local festival, they go early in the morning to the river to bathe and float small oil lamps. Ugadi, their New Year's Day, is also observed in the same manner. Weavers choose not to work on these festival days, but it means informing the masterweaver in advance and losing wages for that day. A part of their small annual savings, if any, are used for festival expenses.

There are no major expenses for Venkataramanamma and her family. They pay one hundred rupees a month as house rent to their landlord, who is a Gowda from a backward agricultural community. Schooling for the children is free, with no school uniform required. Some books are free and others have to be bought. Since there is no water and electricity, there are no bills to pay. Travel is limited to a two rupee bus ride to see their parents occasionally. Narasimha Rao can get about locally on his bicycle and the only long distance journey is to the temple at Vijayawada twice or three times a year.

If handloom weavers want people to use handloom products, why does Venkataramanamma herself wear a machine-woven "mill" sari we asked. "Handloom saris in finer quality yarn are too expensive. Men wear handloom *lungis* but ever since the Janata Cloth Scheme which supplied us with cheap saris was withdrawn we have no choice. Once in a while we used to get a sari and a dhoti through our ration card."

Perhaps the one satisfactory aspect of the wage structure is that men and women weavers are paid equally. Processes such as spinning or stretching of the yarn are done by others and paid for separately. However, there are no weekly holidays, no compensation for overtime, no accident compensation, leave facility or medical benefits. In the normal production process there are hardly any occupational hazards, but if a weaver falls sick and needs cash for medical expenses, the masterweaver advances it against the weavers' wages.

Raw material is provided to weavers at their workplace by the masterweaver. The main problem faced is shortage of yarn. While it is the responsibility of the masterweaver to obtain and supply the yarn, perennial short supply and rising prices affect the productivity and earnings of both the masterweaver and the daily wage weavers. Yarn is bought from Coimbatore where a number of spinning mills are located. However, a regular supply is assured only if payments are made in advance. Since even the masterweavers cannot afford to do so, supplies are intermittent and are usually brought in small quantities to Mangalagiri by local dealers. Sometimes yarn of good quality is not

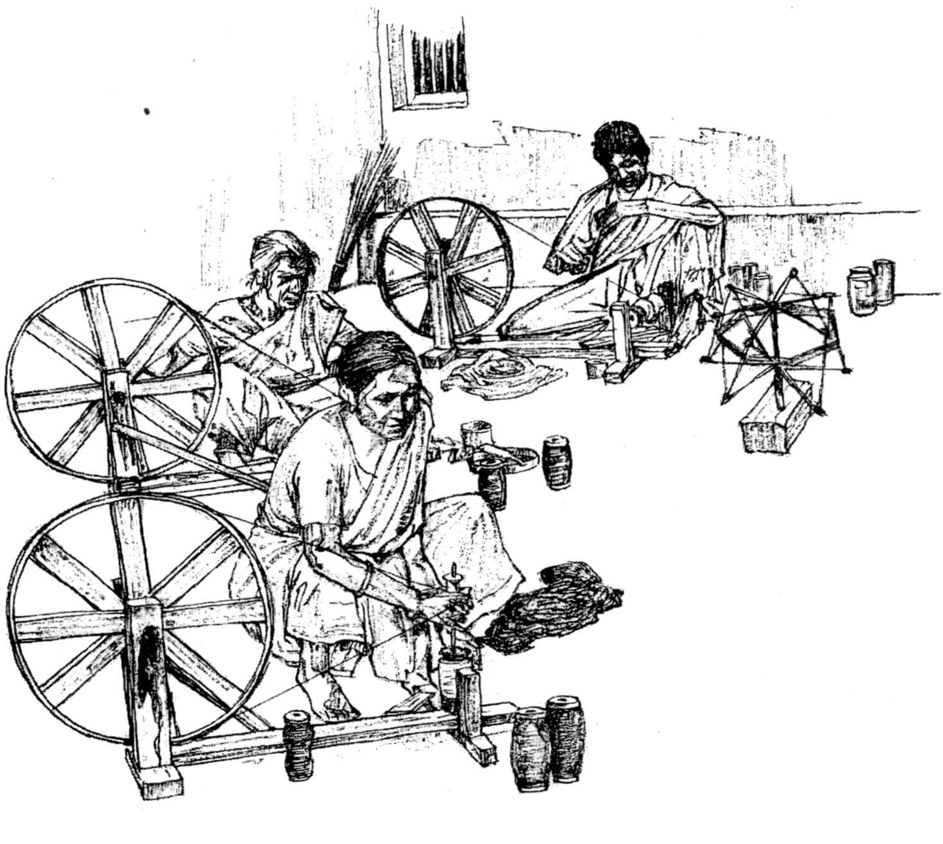

available, and when it is available at a reasonable price, they lack the requisite finance to buy it in bulk. Narasimha Rao said that the availability of an improved "Hyderabadi quality" yarn had made it easier for them to weave "Punjabi" dress material, which had a wider market, and this had improved their remuneration to some extent. The introduction of more varieties of yarn and new designs had improved sales, and hence the masterweaver was able to pay wages to them on time. Venkataramanamma was more comfortable using the improved quality of thread and said that it had helped her to increase productivity and improve her skills.

The masterweaver has often been termed the "middleman," who supplies the yarn and markets the finished product. Observers have often suggested that the way to improve the standard of life of the craftsperson is to eliminate the middleman in the production process. But for the weaving community, the masterweaver – the so-called middleman – is part and parcel of the production process. When one attempts to eliminate him the survival of weavers becomes difficult. Venkataramanamma says: "In the present system of government apathy and primitive marketing methods, this is the only way we can survive. There is no other choice before us."

Venkataramanamma's knowledge of design vocabulary is largely traditional. If given the opportunity and exposure to market trends, skilled and experienced weavers have the capacity to become design experts, but the scope for innovation and creative work is limited when colours and designs have to be followed strictly according to the instructions of the masterweaver. An average weaver like Venkataramanamma offers no creative ideas of her own.

It was the masterweaver who threw more light on design development. Parties who come to him to buy materials advise him according to their knowledge and assessment of market needs. They order the required quantities of cloth but, according to the masterweaver, the production is not just against specific orders because it is not economically viable to halt production at any point. "Since we have to provide work to the weavers for all the 365 days of the year, we continue production," he said. If they stop work the weavers disperse and it becomes difficult to organize them together again when a new order comes.

New technology is too distant even to dream of. Narasimha Rao says, "We have heard about powerlooms and that they are the reason why we are losing our jobs, but we do not know of any improved looms." The Weavers' Service Centre at Vijayawada holds week-long camps to disseminate new technology to weavers but, according to Narasimha Rao and Venkataramanamma, the weavers find that they are unable to assimilate information about new looms. The tools and looms are the same as have been in use for the past thirty-five years, and the changes have been only in the yarn and designs. The masterweaver who maintains fifteen looms has to incur an expenditure of approximately Rs 8,000 to Rs 10,000 per year on their maintenance cost, including repairs. He does not bother to insure them unless he has taken a bank loan for their installation and is thereby compelled to do so.

Various loan schemes have been introduced for handloom weavers but the couple find them unviable. Buying a loom is of no use when they have only a tiny rented house. They are aware of schemes for housing and worksheds but do not know the details. They admit: "We did not try. We do not think we will get it even after wasting time in finding out about it, so what's the use?"

While speaking to us for a while Venkataramanamma felt that she had spent long enough away from work. She rose and left to weave at the workshed about half a kilometre away. Narasimha Rao stayed back to talk.

Since the weaver is inextricably linked to the masterweaver who provides the yarn, the workspace, and the wages, it was thought necessary to establish contact with him as well. Masterweaver, middleman, community benefactor, exploiter, employer, market outreach person, what is he? Vithala Anjaneyulu is a weaver, as was his father and grandfather. He organizes the production and sales of handloom fabric, and also weaves if one of the weavers is absent and there is work to be done. His family includes his wife, three sons, two daughters-in-law, two grandchildren and his mother, all of whom work in the establishment and get the same wages as everyone else. Their home and workspaces provide room for 15 weavers and a scattering of women who spin the yarn. His granddaughter has a sewing machine and does tailoring work in the same yard. They had bought the property very cheap thirty years ago. It was now worth Rs 5 lakhs but "that means nothing to us as we have to live here."

Masterweaver Anjaneyulu executes a sale of approximately Rs 3 lakh in a year, and earns Rs 3,000 a month. Excluding the wages received by working members of the family, this works out to Rs 300 per capita per month, demonstrating that unless the family members worked regularly alongside the weavers they would not be able to sustain themselves.

A strong sense of community is discernible among the weavers. The masterweavers recognize that they are the prime strength in keeping handloom work alive in Andhra Pradesh. "In the shoe trade everyone from different communities competes but a masterweaver who is both manufacturer and salesperson is always from the weaver's community," says Anjaneyulu. He also admits that working hours are long and wages are low for the weavers but that he is restrained from improving their conditions due to the operative market forces. He wants to pay better wages in his own interest to keep the weavers with him on a regular basis. In fact, he said that the masterweavers often change the variety of cloth to a simple weave that can be a regularly sold in order to continues production only to keep a hold on the weavers.

A masterweaver like Anjaneyulu has no capital to invest in the promotion of his textiles. There has been a decrease in the vibrancy of the market because of competition from mill-made polyester material. In Mangalagiri itself, very few can afford to buy a fine cotton sari for six hundred rupees so they prefer to produce "Punjabi dress" fabric instead of just saris. Earlier the yarn provided was usually for coarse 40 count fabrics, whereas now they were able to produce finer cloth of 80 to 100 counts but competition from mills forced them to keep their prices static. As the prices of yarn rise, either the wage component is depressed or the production is reduced. According to Anjaneyulu, in the last three decades, the number of weavers decreased from ten thousand to two thousand in and around Mangalagiri because weavers are moving away to other kinds of labour or occupations which offer them better remuneration. The masterweaver saw himself as a victim of this vicious cycle rather than a perpetrator of injustice against the weavers since he cannot offer the weavers' higher wages and cannot also afford to lose them to other trades. He points out that the problem of competition with the powerloom sector is not only that handlooms are being wiped out by the flooding of the market with powerloom substitutes, but that because of greater production per loom, each worker's wage in the powerloom sector is higher than that of the handloom weaver. He recalls nostalgically that thirty years ago the wage for one unit or *patsam* was Rs 7 whereas now it is Rs 300.

The masterweaver produces, stores and sells from his home, which is also his workplace. He says there is always enough place to stock goods but production is never so high as to justify incurring expenditure on setting up a showroom of his own. He adds 10 per cent as profit on the production cost but if there is a crunch in the market he has to lower the profit margin and sometimes even sells his goods at cost price. Since his house serves as a warehouse as well, he does not incur any storage costs. The "good season" is during March, April and May when marriages take place and it is the harvest season as well. For the other nine months he has to lower his prices.

As sales outlets are varied so is the quality, but prices are not altered according to the market. Once the price is fixed it remains the same whether it is going to a shop or to an exporter. While he uses better quality yarn for export goods, he confesses that he does not really know whether the goods ordered from him for export are really exported or sold in upmarket areas in big cities in India.

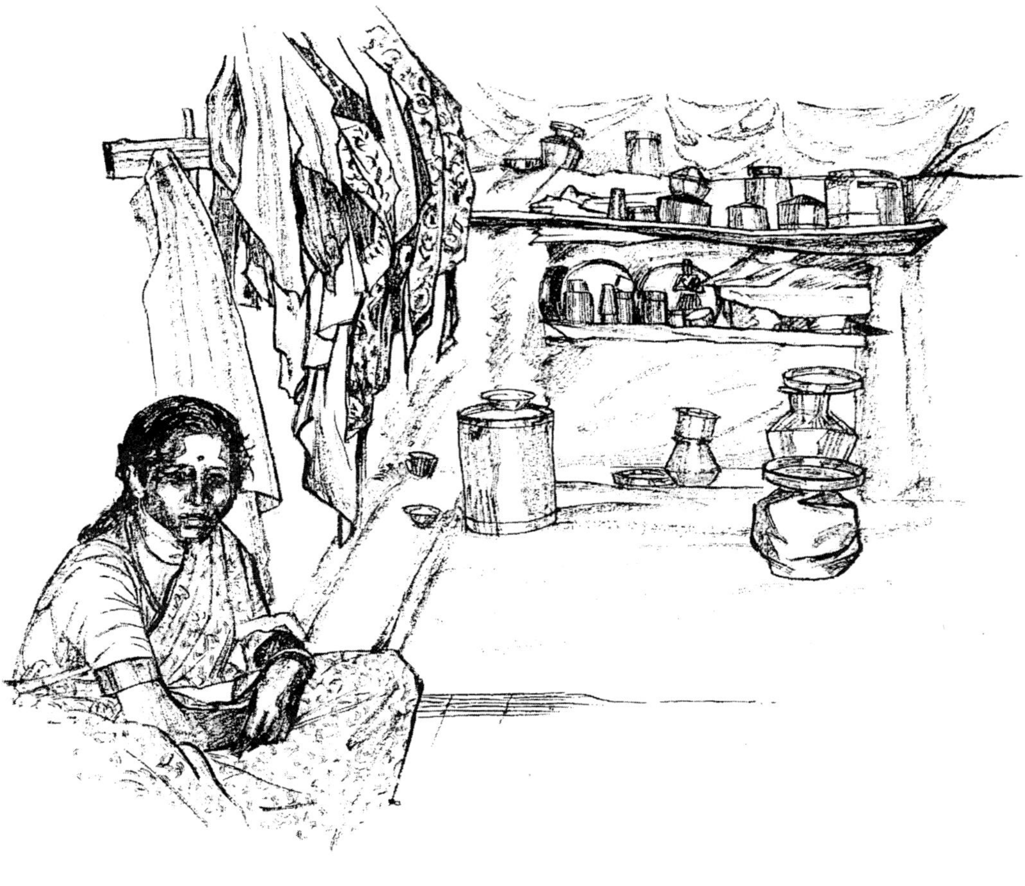

Buyers come to Anjaneyulu's home, where he sells against cash payments if the cloth is taken from existing stocks. On fabrics made to order, he takes no advance from well-known buyers but charges a 10 to 15 per cent advance from unknown ones. Generally everything that is ordered is cleared but in case some pieces are rejected because of defects in quality, he sells them locally at a lower price. Sometimes he goes to Vijayawada and Hyderabad to dispose off existing stocks to private shops, where he has to leave his goods on credit and collect the money after three or four months. Since he doesn't adopt any high profile selling techniques, he uses the jute bags which contained the yarn to pack the finished products.

Despite the crucial role of the masterweaver in sustaining the livelihood of the handloom weaver, as in the case of Anjaneyulu his own outreach is considerably limited and also subject to exploitation. For instance, Anjaneyulu, has never participated in any private or government-organized exhibitions or fair – *melas* – in order to find out the demand and acceptability of his textiles or the prices at which they can be sold. "We do not have the capital to produce and carry enough stocks to a *mela* for sale. We know that people who come here and take our stocks participate in these *melas* posing as weavers but we cannot help it. Exhibitions are usually organized only for societies and we do not fall under that category. I am a weaver but I do not weave much anymore. Even though my family members weave, since the material is largely woven by those who work in the shed, I am no longer considered a weaver.

"The government has listed seventeen societies in this area but there isn't one that is actually functioning. They are only 'societies on paper' No list of masterweaver worksheds has been prepared by the district authorities of the state and central government. How will they know about us or help us?

"We are not educated. Those in our community who are educated do not even bother about us, and are practising other professions."

Between Venkataramanamma the weaver and Anjaneyulu the middleman, the living tradition of handloom weaving seemed to be hanging precariously by a few faded, fragile threads.

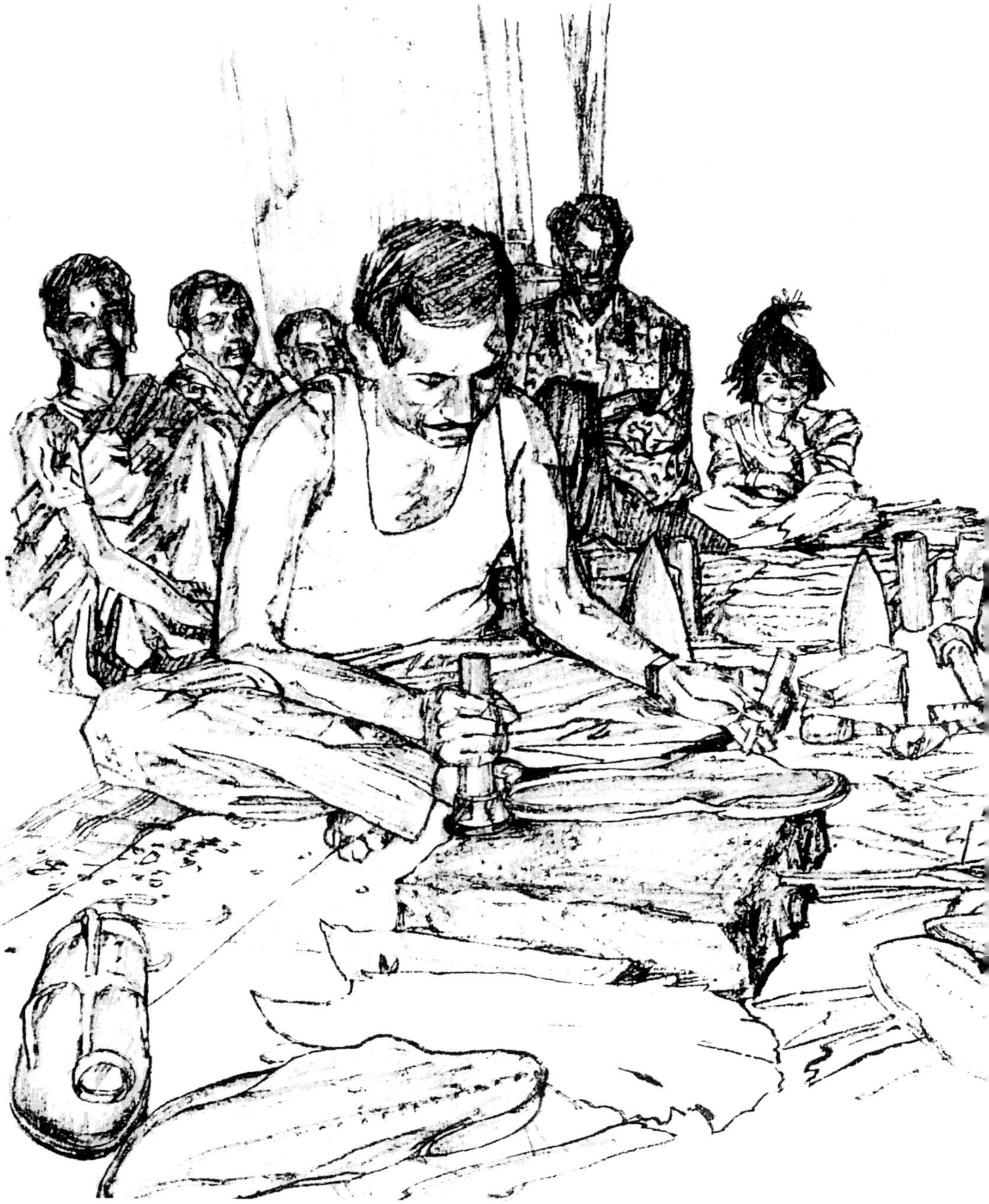

CHAPTER THREE

The Chappal Makers of Kolhapur

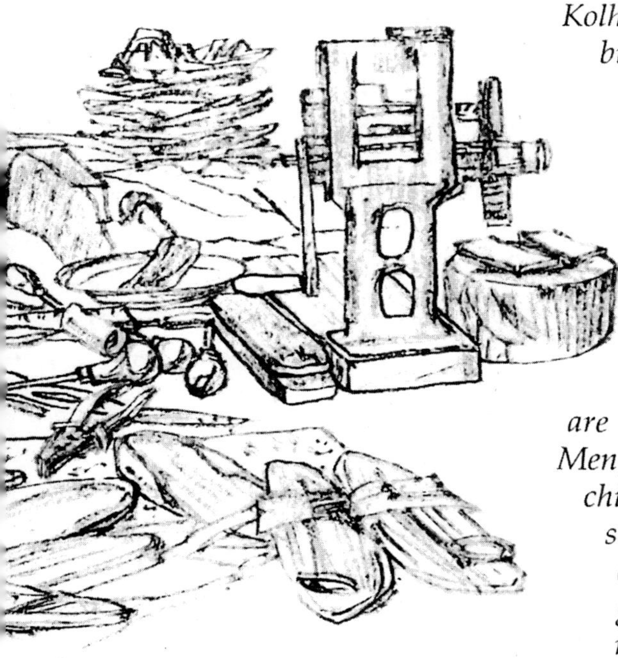

The scheduled caste leather worker in the profile lives in an urban colony at the edge of Kolhapur, a fairly large and bustling town. The family has disengaged itself from its rural surroundings and carries on the traditionally known skill nearer their local market where they supply slippers and sandals to local shoe shops. They are landless, full-time artisans. Men, women, and even their children, who work after school, are engaged in the craft. They have had no grants, training or marketing programmes organized for their benefit by either government or private agencies.

For anyone who travels to Kolhapur in Maharashtra, its association with the *chappal*, the flat traditional leather footwear, becomes immediately apparent. And even if there is little time to shop, a visit to the street of more than one hundred shoe shops at Shivaji Chowk is still a popular activity. On an average, sales reach almost Rs 1 lakh per month at each shop during the peak season. Some of the smaller shops sell only Kolhapuri chappals and its variations while others stock a mix of what are described locally as "Bombay" shoes, consisting of plastic and rubber slippers, sports shoes and traditional Rajasthani *tilla joot*is which are leather slip-ons with decorative embroidery in gold and silver coloured metallic thread. The advent of "modern" styles from India and abroad are reflected in the eclectic range of footwear in the town which was once the exclusive stronghold of the famous Kolhapuri chappal, without which no *kurta-pajama* outfit was complete. The cheapest Kolhapuri chappal has doubled in price from Rs 35 to Rs 70 a pair in recent years, while the average range of most traditional styles with some embroidery sells between Rs 110 to Rs 150 per pair. Buckled sandals, men's semi-closed casual footwear, and the elaborate traditional chappal meant for bridegrooms or royalty are priced between Rs 150 and Rs 200 a pair. Since there is something to suit every pocket, all those who appreciate traditional craftsmanship in footwear still invest in Kolhapuri chappals for all the members of their families.

A few more Kolhapuri chappal shops are scattered around the town. D.T. Satpute, who received the mastercraftsperson's award in 1990 from the President of India, owns a small shop near the railway station. He has framed a large coloured photograph of the award ceremony, along with pictures of himself displaying his footwear at a stall being visited by Indira Gandhi when she was prime minister. The mastercraftsman himself is the proud salesman and, along with his wife and children, poses for a photograph with any visitor he considers a VIP so that it can later go up on the wall, above the little table that serves as his cash counter. The size of the shop is barely 10 feet by 6 feet; it had been constructed from the earnings of a successful sale conducted at a five-day exhibition at the People's Science and Technology Fair held at Powai, near Bombay, in 1992. He had been sent there as a member of the Dastkari Haat Samiti, a countrywide federation of craftspeople who work to develop wider markets for themselves. Satpute's chappals were popular amongst the students and other young people who had assembled at the Indian Institute of Technology campus during the fair to discuss and promote indigenous skills and technologies as an alternative mode of development. A remarkable sale of Rs 80,000 in just five days enabled him to take the major step of opening his own sales establishment.

Another mastercraftsman who also has a shop in Kolhapur is N. Godkar. An export order in the past, and good sales at the Apna Utsav (Our Festival), a cultural event that did the rounds of major cities in the country in the 1980s, helped him save enough money to set up a small shop in the heart of the town, at the crossroads near the Mahalakshmi Temple. According to local information, ninety per cent of all newly married couples in Maharashtra come to worship at this temple. It therefore appears to be a perfect location for sales. Godkar has his small workshop and residence adjacent to the shop. He revealed that he also had a public telephone booth in Bhondre Nagar which supplemented his income from shoe-making. He too had a framed photograph of himself receiving the mastercraftsperson's award from President Shankar Dayal Sharma. Significantly, both Satpute and Godkar declared that the award had in no way facilitated the setting up of their shops, and that it had been possible only from the savings from good sales at special events. The award was in fact just a source of pride. The products in their shops were of average quality and had imbibed the rubber/plastic/sponge high-heeled styles of other shoes.

Of the 6,00,000 inhabitants of Kolhapur city, 25,000 are leather shoemakers belonging to the Chamar caste of tanners and leather workers who have been given a low status in the Hindu social hierarchy. In the entire Kolhapur district it is estimated that there are a total of about 1,00,000 Chamars, and there are still more in the adjoining areas of Sangli, Satara and Pune. Godkar accompanied us to "Bondre Colony" and took us to a small cemented structure that looked similar to others in this unauthorized settlement in a newly developing section of the town which is actually named Balinga, about 10 kms from the heart of Kolhapur town. Here lived Yeshwant Rangrao Pawar, aged 42, a self employed artisan who reflected the average condition of Kolhapur's chappal makers. His entire family including his wife Sulochana, aged 31, and three children participated in chappal-making. The children also went to school; his daughter Vaishali, 16, was in the 11th class, which is termed Junior College; Sharad, a boy of 14, was in the 9th class and the younger son Pradeep, aged 12, was in the 7th class.

Yeshwant's father Rangrao Pawar, 60, had studied, like his son, up to the 4th class, while his mother Harubai, aged 55, was non-literate. He had one brother in his native village, Bhogaon Bazaar, 30 kms away; and the youngest brother, who had studied till the 12th class, was now in Bombay as a conductor with the Bombay Electric Supply and Transport Undertaking, a Bombay Municipal Corporation enterprise. How did this happen? "Well," explained Yeshwant, "we were all in leather work and knew nothing else. We thought, let one of us be educated and get into service. We can't all do the same thing." They had no other businesses or avenues of income.

The Pawar family spends Rs 60 every alternate month on water and electricity bills and Rs 60 on the children's education. Local travel costs were nil and because it costs Rs 10 each way to visit their village only one person went at a time. The sum total of their consumer durables consisted of a cycle and a cassette player. There was no furniture in the house. Sulochana's *mangalsutra*, a pair of small gold earrings, and some glass bangles were her total possessions in jewellery. Her wardrobe of six saris were of either synthetic or mill cotton fabric. A few clothes for the children and some vessels for Diwali were their acquisitions in the last year. They felt fortunate that they had access to electricity, drinking water, adequate ventilation, a toilet facility, and a hospital nearby. These were the advantages they thought they had acquired by shifting to a city.

As a traditional artisan, Yeshwant Pawar had learned his skills from his father and could not even remember when and how their work had originated. Their possessions in the village were limited to a house with four rooms and a buffalo. A tiny cluster of thirty-five houses provided few customers, so ten years ago, in 1986, Yeshwant and his family moved into rented dwellings in Bondre Nagar, where a few relatives had moved earlier. They had gradually been able to buy their present house which consisted of two rooms, of which one was a workplace where everyone sat around against the wall, cutting, shaping, pasting and embossing leather pieces to produce casual footwear.

Yeshwant works from 7.30 am until 8 pm every day. His wife manages to contribute time from 11 am to 4 pm, after attending to the daily chores of cooking, washing clothes and dishes, and attending to the children after school. The children play for half an hour and, having completed their school homework, put in an hour or two every evening helping their parents with shoemaking. With their combined efforts, they are able to produce about 125 pairs of shoes every month which brings them an earning of Rs 1,500 to Rs 2,000 per month during the Diwali season. However, during the rains when sales are low they earn only Rs 1000 in a month. With no other source of income, a maximum monthly earning of Rs 2000 for a five-member family results in Rs 400 per capita per month or Rs 13.50 per day, which is one-third the minimum wage for unskilled manual labour anywhere in the country.

Apart from being nearer to the market, they are also now much nearer to the local source of raw material. What used to take a full day and an expenditure of Rs 10 one way by bus, is now done in an hour, and free of cost on a bicycle. The Jawahar Nagar leather factories provide the cut remnants of buffalo hide while the shops in Subhas Nagar supply fine goat leather suitable for the plaited strips placed across the upper portions of the slipper. The *zari* or metallic gold thread, small red floss-silk pompoms, nails, polish, brushes, glue and other such decorations and necessities were available in Kolhapur city, all a cycle ride away. The only raw material they still brought from the village was the fine-grained black soil taken from the rice fields. The two portions of the leather soles are temporarily stuck together with this clay until the edges are handstitched. Factory glue is used only for sticking rubber soles.

Although they are not registered as a unit with the District Industries Centre nor with the Khadi and Village Industries Commission (KVIC), they were able to obtain a loan of Rs 5000 from the KVIC to buy raw material to prepare a stock of lowers during the monsoon season. The uppers are made later. By storing this produce during the lean season, when they would have been paid only Rs 20-30 a pair instead of Rs 50 at Dussehra-Diwali, they were able to repay KVIC a few hundred rupees every month. They still had some amount to repay but as soon as the due is paid off, Yeshwant intends to take another loan to allow him to tide over another monsoon period.

City living does not, however, assist them in overcoming their single most troublesome problem – the shortage and high cost of leather which affects almost all aspects of production, and thereby their earnings too. Trying to overcome or adjust to the irregular supply of raw material takes up most of their time and mental energies.

The cost and availability of leather needed by the Kolhapuri chappal worker is described by Yeshwant Pawar simply and lucidly. "*Madras paita,* which we need for uppers, used to be Rs 14 per kg two years ago; due to shortage of this material in Madras it is now Rs 35 per kg. If the leather is a little fresh the price increases by Rs 2 per kg. We are hardly left with any profit margin. If we had Rs 50,000 we could go to Madras ourselves. Now, if we take a loan of Rs 5000 we can go to Miraj where the leather from Madras comes. This way we get it two rupees cheaper, so that if we buy 50 kg we save Rs 100. The trouble with taking a loan is that we are required to insure the purchased goods. This implies presenting the original bill of purchase at the octroi post, where we then have to pay the stipulated rates according to a percentage of the bill. This can wipe away the small saving.

"There are other problems also. You see, we can use buffalo, cow, or goat leather depending on how it has been treated. For instance, a high quality piece called *chauhani* or *paper kapshi* is so fine and light it weighs only 100 gms and can be folded and put into your pocket. It is best suited for walking on carpets but we hardly get leather of the required quality to produce this prized item. Tanners aren't getting thick leather easily. Prices have gone up from Rs 35 to Rs 72 per kg because stocks are being diverted to make bags, boots, purses and jackets."

Yeshwant was particularly upset about the fact that leather from Maharashtra is sent to Calcutta and Madras at better rates to make quality goods. He felt that there should be a provision whereby 50 to 70 per cent of Maharashtra's leather should be reserved for local use. He said that they had been making this demand for the past ten years without any success. "During the time of Sharad Pawar's chief ministership, 85 per cent of the state's leather was sent out. Because of all this we only get cut-pieces from Madras now. A whole piece would cost Rs 200 per kg which we cannot even dream of. We are thus compelled to use inferior quality leather which spoils the appearance of the end product. If we could get Maharashtra leather we would get better quality products. Our work would definitely improve."

Talk of inferior quality raw material led to a discussion on the problem of duplication – imitation Kolhapuris had mushroomed in Karnataka, Sholapur, Madbai, Miraj, and in the vast slums of Mumbai. "People put cardboard between inferior quality top and bottom soles, they use nails instead of handstitching, copy the style and sell it as Kolhapuri. Consequently our reputation is tarnished. If the "duplicate" makers can be controlled then the old fame of the Kolhapuri chappal can be restored."

Most of the shoemakers have not been actively pursuing solutions to their problems. Yeshwant described his own efforts: "We tried to get a raw material depot and common facility centre established. We collected Rs 10,000 and prepared a project report with quotations. We formed a society in order to avail of such facilities but it did not last. We called craftsmen from all around. We approached the LIDCOM and Mahatma Phule Maheswariji Vikas Mandal, and also asked KVIC to provide us raw material on payment and to find a market for our products. However, in spite of all these efforts, we got no response from anywhere. In another effort, we submitted a project proposal for Rs 60 lakh to the state industries department, to use leather residue to make taxi seat covers. We even paid the five per cent bribe described as a "commission" but they made us run around for one year before they finally funded another project.

"If only the government would purchase the leather and supply us with stocks regularly we would feel secure and be able to concentrate better on developing our skills.

"We also feel insecure about forming another society or a common facility centre because each family has different needs and expenses. There is no money to form a society again or to buy common machines. We cannot afford to spend time experimenting with these newfangled ideas, when we have to make twenty pairs of shoes in eight days. We cannot do much for our own development."

Investments on instruments were minimal. Each cobbler had around Rs 5000 worth of instruments like *asth, rapi, ladi,* scissors, ten kinds of awls, pincers, pliers, a stone base, brushes, polish, a compass, embossing nails, and a die machine to emboss decorative grooves along the rim of the slipper. A machine to stitch the uppers (good Kolhapuri chappals have handstitched lowers) meant an investment of another Rs 5000.

Monthly overheads on work could sometimes be as high as Rs 200 for polish, repairing awls, sharpening knives at the blacksmith's shop, and goat fat to rub on the tools to lubricate them before use. Except for the die machine which they acquired recently, all the equipment was twenty years old.

The die machine had made the edging work much easier, particularly for the rubber-soled variety which Yeshwant had begun to produce only ten years ago. As a die machine to make soles costs Rs 25,000, he considered it to be well out of reach. While he was eager to acquire significantly better technology, he dismissed the thought with a brief shrug since he could not afford it.

The discussion on training similarly ended in a few moments. No, he had not undergone any formal training. He would like to, but not unless he was given a stipend during that period as he would lose his earnings. No, he had never received any information from government agencies about any training programmes.

Surprisingly, while the traditional Kolhapuri chappal has its unique style and chappal makers produce simple variants of these, there are a large number of design variations that have been introduced through suggestions offered by customers and shopkeepers. Thongs or plaited strips forming the upper portion of beach sandals, heeled sandals and rubber soles have all been assimilated into the generic style of Kolhapuri footwear. Colours could be light or dark, natural tan, or polished versions that could make the slippers rust-pink, mustard yellow or dark chocolate brown. Yeshwant knew of no design workshop ever having been organized by any agency, or the community ever having been provided scientific technical inputs. He asserted that design inputs should be connected to an assurance of orders and a regular market.

While on the subject of design, an amazing and almost unbelievable fact was brought to light by Yeshwant. "Since we get no large orders demanding standardization we are not bound to fix sizes. Each shoemaker has his own sizes and the shopkeeper knows the relevant Kolhapuri size by looking at the customer's foot." A Kolhapuri size 2 could be a Bata size 7. This difference in sizing creates confusion for any customer who wants to buy a pair for someone who is not present and makes bulk buying of specific sizes almost impossible. According to Yeshwant, there is no institution which could help them to standardize sizes.

We took this very important issue to a larger group of shoemakers who had assembled to discuss problems common or specific to self-employed units as well as proprietor-owned workshed units. The discipline of standardization was not required when traditional footwear was custom made. While traditional skills and styles continued, factors related to production and marketing had not kept pace with market needs. Artisans said it was the fault of the shopkeepers. Someone in the group said that an order for 22,000 pairs of shoes had come once from Italy and had been successfully executed. All kind of demands had been met. They used this example to demonstrate that if the customers are specific about their demands then they can produce accordingly. The main problem, according to almost all of those who were present, was the fluctuating costs of raw material. This factor prevented them from being able to quote a firm rate for an order as big as 50,000 shoes to be supplied in three months, unless they were paid at least 50 per cent of the money in advance so that they could buy all the leather at one time. Even in local markets the price paid to them for the shoe remains the same for as long as two years while the price of leather can fluctuate every eight or ten days.

It seemed simple enough to suggest that they could immediately organize themselves to make shoes in standard national and international sizes. A large number of cut-out sole sizes could be made in cardboard, tin or stiff plastic or charts with outlines of sizes provided and widely distributed. The entire group saw the logic and benefit of this step and agreed to start preparations right away. It appeared rather strange that this hadn't been suggested or attempted by the artisans before. If it had, it only demonstrates that even basic technological information and knowhow is difficult to disseminate in a cottage industry, and if it had not, then it shows how such simple needs have never been addressed by any institution set up to develop leather footwear among traditional artisans.

Yeshwant requires storage space only during the rainy season, when he manages to stock the lowers till the festival season which fetches him a better price. Otherwise, production and delivery at shops are almost simultaneous. Also, since he cannot afford to buy leather in bulk and stock it, there is no storage problem. "To stock the raw material one needs finance, but a loan at 4 per cent interest requires a bribe of at least 5 per cent to get it. Even to get subsidies from the government, a part has to be given as a bribe," explains Yeshwant, while everyone around nods in support of his statement. Corruption is viewed as an established government norm.

Typical of most small self-employed artisans, Yeshwant's system of fixing a price for his product is based on the premise that "*karigaron ke liye mazdoori munafa hai*" (for craftsmen, their labour is their profit). For the leather slippers made at his home it is the number of finished products that matters, rather than the hours spent or the number of people who work on it. Consequently, the actual cost of materials plus an average wage of Rs 15 per pair is the price at which he sells his shoes. "There is no value attached to our work. The shopkeeper tells us that he has spent five lakh rupees on his shop and asks me, 'What have you spent other than your labour?' The cost of a pair of shoes is eventually determined by the shopkeeper or trader. There is no point in our determining it, as it won't sell at that price. Since the state government hasn't taken any step to waive octroi, if the cost of making a pair is Rs 40 and the shopkeeper gives us Rs 45 or Rs 50, all our profit, transport, etc., must be included in that." Yeshwant offered further insight into their marketing problems: "All shopkeepers raise rates simultaneously, they also pay us at the same time. The shopkeepers have a control over rates and work like cartels. But the same does not work for us who make the shoes."

These are the obstacles in getting a fair price. In the group discussion, it emerged that those who manufacture under workshop conditions find that the self-employed artisan sells his products cheaper than the shopkeeper, especially if he happens to have some land or alternate form of assets. The members of the group felt that "sellers of our *samaj* are out to cut us. All the shops in town have to serve all of us in Kolhapur as well as those who manufacture in the villages.

"KVIC only orders 30-40 pairs a month. That is not enough to keep us going. Where do they buy their Kolhapuri chappals from, if not from Kolhapur?"

Yeshwant and others receive payments in cash on the spot, or weekly, or in portions spreading over a few days. Occasionally, he manages to secure a regular order but for this he has to spend time going from shop to shop.

As he sat working on the leather in front of him, looking around at his wife and friends while answering questions, he summed up their situation: "We all work hard but we don't get any value for it in the shops. They keep finding fault with our products by saying the size is not proper and making various other criticisms aimed at humiliating us. That's how a person's spirit is broken."

Yeshwant had an opportunity to search for markets outside Kolhapur when he became a member of the Dastkari Haat Samiti, a marketing society. It cost him Rs 250 to become a member and another Rs 60 as annual membership fee. The Samiti has 570 members from all over the country, and includes co-operative societies and associations. About four times a year it organizes exhibition-sales called Dastkari Haat (crafts market) in different cities, with a grant of Rs 1 lakh from the Development Commissioner, Handicrafts, of the Ministry of Textiles, Government of India. These bazaars provide an opportunity to propagate handmade crafts and textiles. They also educate crafts-persons about consumer preferences and the sales potential in different parts of the country to enable them to get better prices for their products. Yeshwant had gone to sell at Dilli Haat, a crafts marketplace, and a fair at the Pragati Maidan exhibition grounds in Delhi, and at Dastkari Haats in Baroda and Hyderabad, and he had recently returned from a successful sale at Goa. He found it difficult to pay travel costs but conceded that taking travel subsidies from government was not the answer as only a limited few would eventually benefit, and it falsely depressed the selling price of their product. However, he pointed out that if there was privatization "everything would become more expensive for us. If we add all this to the cost of the shoe and charge Rs 400 per pair who will buy them?" Shoes in Bombay shops were selling from Rs 600 to Rs 2000 but he did not know how to catch up to get into that market. All he could say was that a levy rate and a raw material depot at Kolhapur, or assured marketing avenues were desperately required before any change could be brought in his life.

Until that time, he and his family continue to rise at 6.00 am and work till 8.00 am, when they break for a cup of tea. Before the children leave for school they have a meal of *bhakri*, rice, vegetables and *dal* at 10 am Another cup of tea at 1 pm and dinner at 8 pm consisting of the same items as lunch, but freshly cooked, completes their food for the day. Depending on their earnings, they cook mutton twice a week or once a fortnight. He said that 70 per cent of the Chamars drank alcohol

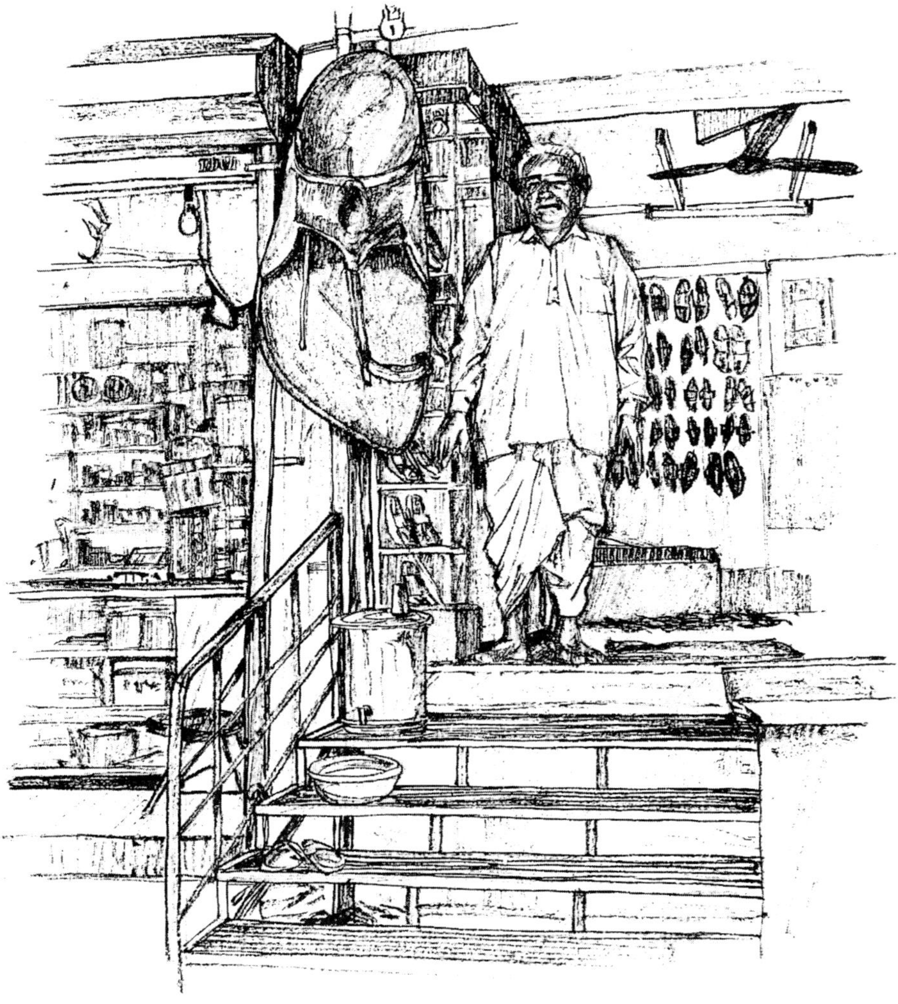

when they cooked non-vegetarian food. This was seen as a form of escapism, "because they did not hold much hope for the future." "My entire family does not drink alcohol, nor do I have *beedi* or *paan.* A visit to the cinema maybe just once in a year. We work for twelve months of the year, except for two days during our main festivals, Naag Panchami and Vishvakarma Puja at Dussehra. Ganapati is our main deity. We shoemakers do not go anywhere for entertainment.

"At festival time it costs Rs 150 to buy new clothes for each child. We often have to pawn or sell something. Just yesterday, we released Sulochana's earrings from the money lender."

For the Kolhapuri chappal maker, life is simple and stark. The close relationship between members of the family provides emotional sustenance in a world where survival means having to run in order to stay in the same place.

"Sometimes sorrow and sometimes joy – life goes on like that. Still, we are happy. At least we are better off than those who live on the footpath," says Yeshwant with a brave smile.

The potter of Panchmura, in Bankura district of West Bengal, presents a case of a traditional craft skill being practised in a distant rural setting by a backward caste community. The potter family lives in a joint family system and owns some land. It is a household activity in which menfolk perform the actual moulding work while women assist in the supplementary activities of collecting clay and painting the moulded object. Recognized by the government for their skill, they have undergone some government-organized marketing programmes. However, in spite of this, they have no regular support from government or voluntary organizations. Given the nature of their products, exports are also non-existent. They balance their products between traditional festive needs and the awakening urban interest in and demand for, decorative terracotta crafts.

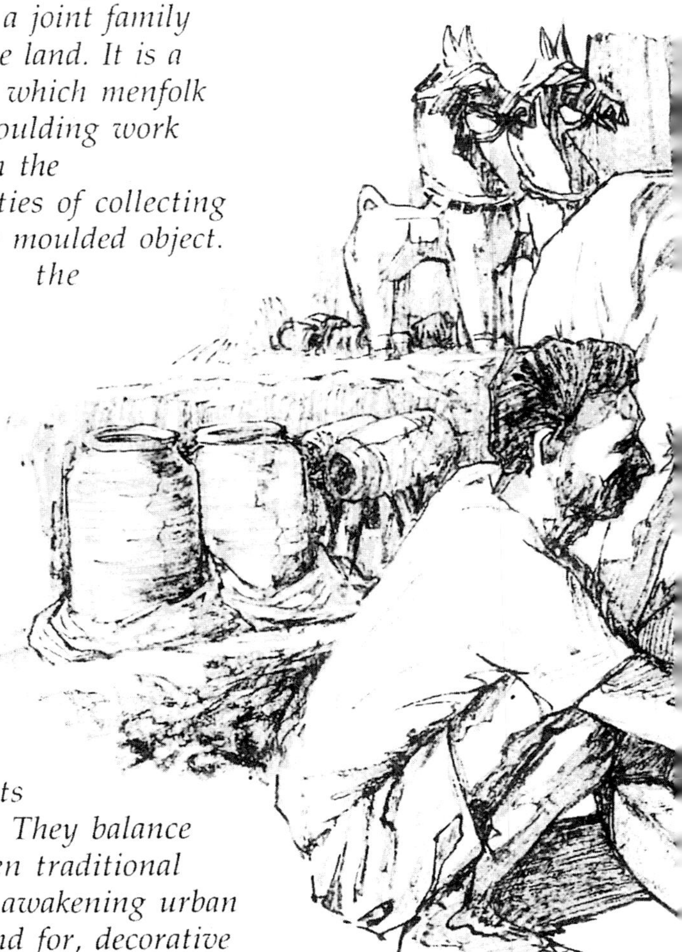

CHAPTER FOUR

The Potters of Panchmura

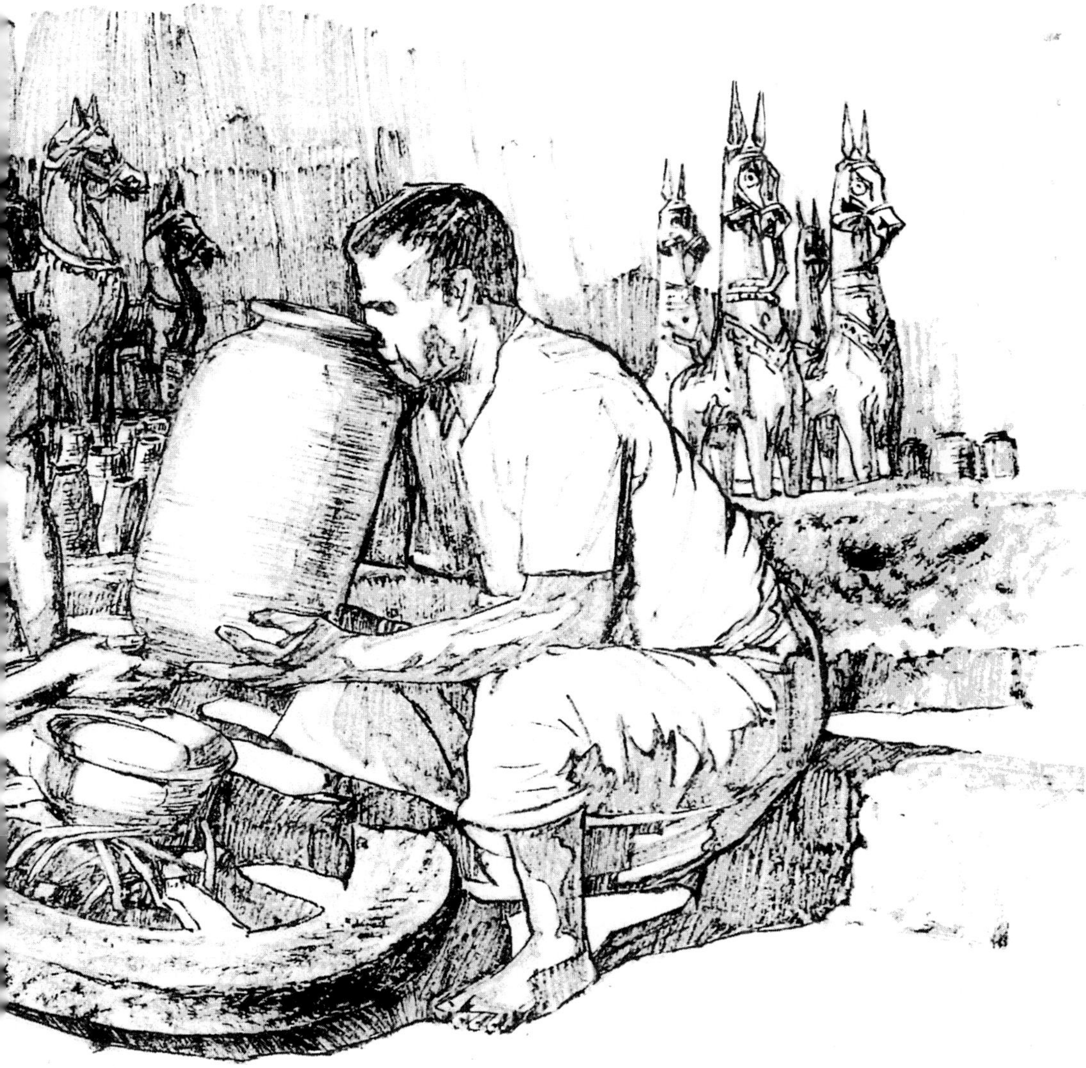

The Kumbhakars or potters of Panchmura village near Vishnupur in Bankura district of West Bengal are tucked away from the world, practically out of sight. Reaching them takes a three-hour train journey from Calcutta to Durgapur, a five-hour bus ride to Vishnupur, and then one and a half hours by taxi on a bumpy road through paddy fields and sleepy villages. There is no milestone to herald one's arrival at Panchmura. The village community consists largely of families who earn their livelihood through the family tradition of making clay horses and elephants, with a combination of wheel-thrown and hand-modelled terracotta techniques.

Pasupati Kumbhakar is a bespectacled, fast-aging 63-year-old, slow-paced though mentally-alert. Parni, 45 years old, has been his wife and life companion for thirty-two years. Of his three sons, the eldest, Baul Das, 30, is married to Lobita, 20, and has two children, Suman Kumar, a three-year-old boy, and Shravani, a girl aged one. Of his other two sons, Chandidas has not passed his matric and is unmarried at 26, while Gurudas, the youngest at 20 is a bright student. He obtained a first division at school and is presently in the first year of his bachelor's degree in economics. He has also received training as a primary school teacher and desires to make teaching his career.

Conversations with Pasupati Kumbhakar's son, Baul Das and nephew Buddhadev Kumbhakar were spread over many hours. They took place sometimes out in the open or in the verandah amidst his tools and stacks of terracotta horses, and sometimes in the small "furnished" room inside his home, while the rest of the family was busy elsewhere. While the prepared questionnaire served as a springboard for discussion, the conversation traversed many side-lanes. Personal stories and reminiscences of ironical twists of fate gave an insight into their lives. Most of the craftsmen are self-employed, and thus regard any time spent on talking to visitors and posing for photographs or conducting a visiting film unit around the village (as was the case that day) as valuable time taken away from work. Yet, in a civilized and dignified manner common to all rural people, they were very accommodating, not putting professional earnings ahead of human communication and hospitality. They readily listened, reflected, and responded to a varied range of questions with wisdom and equanimity.

Ever since they can recall, the Kumbhakars have lived in Panchmura village, situated in Taldangara Block of Bankura District. The exquisite 15th century terracotta temples of Vishnupur are barely 60 kilometers away but the potters were unable to say with any certainty whether it was their own ancestors who had made the moulded terracotta tiles which decorate these temples. While they make replicas of some of the tiles, apart from cooking vessels, ornamental horses, elephants, and the elaborate *Mansa Jhad* – a decorative ritual item – they seem unaware of their physical proximity to the wondrous temples which belong to an eclectic architecture of earlier times. The booklet published by the Archaeological Survey of India on the temples makes no mention of the living traditions of terracotta at Panchmura village. The potters know of no other place of origin, and have professed pottery as their main source of income ever since they can remember.

The craft activity in Panchmura is purely family-based. A few years ago, some of the Kumbhakars including Baul Das had attempted to create a co-operative society, but they had to suspend their efforts because of a limited understanding of the role and functions of a co-operative society. They were unable to resolve issues such as problems arising out of a lack of uniformity in the quality of work done by the members. Mistrust amongst those who were unsatisfied with the sale of such products was also responsible for the initiative being aborted. Today, although they are registered with the Cottage and Small-scale Industries Department of West Bengal, they derive no consequent benefits. The rather fatalistic reason for continuing with their work is that it was a family tradition. They had simply grown up helping their father. Having received no specialized education they have no scope to find other jobs. Even if the demand for their products was negligible they had no alternative options since the skills acquired through the family were the only one with which they were equipped.

Pasupati Kumbhakar's family lives in the state of West Bengal which has implemented land reforms, and it is relatively better off compared to those of artisans in other states who possess no land at all. The family owns five *bigha*s of land on which they usually cultivate rice. If two crops are harvested annually, it covers the family's needs, but in years of low rainfall or other vagaries of weather they have to buy rice to feed themselves for three months. They also plant wheat on their land, but not necessarily every year.

Drinking water? "There are three or four tube-wells in the village provided by the *panchayat*, but the one nearest to us has the sweetest water, so there is always a long queue" said Baul Das. The tone of his voice implied a felt sense of magnanimity in allowing others to use the well. They have a primary health centre at the block headquarters and a government hospital two kilometers away which they found satisfactory for treating minor illnesses.

They also talked about their personal expenses and lifestyle. "We have *muri* (puffed rice) and tea between 6 and 7 am; *muri* again with chopped onions and some rice left over from the previous day at 11 am Between 2 and 3 pm we have rice, *dal* and vegetables, and occasionally some fish, and the same *dal* and vegetables at 9 pm, with *roti* instead of rice. We do not make tea in the evenings and buy fruit only occasionally for the children or if someone in the family is sick because it is expensive and we do not really feel the need for it.

"School expenses are not much till the 5th class, because there are no fees and the textbooks are given free of cost. Even though there are no fees up to the 12th class, books have to be bought. In the 6th class, books cost about Rs 500 a year. Beyond school the cost is much more."

What did they do for leisure and entertainment? "Well, a visit to the cinema not more than three times a year." They were amused at the question, but they spoke with animation about the Nabo Jagrato Yuva Sangha, a youth club of which they were members. They played carrom and card games and organized cultural programmes with songs and music. The club organizes its own Durga Puja procession and a programme for Saraswati Puja. They spend almost nothing on tobacco and alcohol. "In fact we are against drinking" said the gentle Baul Das. "About twenty per cent of the people of the village drink. When the liquor shop was set up, our club had objected, but what could we do, the government gave it the license. We put up a fight to prevent it but the local political parties helped them, so we had to give up our fight." Other family expenses include Rs 300 every six months for the meagre supply of electricity, and an average of Rs 200 a year on local transportation to deliver goods to the private shops in Vishnupur or to visit relatives if they were ill or on some special occasions.

The family's workshed and residential quarters stands on five *kattas* of land. The home consists of three rooms, a verandah, and a kitchen. Across the courtyard is a granary and prayer room made of mud with wooden beams. Baul Das could not recall when this old part of the house was built. The workshed, farther away, came up much later and was made of cement. This extra construction became necessary as the children grew up and Baul Das had his own family. One bed in the "office," goods stored in the thatched extension of the workshed, and workspace and storage in the 8' x 8' verandah is the most they could manage for both work and family needs. They also own two bullocks and three cows. The family buy utensils at times of need and jewellery only at the time of weddings. In terms of furniture, they own a bed, two chairs, one table, and three *charpoys* (string beds with wooden frames) which are also used for outdoor seating. These simple assets are not always permanent. They sleep on the floor. They possess no cupboards and hang their spare clothes on a string held up by two nails on the wall. The word "lifestyle" as it is used in modern urban parlance cannot be applied to this rudimentary and uninhibited way of life.

After the usual expenses on rations, cloth, packing materials, sweets, hardware and medicines, the savings made over the past five years had enabled them to set up a small *gobar* gas bio-digestor to provide fuel for their kitchen. This is their most prized possession. The womenfolk look after domestic chores and help in taking the articles out of the kiln for drying. They also apply the yellow and black coating on the terracotta figures before baking.

Some land had been sold for one daughter's wedding and again, more recently, to cope with a family member's medical expenses.

Financial transactions are minimal. The loan of Rs 3,800 taken from the Khadi and Village Industries Board to make a shed for the kiln and buy a potter's wheel with ballbearings was returned "timely." Baul chose to use an English word. Transactions with the outside world seemed to have compelled them to adopt the words of a foreign language, although they conducted the rest of the conversation in a mixture of Bengali and Hindi.

When the co-operative society in Panchmura was still attempting to function, they had obtained a grant and a loan from the Khadi Board to buy land approximately two kilometers away from their village. They transported the clay from a pit dug in this land. The pit had grown very large and a lot of mud had been used up, leaving them with no suitable raw material nearby. They had brought the problem to the notice of the District Industries Centre, which had offered to provide funds if they could locate suitable land. They view this predicament as serious and believe that this problem will only increase in the future.

A problem faced by almost all potters in the country is increasing non-availability of suitable clay.

Potters normally accumulate clay in their houses once a year, when there are no rains and the fields are dry; otherwise, they bring it from around their rice fields. Depending on the need and the storage space available, the family transports about ten to fifteen bullock carts of mud to their house. "We have to stock the clay, and work and live in the same place" smiled Baul Das. All the work of digging up the mud, transporting it to their workplace, and re-filling the deep pits created in the fields is executed by them. One load of clay by bullock cart costs Rs 25. However, nowadays, a three-wheeler cycle cart costs Rs 30 per trip, although it transports a slightly lesser quantity (two and a half to three quintals). They also need another kind of mud to coat the terracotta objects, one in yellow, another in black, before baking them in the kiln. The land from which they used to obtain this mud has now been converted into a fish breeding tank by its owner. As a result, they have to fetch mud of inferior quality from a distance which engages them the entire day.

The collection of fuel to fire the kiln is also a major problem faced by the potters. In earlier times, a *sal* forest located nearby provided the leaves they used as fuel. The leaves fall only in springtime, and, although they give a nice colour to the product, the intensity of heat is not very strong. The forest officer used to give them permits to carry away the leaves on a "per cart" basis. "We ourselves cut down the firewood in the forest, and are now faced with a problem!" Buddhadev Kumbhakar admits, laughing. For the present, private and government eucalyptus plantations provide an alternative. The dry leaves of these trees fall throughout the year, the trees grow quicker, and the burning of their leaves generates more heat but also more smoke. Unfortunately, the colour of the baked terracotta is no longer as bright, and they have to engage in the task of collecting leaves throughout the year. They now obtain the leaves at no cost, and this has reduced their expenses to some extent.

The famous "Bankura horse" which they make, with its long neck and upright ears, has been the symbol of the Central Cottage Industries Emporium (a Government of India enterprise to market handicrafts nation-wide) since the inception of the organization. The ears and tail are detachable to facilitate packing. The body is composed of two tubular parts made on the wheel, and the decorations are added on by hand. Until 1988, the Bankura horse was unembellished. The change to decorative trappings was a milestone in itself. While the horses are preferred by customers in a rust-red terracotta shade, elephants are generally made in black. Sizes of the artefacts range from 6 inches to 3 feet. They vary the sizes according to the size of the kiln. Since they have twenty days between each firing they cannot spend too long a time in making enormous figures. Whatever production is possible during this period is sent to the kiln for firing.

However, their entire range of products, at present, indicates that any extraneous design input has been negligible. The same traditional form of the horse, elephant, once popular as votive objects, and vessel or moulded tiles continue with only very minor variations. They have received no new designs from any institutional source. The design range is provided largely by customers' suggestions and their own new ideas. Baul Das has a practical explanation for their minimal range of products. "We cannot risk making something new in case it doesn't sell" he says with quiet finality. Both Baul Das and Buddhadev expressed the need for access to and interaction with designers who could help them to create more utilitarian products rather than just decorative or ceremonial ones.

The provision of electricity is sometimes more important to artisans than any other type of infrastructural support. A simple electrical connection doubles, if not trebles their output. A major technological innovation that has increased production, eased drudgery, and augmented their earnings has been the advent of the ballbearing wheel system which was adopted in 1975. They expressed a strong desire to acquire an electric wheel but electricity had been provided in their village only in 1995. Persistently low voltage and long hours of load shedding made the purchase of the electric wheel which could remove the burden of hand operation unviable. They described at length the saga of getting electricity connections to their homes. "The department put up three or four poles in the marketplace" said Baul Das animatedly "and when we asked for connections to our homes they told us we had to arrange for the wire and poles ourselves." So, the village panchayat contributed Rs 30,000, and with each homestead contributing Rs 400 to Rs 500 they were able to collect another Rs 24,000 and thus were able to bring the feeble and often dysfunctional electric line to their homes. The low voltage could not make anything work other than the fan and the bulb. During the entire period of our discussions we sat either in the heat of the day or in the darkness of evening.

Against such a background, they admitted that they had not even tried to acquire any new technology through the District Industries Centre or the Khadi Board. They were, however, able to enumerate the areas in which they needed better technology. "We would like a better system to process the mud. We presently mix the mud and sand with our feet. If there was some machine to mix the two more smoothly it would be good for us". The problem in the acquisition of any new technology was the inadequate markets for their finished products. "If our market is not adequate now, how can we afford to spend money on searching for new technology and investing in it unless we can be certain of better sales?" It seemed like a chicken and egg situation in which no agency has intervened as yet to break the deadlock.

The potters are not willing to take the risk of investing any further either in acquiring new technology or in training. Buddhadev Kumbhakar had been trained at the Khadi Board in glazing techniques but because these techniques needed investment in a separate kiln, more fuel, glaze grinding machines, etc., they could not afford them. Even if they took a loan, they were unsure whether they would be able to sell enough to repay it. The present circumstances of their production and marketing do not instill in them the confidence to take such a risk.

They incur losses both when the weather turns wet and while the kiln is being fired. If the raw pot is uneven they can always demolish it and re-use the clay, but if there is breakage after the article has been fired they can now repair it with Fevicol, a popular brand of adhesive. "This is a very good new thing for us" said Baul Das, happy with the advantage he had obtained from this product.

We entered into a long discussion about the nature of training programmes they had undergone. They felt that the techniques they had learnt or the information they had gathered through these programmes were isolated from their area of expertise. The training programmes thus lost their relevance and effectiveness. None of the agencies followed up the training programmes by assisting them in marketing the new products they had learnt to make from the training courses. The task of raising institutional credit to equip themselves with new infrastructure necessitated by the training was also left unaddressed. For instance, even if they learned glazing techniques, the new raw materials and higher fuel heat required were unaffordable. The products designed during training did not take into consideration the fact that this would serve only a specific set of consumers. The trainee was thus psychologically unrelated to the user of the end-product. There was no supplementary guidance offered on how to cost the new product or promote its sales. At the end of the training they were not even remotely aware of any of the new concepts in marketing management that are taught in management institutions.

"We do no *hisab* – no costing and pricing exercises," said Baul Das and Buddhadev in unison, smiling at the onerous and almost impossible effort this would entail. "Whatever we earn gets spent. We do not even accurately cost our own products." Pressed to describe roughly how they balanced their budget, they embarked upon a convoluted calculation. "Look, if Baul had a job, he could earn three thousand rupees; but if we price our clay horses in order to ensure this kind of an income every month our horses would not sell. If we had government jobs, our salaries would cover Sundays and other holidays, or give us leave benefits and an opportunity to visit our relatives. But in our kind of life we have to cover all these costs. Actually, we work for eight months in the year, and rest only at the end of *chet* (Chaitra month of the Bengali calendar year, i.e., mid-March to mid-April), when we put a *shivalinga* on the wheel for one month. We do not work during April. We pray on the first, third, fifth and ninth day of the month, starting on the first Saturday. This is our tradition. Then there are the twelve days of Durga Puja/Dussehra, when we do not work. Kali puja takes three days and then there is Mansa Puja. The wheel cannot turn on these days. There is also the rainy season, when work slows down, although it does not stop. Goods have to be stored inside the house during the rains, and since we have limited space we have to reduce our production. Also, fewer people come to buy our terracotta during the rains."

The method of arriving at a selling price for their

products was simple, almost primitive, but based on the realities of their condition which was directly related to the situation of their markets. Market price, input cost, production cost, were all reduced to the simple formula of a day's required income. They calculated Rs 50 per day as a day's required income, not accounting for the helper's earnings but simply according to the time spent in making the object. "If we increase the price of the product according to the rise of prices of other goods in the bazaar we would never sell our goods" Baul explains good-naturedly. If they use a cycle van for transportation to Vishnupur, it costs Rs 110 per journey. This is paid by the retailer. All the packaging material is collected after delivering the terracotta wares, and brought back home to be re-used. There are hardly any packaging costs, as a lot of recycling takes place. A 12" horse and a 10" elephant are sold at Rs 20 each locally. "We know that we could get Rs 40 for it in Delhi, but we cannot ever dream of getting this amount here because a local customer would never pay that much."

With depressed costing and restrained production, was it worthwhile pursuing this livelihood?

"Our experiences so far have shown us that there is no option" they both replied, and described attempts by Baul Das to find a job at the Durgapur Steel Plant. He had applied for the post of a cashier in the clerical section and gone for the interview. He had no idea why he did not get the job, whether it was because he lacked the qualifications or the personality, or whether it was due to the Rs 80,000 that he had heard was the sum paid as a bribe by the person who eventually got the job. As far as he was concerned, the episode had dampened his enthusiasm to pursue similar endeavours. He had also gone for an interview to the Khadi and Village Industries office for the job of storekeeper but read in the newspapers some days later that there was an injunction against filling this vacancy. "There must have been some underhand dealings, that's why someone went to court" surmized Baul Das. The use of the English word "injunction" again placed him in the alien world where such situations occur.

As we spoke, the light drizzle had turned into a heavy shower. The electricity had been off since morning. Darkness enveloped the courtyard and us. We moved into the verandah amidst the clay horses and elephants, and a large blue plastic sheet was spread over a part of the verandah and steps to prevent the rainwater from splashing in.

It was on the subject of marketing of their products and its related activities that both Baul Das and Buddhadev became most animated.

What was the most frequent source of their financial problems?

"Marketing," in English again, was the loud and unanimous answer.

What were their fears concerning loans and mortgages?

Their inability to pay back, if the market for their wares was not adequate.

A major problem was the lack of easy physical access to the market at large. They frankly admitted that they lacked confidence during this process, because a train journey to the capital city of Calcutta was a saga of harassment by the railway officials and police. Customers who visited them and bought their goods in bulk did not wish to carry their purchases. Both private shopkeepers and individual buyers expected the potters to deliver the goods to them.

When packed, two terracotta horses, 3 feet in height, make fairly large packets which instantly arouse the suspicion of authorities at Howrah station. "Why such big packages? Open them and show us what's inside" they were ordered once. Having arduously packed the horses in straw, old newspaper, old corrugated board, plastic, string, and sturdy cardboard cartons, they feel most disheartened when they have to unpack them in the middle of a journey.

"It is at times like this that we feel we should give up our work with Mother Earth" says Baul Das.

The fleeting moment of sadness gave way to concrete and sensible suggestions for the transportation of their goods and for ways to overcome breakage during transportation. Since they faced obstacles from government agencies while carrying goods for personal delivery, they wanted government organizations who made purchases from them to send a person to accompany them.

"We would pack, travel and deliver the goods wherever they want, but at least a government representative needs to be with us to tackle the harassment en route."

While government agencies invite them from time to time to take part in "exhibition-sales" at craft festivals and bazaars in the cosmopolitan cities of the country, the authorities give no thought to packaging, cartage, and the problems of travel with fragile goods with obstructive and corrupt officialdom along the way.

Their other suggestion was that they should be allowed to carry clay and their wheel to the venue of the exhibition and be permitted to sell what they produce. This idea was rejected during the course of the discussion as unviable because they would still need a kiln, fuel and extra hands, not to mention a sufficient quantity of goods each time to fill the kiln for making the quantity economically feasible. They fell into deep thought wondering who could help them to surmount these problems.

For the present, most of their goods are taken only as far as Vishnupur and Bankura because these are tourist spots. Orders emanate from the fifteen little shops located in the crafts complex near the Vishnupur Tourist Lodge. During a good season, they are paid the full amount in cash on delivery but at other times they receive about 80 per cent of the money, and the rest later. There is no attempt to even address the issue of interest that would accrue on goods lying at any place prior to sale.

They have some marketing links with Manjusha, the West Bengal State Handicrafts sales outlet, and the Central Cottage Industries Emporium, both of which have branches nationwide. The potters expressed great regret that their goods were not supplied to branches other than those in Calcutta. Their sales to these organizations amounted to not more than Rs 2000 a year, covering not more than two or three consignments.

Production and demand need to be co-ordinated. In the case of the Vishnupur potters, production has to be restricted in the absence of demand or a better market reach. Buddhadev confidently assessed that if the entire village worked arduously, they could jointly produce five hundred small and medium terracotta pieces per day. Again, the wry laugh: "but how will we sell them all, if we made so many?"

Some sales were made locally to those who needed items for *puja*. Contractors and interior decorators arrived occasionally to give special orders for wall plaques, moulded tiles, or garden decor. On the subject of exporting their products, they had obviously come to the conclusion, after considerable experience, that it was not possible. "Not that our items are not in demand" Buddhadev explained, "but demand is never linked to the supply of the requisite quantity with uniform quality. Exporters come and say they want thousands of pieces in fifteen days. Samples are taken and approved. They feel that, since there are so many potters, we can produce large quantities very quickly. They do not realize that all artisans do not maintain the same quality and standard and therefore the end product will not match the approved sample." Baul Das described this failure of being able to respond adequately to export possibilities as lack of "business matching," using English words again.

The biggest order they had executed was in the year 1995-96, which involved a month and a half's work and brought them an earning of about Rs 3,000 per month. It was not really such a large order if one noted that the goods took as much as fifteen days to dry. The only regular orders come from Vishnupur shops, which are not more than roadside kiosks in size and style.

Did they ever use their own products? "The extent has reduced with the advent of steel and aluminium vessels but we still use our own water pitchers and grain storage vessels." Festivals such as Durga Puja and Makar Sankranti called for a new set of earthern vessels in their homes.

Thousands of craftspeople, especially potters, have never attended prestigious, highly publicized festivals and fairs organized by government agencies to market their goods. Pasupati Kumbhakar's family was fortunate that it was quite well known outside the village and was on the "circuit," because their names were on lists of government departments concerned with the development of handicrafts. They had attended the Apna Utsav festival in Bombay, the Surajkund Mela in Haryana once, the Crafts Museum's Skill Demonstration Programme at Pragati Maidan in New Delhi, and the SAARC festival in Chennai, courtesy of the Lalit Kala Akademi. They were also guests at a private sector programme in Baroda on an invitation from Hindustan Petrochemicals. At all these places, they had set up a stall and were paid an allowance for travel and a daily allowance commonly known as "TA/DA" without which many craftsmen do not dare to undertake long distance travel to participate in any marketing event. They explained that transporting their goods to these bazaars was extremely costly for them. A truckload of their wares costs as much as Rs 10,000 to transport.

Baul Das had even travelled abroad on government invitation, but while they were lauded for their skills and the continuance of the country's

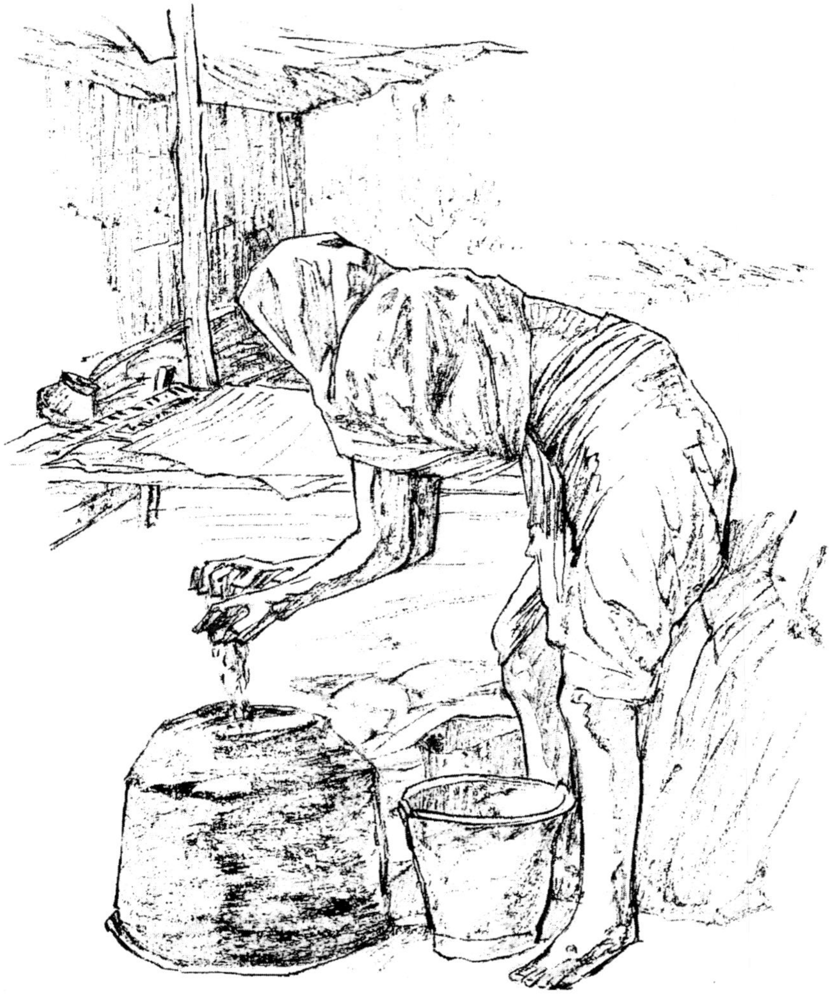

glorious heritage, financially and culturally their gain was minimal. At the Festival of India in Russia, they were paid in roubles and spent all the money there, returning empty-handed. In West Germany, they received 100 DM per day for 21 days. After paying for their food, they were able to save about Rs 5,000 which they brought back and used for house repairs in 1985. This was approximately the equivalent of two months earnings in India. They felt that such exposures had not taken them very far.

Pasupati Kumbhakar hardly works on the wheel anymore. Even with his spectacles he cannot see too well. He proudly held up a framed photograph of his father Rashbehari Kumbhakar receiving the

National Award for Master Craftspersons in terracotta in 1968-69 from Dr. Zakir Hussain, then the President of India. Baul Das is trying to follow in his grandfather's footsteps.

Last year he sent an item to Delhi to be considered for the award. It had to be approved by the local District Industries Centre, after which, if approved by the state of West Bengal, it was to be sent to Delhi. It was packed in the village and despatched by the potters while the transportation costs were borne by the government. The District Industries Centre later informed him that his work had broken on the way to Delhi. He had to bear the burden of this loss as the terracotta piece itself had not been paid for by the state government, nor had it been insured for breakage during travel. He accepted the situation calmly as a part of the vagaries of their lives and related the story without any feeling of regret. After some moments of silence, Baul Das philosophically answered a question he had not even been asked "Well, we will carry on as we are, but if our children want a future, they should do something else – business or service perhaps, because if there is no demand for what we produce, what can we do?"

The Karnataka sandalwood carver is based in the cosmopolitan city of Bangalore. He is recognized by state government institutions and holds a full time government job as a designer in the State Handicrafts Development and Marketing Organisation. In his leisure time, he carves sandalwood figures for private customers and a fixed proportion of his production is bought by the state government. The latter is calculated according to the strictly controlled quantity of sandalwood that is allocated to each artisan. The diversion of sandalwood for export has raised its price and reduced its availability to small producers. He works alone within a family unit and maintains links with his extended family in the village.

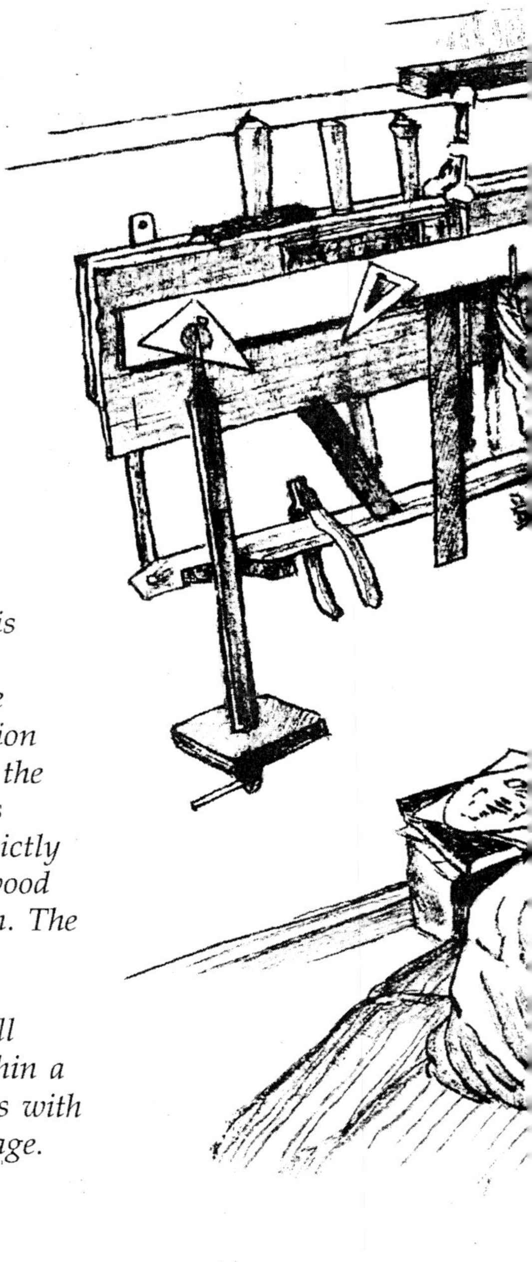

CHAPTER FIVE

The Sandalwood Carver of Bangalore

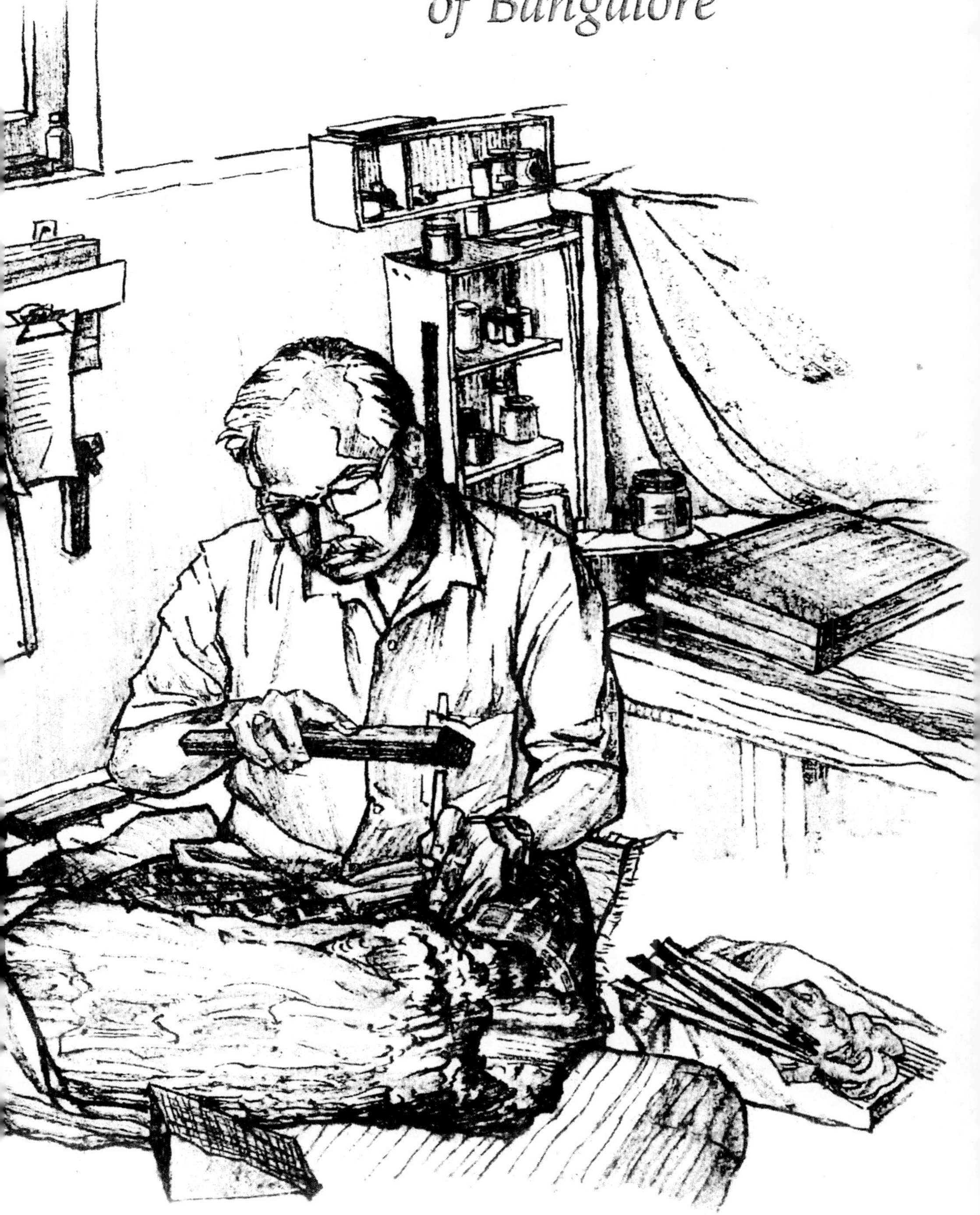

Nagaraj, S.G., June 9, 1947, Sorab, Shimoga District, Karnataka, DIP in DRG and PTG. Cultivated the family avocation of wood carving and sculpting."

The opening sentence is part of the bio-data of a highly skilled designer and sandalwood carver, design artist with the State Handicrafts Development Board, Karnataka, and winner of many awards. The impressive abbreviations simply meant "Diploma in Drawing and Painting."

With quiet pride, Nagaraj handed over two typed pages of his bio-data which he had dictated on his own, in English. Since very few craftspeople speak English, and as he wished to express his concern for the propagation of the traditional skills of his Gudigar community and to elucidate his educational and artistic qualifications, it would only be fair to reproduce his bio-data verbatim:

"I belong to a family of great artists who have dedicated their entire life to the noble cause of creating invaluable materials to enable us to imbibe and follow their food-stuffs (*sic*, read "foot-steps") in this field. The creations of these great artists can even now be seen in the Mysore Palace, Jaganmohini Palace, Bangalore Museum and Vidhana Soudha. Even in the recently established museum at Shimoga can be seen some of the creations of these artists. Some of the artistic creations made out of sandalwood, ivory & wood by these great artists of my family have certainly enhanced the image of our country, world over.

I have also been able to imbibe, to some extent, the great zeal and enthusiasm exhibited by my elders in this field. So, along with my education, I also developed an artistic bent. My elders, particularly my father and uncle attracted me whenever they were at work. I also sat with them and worked with them, thus assimilating knowledge of their work. Sri K.G. Shantappa, who has earned a name as an artist, became my tutor, some years later. I always had a desire to learn more and more. During the 12th year of my life, some of my artistic creations were displayed in the Dasara exhibition at Mysore.

In the year 1959, I had sent some of my works for Dasara exhibition at Mysore and I was awarded a silver medal and a commendation certificate.

I accompanied my father to Bangalore for the 5th All India Handicraft Week held from 20th December, 1959. We took this great opportunity to demonstrate our exhibits and were very highly appreciated. From then on we settled in Bangalore. We got more and more orders from Kaveri Arts and Crafts Emporium, Bangalore,

Chamarajendra Technical Institute, Mysore, Victoria Technical Institute, Madras, and CCI Emporium, Delhi. Now we are sending finished materials against orders from Delhi, Bombay, Ahmedabad & other places also.

We have received many prizes for our exhibits in the Mysore state Lalitha Kala Academy exhibition for the past two to three years. There was a radio programme on 14th July, 1971 in the Taruna Bharathi programme about my life dedicated to the propagation of traditional Arts and Crafts. Since, my regular education was discontinued due to several factors including my sudden leaving for Bangalore, I had to start my education afresh. I was admitted to Design Centre with a view to learn some more techniques. It is because of my young age that I was unable to get stipend. I worked there without any stipend for three years and learnt the work with special permission of the Director. Shri D. Dahiraj was the master craftsman and Shri C. Parameswara Acharya was the Assistant Craftsman at that time. Once again I returned to school after attending the course. The Director of the Design Centre, Sri Hariharan inspired me to take up the creative artistic work of my family.

When Sri Hariharan became the Director of CHDC, he gave me an opportunity for undergoing a training for one year and employed me there as a skilled worker. I later realized that regular education was more important and again made an attempt to gain admission in school and completed my S.S.L.C. (Secondary School Leaving Certificate).

For my wood carving of "Ugra Narasimha," I got the state award in 1971. I have also completed five year Diploma course in drawing and painting and come out successfully with 2nd class. I am continuing the same profession even today. Some of my artistic creations have been bought by the Bangalore Museum and some others by the CCIE, Delhi."

Nagaraj belongs to the Gudigar sub-group of the Asari community, listed among the backward castes of Karnataka. His father S.P. Ganapatappa passed away two years ago, leaving Nagaraj the head of the family. He has a sister who is married and two brothers – Venugopal, aged 37, and Anil Kumar, 30, both sandalwood carvers. His mother Vimalamma, aged 67, joins the family work by making small items and flower garlands out of the sandalwood shavings. Nagaraj married late. His wife Usha is 37 years old, and they have a daughter, Bhavana, who is five. Usha is an artist of repute as well, specializing in the Mysore style of embossed gold leaf painting. She too has a state award to her credit.

With tools, brushes, paints, half-carved sandalwood figures all over in the small double storeyed house, the mood is quiet and industrious. The young women of the household were working swiftly and silently in the kitchen. The only noise was of little Bhavana with her cousins Ankita and Ankush, who sat on the two-wheeler Luna vehicle parked in the corridor, singing film songs, each trying to drown out the others' voice.

Nagaraj had been working in a vest and *lungi,* but when he came to converse with us at length about his life and work, he donned a bush shirt over his lungi. With his greying hair, spectacles, and a pen in his pocket, he looked more like a school teacher.

His home is in an urban residential locality called Parsi Garden Layout, in Swimming Pool Extension, in the southern part of Bangalore city. Nagaraj's neighbours are employees of the Post & Telegraph department and bank officers, unlike in the village where he would be surrounded by fellow artisans from the Gudigar community. Do the neighbours appreciate your art? "Good question" replied Nagaraj. "They come, sit, watch and appreciate the art but if I had been a stone carver who made a lot of noise breaking stones, they would complain. My room is quiet and scented with sandalwood so they like to sit here."

The entire extended family of eleven members, including his sister's husband who stayed as a paying guest, lived together. The women did the cooking but they left it to the menfolk to bring vegetables every day on their way back from a visit to a nearby temple. Very rarely did the womenfolk buy jewellery. Purchases were more family oriented, such as a television, radio, two-wheeler Luna, and a refrigerator which they bought three or four years ago.

Nagaraj and his family rise usually between 6.30 and 7 am, when they all drink filter coffee from steel tumblers. Breakfast at 8.30 am consisted of chapatis, dosas or idlis with chutney and more coffee. If lunch was at home there would be sambar, rice, vegetables and curds. Fruits and sweets were reserved for functions and festivals. Bananas and coffee were usually offered to visitors. Tea time was between 4 and 5 pm, and dinner was served at 10 pm and had almost the same constituents as lunch.

The family celebrated all the main Hindu festivals, Ganesh Chaturthi, Sankranti, Janamashtami. The women did most of the puja with the men joining them only in the mornings. Nagaraj emphasized that they observed no holidays, and stopped their work only when someone came to visit. His health was not satisfactory since he had fractured his back, but he still worked till midnight. Of course, it depended on orders and customers. Purchases for festivals, such as new clothes for the whole family, cost Rs 4-5000, and a visit to the village if everyone went together cost a little less than that. House repairs and whitewashing every two years required another Rs 10,000. Luckily, his brothers were able to contribute towards family expenses, since the youngest taught at a private school, drawing a salary of Rs 2,000 per month, and the other brother earned between Rs 2,000 to 4,000 from his sandalwood work as well.

The family pays Rs 450 for electricity every month, Rs 150 for water, and a municipal corporation tax of Rs 750 per annum. The three children of the family went to a private school by autorickshaw, which cost them Rs 250 per month.

The Nagaraj family are members of the Gudigar Samaj, their community organization in Bangalore. Every year they organize a programme on Republic Day and for Satyanarayana Puja, "without fail" he repeated twice, in English. They had also organized a *rangoli* camp for women, sports for the youth, and a fancy dress competition for the children. His wife, sister-in-law, and the children had won prizes at these events, recounted Nagaraj, smiling broadly at Bhavana who was listening, peeping from behind a door. He regretted, however, that there was no society which could discuss the artisans' problems. There are "family guiders" and elders' advice, but that is all. He wanted recognition of the craft skills of his family.

The family had lived in rented accommodation from 1958 till 1971, when they bought a piece of land measuring 15 feet x 45 feet, out of a larger plot. They had paid Rs 3000 for the land, and at that time they could not afford to buy the entire plot. Nagaraj described the days when they were in the process of building the house as very hard. "We took food only once a day. At night, we held our mother's hand for support." The year they built the house, he won a state award for his sandalwood carving of Ugra Narasimha. They feel the house has brought them good fortune.

Nagaraj rose and pulled out a pile of albums from the cupboard behind him. Coloured photographs of sandalwood pieces designed and carved by him. "There is *Dhanwantri*, *Vishwaroopa Darshana*, Japanese Buddha. I used to get many orders for these in those days. In 1969, I went to Delhi, here is a group photo with Indira Gandhi and President Zakir Hussain. How? Because I designed the Republic Day tableau for the state. It was a papier machie float of the *Khedda* operations. I have good knowledge of all crafts, clay, paper and wood. Here is the *Kalabhairava* in teak wood which was bought by the government museum in Bangalore. I have photographs of other pieces also. Here is the bust of Dr. Olsen, the U.S. dignitary in India between 1970-75, I don't remember exactly. Here is a leather puppet scene copied in yellow teak wood. This was purchased by Government of Karnataka to present to Todor Zhivkov,. State Council of People's Republic of Bulgaria."

"This is my famous *Purandaraswaroop, Adisi Dhale Yasodhe, Jagadodharana*.

"This piece is of Yashoda playing with Krishna. Carved forest, Adishesha in tree along with parrot and deer. The photo of this piece came in Marg magazine but they only published the figure and not the elaborate side carving – they are editing according to their own whims and fancies," he laughed a little ruefully.

The piece for which he won the state award is an innovative three-foot tall piece in ordinary wood of Hiranyakashyapa and Narasimha coming out of a pillar in the half-man half-lion form. On the wall was framed his *Nruthya Tharanga*, which showed a dancer and drummer wrapped in waves of sound. From the adjoining room, which served as a store, he brought out a dust-laden "modern art composition" of a woman half-human half-bird. He wiped it carefully and set it up for display, but it was clear that his forte lay in traditional themes.

There were faded black and white photographs of a tableau he had created for the Janata Housing Scheme in Karnataka, where they had wished to exhibit models of old and new housing designs. The carvings ranged from religious figures of a Hindu, a Muslim, and a Christian for the Jindal Aluminium Factory, a Hoysala style Ganesha still unfinished, mixing sandalwood rosewood and inlay work, door frames, wall brackets, boxes, and so on. There was nothing Nagaraj had not designed or carved, once the idea or order came to him.

The albums were coming to an end. "Here is my father at the Mysore Darbar. This was an order from Health Department, Karnataka to publicize breast feeding. My wife also worked on it with me. I make the annual trophy, the Aikya Mandapa of Bijapur, for the Basavappa Memorial function there. It is better to give this kind of work to artisans instead of silver-plated trophies. I am doing art works regularly for the Information Department of the state and various other government departments."

So, is the government good to Nagaraj? "No, the supply of sandalwood to me and all sandalwood artisans is inadequate and is a very big problem. There are about 2000 artisans in Karnataka. Bangalore itself has about 400 sandalwood carvers requiring raw material on a regular basis. The government of Karnataka has an elaborate and systematic scheme for distribution of sandalwood which is in short supply, and it is supplemented by the wood that comes from Tamil Nadu through smugglers," informed Nagaraj.

Elaborating the system of distribution of sandalwood, Nagaraj said: "All sandalwood to artisans is released only through the state handicrafts corporation, Kaveri, at a reduced rate, while private manufacturers can buy it directly from the Forest Department at higher rates. Each artisan has a quota of 9.5 kg of sandalwood per month, but because of inadequate supply we usually manage to get only 5 to 6 kgs. For the past eight months, we have been deprived of the regular supply. The procedure to procure a permit from government authorities is a lengthy one. First, we have to get a permit from the Forest Department, then we have to select the logs, and at the third step, these have to be treated and cut."

Both Kaveri and the artisans need storage licenses to keep sandalwood above a stipulated quantity. They also have to maintain a stock register. "In spite of our compliance with the tedious procedure to acquire a permit, there have been many instances when we did not even get our quota of 9.5 kg. Rules are only for the poor. Many artisans know that Mahalakshmi Flour Mills and the Khoday Distilleries get 100 tonnes of sandalwood from the Forest Department in the name of exports. How? Why? We need it for our food and to preserve our craft heritage. Since logs are not allowed to be exported in their raw form, big companies do a bit of superficial carving and send them out as exports. If artisans get larger orders they need 25 kg of sandalwood, but big people get it instead since exports are promoted. The government easily gives licenses to sandalwood oil factories who crush tonnes together for domestic use and export. But first the government should keep its assurances and promises to the craftsmen. Can artisans spend all their time chasing documents and procedures instead of carving?"

"We are allotted one permit card per artisan. We had three cards, including one for my wife", explained Nagaraj, "but since I work at Kaveri they cancelled my card saying I cannot carve on my own if I have a job!"

"There are many procedural complications. The log doesn't always weigh 9.5 kg. We have to make do with whatever is available. If the quantity with the Forest Department is less, we get only 4 to 5 kgs monthly. If no wood is available, the quota lapses and we cannot go again for two weeks to get more."

The Forest Department at present has sandalwood depots located at Mysore, Dharwar, Shimoga, Tarikere, and Kushalnagar. When the Forest Department depot was located at Malleswaram, it used to be easy to get our full quota and good quality sandalwood, but some 10 years ago it was all routed through Kaveri because of "some distribution problem."

There is a rotational chart with a list of four qualities of wood. It is disbursed on a first come-first served system, but big companies manage to make "some arrangement" and get plenty from the Forest Department. "For artisans, the subsidized rate is Rs 175 per kg, and the open market price in January 1997 was Rs 550 per kg. The government must ensure that we get our full quota every month."

At a workshop on "Wood for Crafts: Crisis and Opportunity for the Southern Region," held in February, 1993 and organized by the Crafts Council of India, two interesting observations were made and recorded in the report:

"Shri C.C. Aiyappa, Regional Director, Office of the Development Commissioner (Handicrafts), Southern Region, recounted that the card system in Karnataka was working satisfactorily until the Handicrafts Development Corporation took over, after which craftspersons receive only three month's quota for the whole year. With 3000 craftspersons requiring 200 tonnes of sandalwood, only 20 tonnes was procured last year. Unless this system is reformed, the craft community would perish once and for all. He suggested the setting up of a high-level committee which could streamline the procurement and distribution system for all the four states. This would be essential to stop the drift away from the crafts. (1.9.3)

Shri A.K. Goel, IAS (Managing Director, Andhra Pradesh Handicrafts Development Corporation), said that for all the three scarce wood types under discussion, the total requirement was only

1000 tonnes. This means 1000 acres of land in the entire southern region – approximately 0.0004 per cent of the land available, or the area of five villages in a region of one lakh villages! The main issue was to control the corruption within the existing systems (1.9.4.)"

When these observations were brought to Nagaraj's notice, he smiled and nodded silently in agreement. What was the nature of Nagaraj's job that denied him a quota card for sandalwood? He was appointed as Kaveri's craft design artist in 1978 on a basic salary of Rs 1400. He brings home almost Rs 4000 per month. He explained that if you had a card and took the full quota, you had to supply Rs 2500 worth of goods back to Kaveri. It was not really part of the rules but "Kaveri people demanded it. When you do not get the full quota, about Rs 1000 worth of goods are to be given."

"If we get an order, we can get wood from the Forest Department at full rate, but not more than 3 kg. If we need more than the ceiling, we need a government permit and have to maintain a storage register and stock register. When sandalwood supplies are reduced, we cannot maintain order schedules with the Central Cottage Industries Emporium or exports."

As a design artist Nagaraj had not just photograph albums but a file of designs as well. Fine line drawings in ink of wall brackets, doorways, paper cutters, boxes, book markers, and photoframes. All designs are supplied to Kaveri which gives them freely to other artisans. Many individual customers also give him ideas for designs. He welcomes any new idea he can get and, despite being an artist in his own right, he is receptive to new designs or ideas to improve his products.

Nagaraj found banks more helpful in earlier days. He had taken loans from Canara Bank and other banks and repaid all of them. The Mysore Bank had once given a loan to his father at an interest of 4 per cent per annum when shown an order for sandalwood carvings. "Now we are not taking any loan but are managing with what we have."

Nagaraj packs his most prized items in transparent paper and polythene. For long distance journeys they go into a light wooden box with paper shavings. "By registered post, "handle with care" is enough. I take the big items personally to CCIE. For the rest, they pay postal charges." Nagaraj had no time to waste in looking for fancy packaging.

Nagaraj's tools and machinery are well-ordered and immediately at hand in his small workroom.

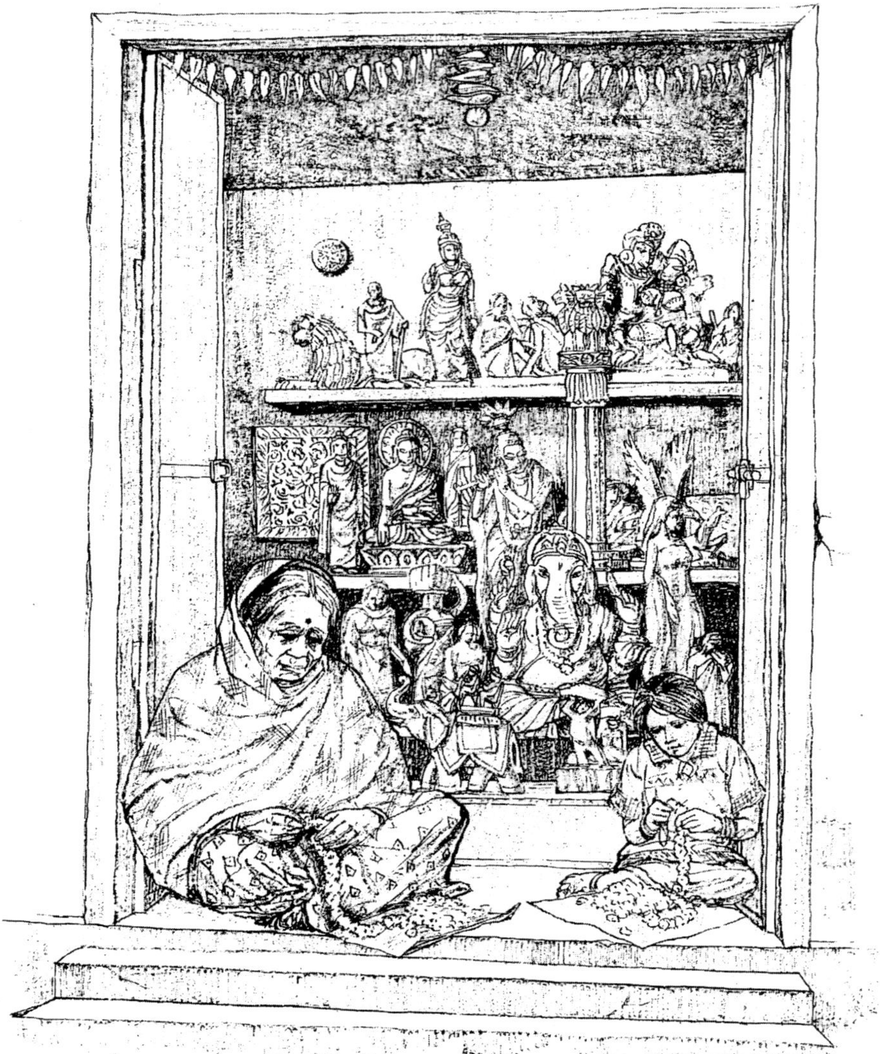

Initially, he had no machinery but later got a polishing machine and a multipurpose lathe through the Design Centre of the Office of the Development Commissioner, Handicrafts. He had recently acquired an electrical drill and jigsaw. His kit of hand tools cost Rs 10,000. Repairs and replacements, such as filing and sharpening, cost him anything between Rs 200 and Rs 500 each month. His younger brother assists him with the paper work in business matters and searches for samples, items, books, files and drawings. Since the main work is by hand, electricity blackouts are not a problem. They have very little need for power.

At his workplace at Kaveri headquarters, Nagaraj has a bright, well-lit corner with a large table. He carries himself with an authoritative air and converses less expansively. He had prepared a sheet of the monthly sales figures for sandalwood through the Kaveri Emporium in the past year. He described a tour to Bidar, Sagar, Sirsi, Mysore, Kumta, and Chennapatna, within Karnataka. The purpose of his tour was to meet and guide local artisans in working on new designs, and to show them samples of new products. Here was a different Nagaraj, a government employee with status, dignity, and a provident fund to ensure financial security after retirement. Alongside, he chooses to carve pieces for private customers because the economic gains were more. But where was the sandalwood? His excursions into the world of exhibitions, bazaars, sales, and *mela*s was somewhat restricted by the fact that he never had enough stock to sell, and had to limit his participation to giving demonstrations of his craft skills, which gave him an audience but no customers. He attended the Mysore Dasara exhibition every year and had been to the Lalit Kala Akademi and Pragati Maidan exhibition grounds at Delhi. He travelled to Mussoorie to the National Academy of Administration to demonstrate the craft. His cousin, Ashok Gudigar, had created the ceremonial gate at the Surajkund Mela when Karnataka was the theme state but although Nagaraj had tried to participate, he had not been selected.

Vimalamma, Nagaraj's mother, came in and sat on the floor nearby as the evening drew on and our discussions were coming to an end. Silently, she sharpened a flat metal spatula under her feet and oiled it against her hair. With it, she peeled a strip of *shola* pith and cut it into small rectangles. These were piled together in layers. She cut around them to make them oval shaped and rolled some to form a stem which she wrapped with thread. Into the stem, she layered the oval pieces in steps to form a perfect imitation of mogra flower buds. With some more oval pieces she made rose petal shapes and tied them to the stem. Their edges curled like real petals. She dipped this flower in a glass of water to soften it and gently tied it in my hair, while Bhavana sang the popular lyric "Made in India" softly and delicately in the background.

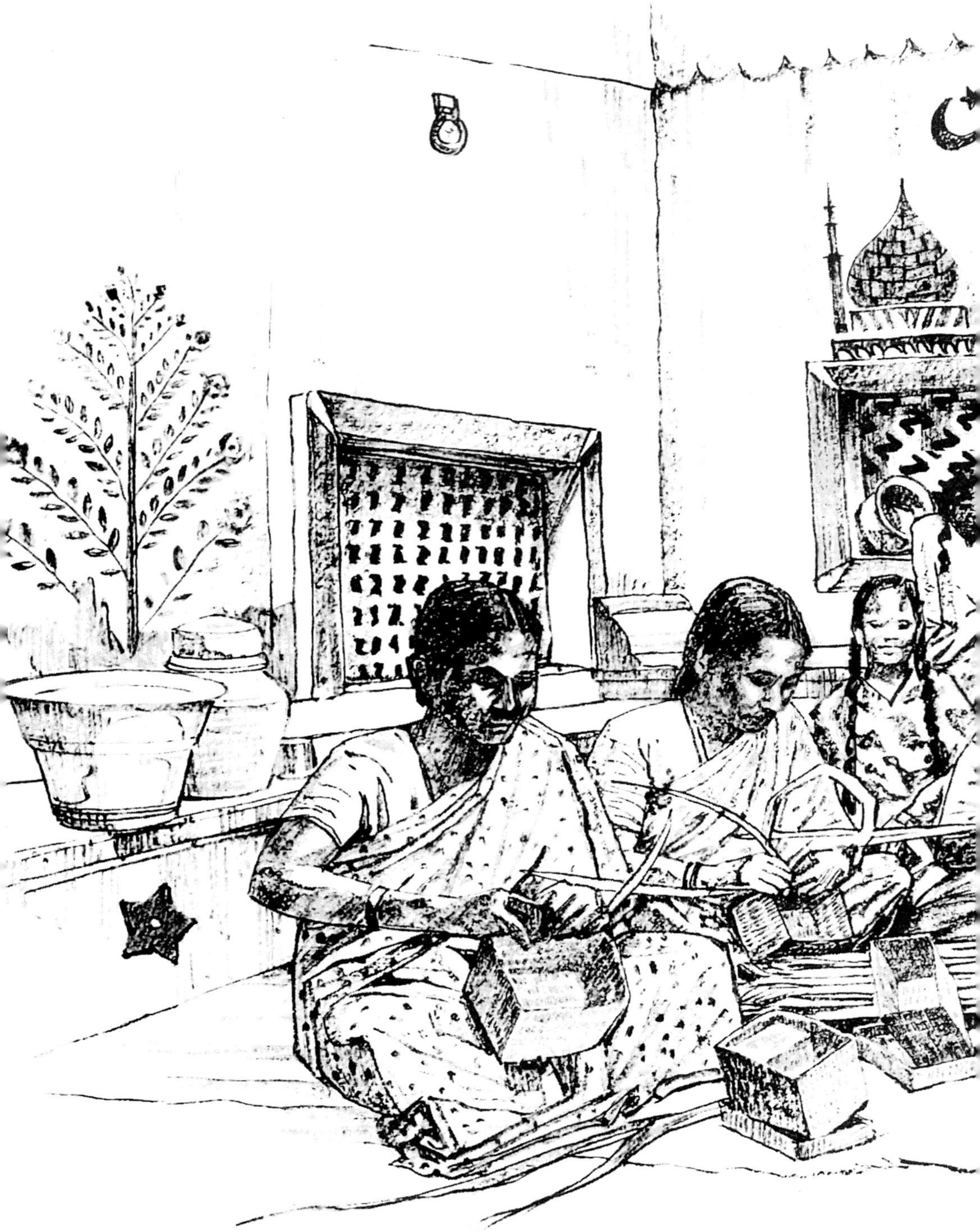

CHAPTER SIX

The Palm Leaf Basket Makers of Pulicat

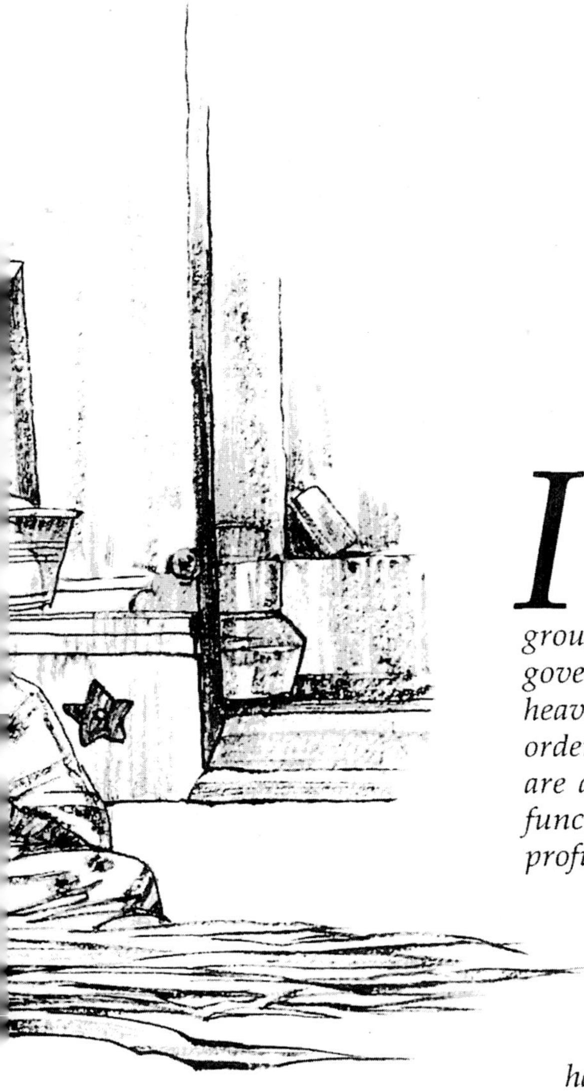

In the southern state of Tamil Nadu, the Pulicat palm leaf basket makers represent an all-women group supported by non-government organizations and heavily dependent on export orders for their survival. They are a well-organized, actively functioning society. The study profiles one of its leading women members, who. belongs to the Muslim community. The family possesses no land, and the women have become the main breadwinners in the changing life pattern of Pulicat.

"Stop at the Indian Bank and ask for the way to the Society office." Pulicat is quiet on Fridays during Ramzan, the month of fasting in the Muslim calendar, with most shops and establishments closed except for the Indian Bank, the vegetable vendors on the pavement in the heart of the bazaar, and one other establishment. In a back street, there is a small old house constructed in traditional style with wooden pillars and an open courtyard. This houses the office of the Pulicat Women Palm Leaf Cane and Bamboo Product Workers Industrial Co-operative Society Limited. It is commonly referred to as the Palm Leaf Society.

The Palm Leaf Society is situated in Ponneri Taluk of Chengalpattu district of Tamil Nadu. Pulicat, also known as Pazhaverkadu, is 19 kms beyond Ponneri towards the Andhra Pradesh border. The presence of a small lake has made it a minor tourist spot. A majority of the population of Pulicat subsists on trading fish caught in the lake.

Khaja Mohiddin is 55 years old, has studied up to the 5th class and works as a coolie, carrying fish amongst blocks of ice on his head for the big traders. He used to catch and sell fish himself earlier, until big agents came on the scene, and from then on he has been reduced to working as a porter, earning between Rs 30-40 per day, about Rs 1200 a month. On days when the catch is low or the supply of ice for storage is scanty his earnings are also reduced. Once a major centre of textile manufacture and export, Pulicat's economy now hinges on the fish trade and palm leaf products. If there was no fish trade, Pulicat would have perished.

Khaja Mohiddin's wife is K. Rahila, President of the Pulicat Palm Leaf Society.

Prior to 1959, local women made rough palm leaf baskets for their household shopping and small containers to keep packets of *beedis*. In 1959, a local teacher set up an informal society with thirty women members to manufacture palm leaf baskets in an organized manner. It grew slowly and in 1962 it was registered as a society equipped with a secretary and other staff. By 1972 they started getting small orders through the South Indian Producers Association (SIPA) which took a few sample pieces for export.

Inside the building, a dozen young girls are being trained to strip the palm leaves into half-inch ribbons and weave them into square and round baskets and small trays. The office-cum-training centre conveys an air of orderliness and calm efficiency. Blackboards are full of information and many instructions have been pasted on the walls. Their export-oriented marketing links are evident from the posters advertising The Body Shop, a Britain-based company that orders their palm leaf baskets as containers and packaging material for its eco-friendly creams, soaps and other cosmetics. The main blackboard tells us that the society started functioning on 25th September, 1959 and has 287 members. With a share capital of Rs 14,970 and a reserve fund of Rs 6,375, thanks to the regular export orders in the past year, it achieved a total sales figure of Rs 3,75,629 and is expected to reach Rs 4,30,105 after the completion of the present Body Shop order which was in its final stages. The society had taken a loan of Rs 1,94,999, of which it has repaid Rs 87,000. It was providing training to the workers under the Training of Rural Youth for Self Employment (TRYSEM) scheme and was presently in its second phase. All this was written in chalk on the board for anyone to see. Unfortunately, even though the second phase had been sanctioned and was underway for the past 3 months, the society had not yet received any funds.

In the initial years, the women earned a meagre two or three rupees per basket when they produced about fifty pieces a month. Now, with export orders coming in regularly, they earn ten rupees a basket on an average. Since there is plenty of palm leaf available, production has never been a problem. Now they have orders from The Body Shop and the Oxfam shops. Some orders come from Switzerland, some from within the country, from cities like Delhi, Bombay and Bangalore, mainly routed through NGOs like the Crafts Council of India, Almas-India and SIPA. The bulk of their production is geared towards export, and since they are paid better prices for the baskets by their foreign buyers than through sales in the domestic market, the women spend most of their time fulfilling these orders.

The secretary of the society is Chengalvarayan. He travels to Chennai to finalize orders and does the office work. Thirty-three-year-old K. Rahila is responsible for organizing the members for production and conducting the meetings of the society. Kokila supervizes the distribution of raw material, training, production and packaging. Kokila and all the members of the society have a smooth and pleasant relationship with Rahila, full of humour and camaraderie.

Rahila belongs to Pulicat but had grown up in Chennai with her grandfather. She returned to Pulicat after her marriage at the age of eighteen. In a rather unusual situation, she lives with her husband Mohiddin and children in her own family home, along with her three brothers, three sisters, and their families. Only one of her brothers is unmarried. Her 70-year-old father also lives with them. Her mother passed away recently. Rahila's husband has only one brother who lives apart from them. She was the eldest in the family. Rahila and Mohiddin have five children, Mohammad Bilal, 19, Jamila, 18, Nasima, 16, Abdul Alim, 13, and Naseem Banu, 11. It is a large joint family. Their house is not too large but has many open spaces and plenty of light. A framed picture of the mosque at Mecca and a star and moon adorns the outer wall of the kitchen. A grass mat is spread on the floor in the front hall. A shelf running along the wall holds the palm leaf strips. Many nails on the wall hold up everyone's spare sets of clothing. On our arrival, the floor was swept clean and everyone sat down to discuss how their daily lives and the palm leaf baskets were woven together. While a dozen members of the society along with Kokila sat with us, it was Rahila who spoke for herself and all the others, with an occasional intervention, humorous or informative, being thrown in by the more confident and extrovert Kokila.

Rahila said she rose at 5 am unless she "felt lazy" and chose to sleep until six. After going to the toilet and completing her wash, she would have a glass of coffee and begin the day's cooking. Her housework would get over by 10 am, after which she worked on making baskets until lunch at half-past one. After lunch she went back to work till 5 pm Then came the cooking for the evening meal, which was at around 8 pm. After dinner Rahila worked again on the baskets till 10 pm. If there was a big order she would continue working till midnight. Rahila was always at work, whether it was crafting baskets or cooking.

With the combined income from her husband's porterage and her basket making, the family could eat fish every day, apart from *sambar* and vegetables with rice. Fish was more costly now at Rs 15 to Rs 30 per kg because it was being sold outside their village as well. Rahila recalled that about fifteen years ago fish used to cost only Rs 5 per kg. Meat was a luxury which they could afford only about once a week. Most vegetables cost Rs 20 per kg, so along with tomatoes, ginger and green chillies, they spent Rs 10-20 per day on them. All the brother's wives cooked separately in different corners of the house.

Not much money was saved. They had some steel and plastic vessels for cooking and storing water. They managed house repairs only once every three or four years. The last such addition was when they had made cement walls to surround a small bathing space. The family shared a small television but watched it only when they had time. Nobody went to the cinema, especially not during Ramzan. Rahila was conscious of the fact that she was staying at her parental house because she and her husband could not afford a home of their own. "If my brothers ask me to leave tomorrow I shall have to go," she said matter-of-factly.

In this house which was not hers, the family had electricity for which they paid the panchayat once in two months. It worked out to an average of about Rs 250 according to the units consumed. "Sometimes there is no electricity for a week or ten days continuously. Most of the time it is very dim." Someone remembered just then that they could bring out the table fan and turn it on to blow away the flies. It worked desultorily for a little while and then the electricity failed.

Drinking water had been a major problem until recently. It was only during the panchayat elections, held two months ago after innumerable postponements, that water supply was provided for those who had taps in their homes. Rahila laughed as she pointed out that it was useful to have elections as this way the politicians provided them with some basic amenities in a race to please the local people to get their votes.

Only some houses had access to toilet facilities, and Rahila's was not one of them. All the women launched into a vivid description of their problems in having to answer calls of nature either before 5 am or after 7 pm, as they became visible to passersby at other times. "If we all had toilets there would be no such problem. We are now going to ensure that we have access to this basic service through the panchayat."

Rahila had no expenses on travel connected with work. Since most of the family lived together, there was no need for visits to other towns or villages to meet relatives. The community sometimes went to a mosque at Nagercoil or visited Kovalam or Nellore, in which case they either hired a van for everyone to share the expenses or they all went by bus or train.

The family owned ten hens, a television, a table fan, the house, and the workplace. None of these were Rahila's personal possessions. There was no furniture in the house other than two old metal chairs. They did not even possess an *andavu,* the typical traditional copper or brass water container found in most homes in south India. Plastic jars and buckets demonstrated both industrialization and poverty.

Rahila's earnings went towards the school fees of the children who were enrolled in the Pulicat Government School. She paid a sum of Rs 500 a year for Bilal in the 9th class, Rs 350 each for Jamila, Nasima, and Abdul Alim and Rs 300 for Naseem Banu.

Despite this rather vulnerable personal situation, Rahila and the other members of the Pulicat Society knew that they had ample work and were getting better returns through exports which were securely spread throughout the year. A basket of size 6"x3"x4" to hold a jam bottle fetched her Rs 20. If she could make one such basket a day it brought in Rs 600 per month minus the Rs 100 for the *ola.* A set of three baskets called toffee baskets requiring one bundle of wide leaves and two bundles of narrow strips, fetched her Rs 35 in wages but took three days to complete. The broad leaf is used on its own to make tea baskets, 2"x3" square but earns her only Rs 5 per basket. Wages are calculated per piece and all payments arrive by cheque to the Indian intermediary agency which sends a draft to the Indian Bank at Pulicat in the name of the society.

Rahila keeps about Rs 200 worth of raw material at home, stripped, cleaned and stacked on a shelf, covered in plastic and protected more carefully than her saris. The palm leaves come by all modes – truck, van, cycle or carried on top of the head from the other side of Ponneri, from Gummidipoondi, Elavur, Reddypalayam, Somareddypalayam and Karunguzhi, to Pulicat. They are sold at Rs 5 - 7 per "fan" according to their size. Palm leaf is difficult to get in November, December, and January as the rains discolour the leaves. Instead of a pale ivory, the leaves turn dark yellow and can be used only if they are dyed.

Since they are strongly in favour of production for exports, design is an important and indispensable factor to which Rahila and her co-workers give considerable attention. Baskets have many uses and a variation in height, width, shape, and colour produces a fairly wide range of choice. The women display a remarkable sense of confidence when they describe how they have evolved many new designs by just sitting together and discussing their individual ideas and possibilities and improving upon them in the course of their discussions. "We also get ideas from books given to us by the CCIC and when export orders come they tell us their requirements. We are able to work out a majority of our problems easily on our own, but if something complicated comes up it takes a little longer for us to understand and resolve it. Recently, we were asked to make very small-sized boxes. We had to refuse because it would not have been practical or comfortable to try and shape something so tiny." As women, they had many ideas about the kind of palm leaf baskets in which household goods could be stored. They were confident about being able to get dyes from Chennai and dye the palm leaves at home if coloured boxes were needed. Designs were never a problem since they were comfortable with experimentation.

Palm leaf crafts hardly need any machinery; although Rahila has a machine which helps to split and clean the leaf, she is so used to doing this by hand that she hardly uses it. All the women prefer to use a small pen knife with which they deftly cut the leaf into strips of even width. "The machine cost me almost Rs 100 and if I keep using it I will have to keep changing the blade and maintaining the machine which I do not want to do," Rahila smiles to explain her disdain for technology.

There is, however, one small innovation that has come into their lives – the measuring tape which they call 'inch tape.' Earlier their measuring and sizing was an ad hoc affair but now this tape helps to measure sizes, and thereby reduces costs more effectively. Since this is all they need, apart from scissors, a pen knife and dye stuffs, there are no expenses of a regular nature that relate to instruments. Rahila was clear and categorical that these minor inputs were sufficient to increase their productivity and earnings, while quality and the final appearance depended entirely on their own efforts and skills.

Would a training programme not help in augmenting their skills? Rahila was already a highly skilled craftswoman who had been an instructor in the TRYSEM programme before she took over as president of the society. The society had already conducted seven programmes funded under TRYSEM to teach batches of women aged between 18 and 25 years for six months at a time. The trainees received Rs 350 per month as stipend. They were introduced to the programme through Chengalvarayan, the secretary of the society, who applied for the funds and involved the society in conducting these programmes. As the demand for baskets increased, the trained young women joined the society and became its work force. In this manner the membership of the society had now increased from eighty to a hundred functioning members.

The old and inactive members still meet every year at the general body meeting and enjoy a good feast of *biryani*, along with everyone else. "They are happy with that and it is the least we can do for those who are a part of the society, even if they do not contribute or earn any longer," laughs Kokila, with Rahila nodding in agreement.

The women had not received training in any other aspect of their work such as design, costing, marketing or raising institutional credit. Export specifications and suggestions from local buyers provide them with the required input to vary their product design. "Many people come from Chennai to enquire about our baskets to serve as containers for gifts such as Dussehra sweets or for weddings. A doctor from Apollo Hospital had ordered 20,000 small baskets for his son's wedding"

How did they work out the cost of their baskets? Rahila explains cautiously, "When an order comes, some members sit together and discuss the cost. Raw material cost plus the number of days it would take to make, at a rate of Rs 10 to 15 per day, plus 5 to 10 per cent to the society plus packing, labelling, and transportation costs." Their prices change according to the prevailing cost of raw material and the size and style of the basket. The standard formula works in both domestic and export orders, except that the wage component is usually higher in the latter even though the products for both markets are more or less the same.

There is plenty of wastage while working on palm leaf if it has been discoloured during the rainy season. Storage is done at home for two to three days while production is under way. After that stocks are kept at the society office. A lot of baskets could be rejected if the size or quality does not match the requirement. This creates auditing problems and since they were usually unable to sell these rejected products elsewhere, the society has to simply "write off" that amount. Rahila used the English accounting parlance.

Rahila calculates that in the past year the society had sales amounting up to about Rs 5 lakhs, including the Body Shop order which consisted of 3,720 sets of baskets which they began in October and supplied in January. She expected a continuous order, in which case they would make a sale of Rs 5 to 7 lakhs in the coming year, failing which the sales could drop to Rs 3 to 4 lakhs, including sales in Chennai to the Victoria Technical Institute, Poompuhar, the state government emporium, and through a member of the Crafts Council who runs shops for contemporary crafts in Bangalore and Chennai. In Delhi, Rahila is aware of supplies going to Oxfam but not to any others. In fact she is not really aware of the final destinations of the orders. She is involved in production, training and organizational work. Export orders come either through SIPA or Oxfam.

What is the role of government institutions? "No one has ever come to us." "How then did Poompuhar get its supplies?" She did not know. Local sales in Pulicat or in neighbouring villages and towns were almost nil. They have neither developed a local marketing network, nor did they feel that the local population would be interested in their products. Why not? "We don't use our own products, we don't feel like it at all, even to bring vegetables from the bazaar." What did they use instead? "Plastic."

Even while the marketing of their products is handled by others and the majority of their products go to far-off places, the women of the Pulicat Palm Leaf Society have involved themselves in some of the processes of domestic marketing. Rahila and her friends have attended exhibition-sales and fairs organized by the Crafts Council of India and Oxfam exhibitions at cities like Bombay, Delhi, Calcutta, Tanjore, Coimbatore, Bangalore, and Madurai. While in all cases their travel costs were paid, the raw material and transportation costs were borne by them in the hope that they would be recovered from the sales. For this reason they add a rupee more to the selling price of each basket for exhibitions.

Rahila recalls that sales at Bangalore, Bombay, and Coimbatore had been good, and they had received enquiries from new buyers and exporters. However, they did not visualize this as an activity that they would prefer, as exports were more secure and easier to manage since they only had to make the baskets and deliver them at the society office to be packed. Packing the baskets at the society office was a joint effort of the staff, members, and trainees. The society stacked their baskets or sets of baskets in lots of five, bound them in plastic

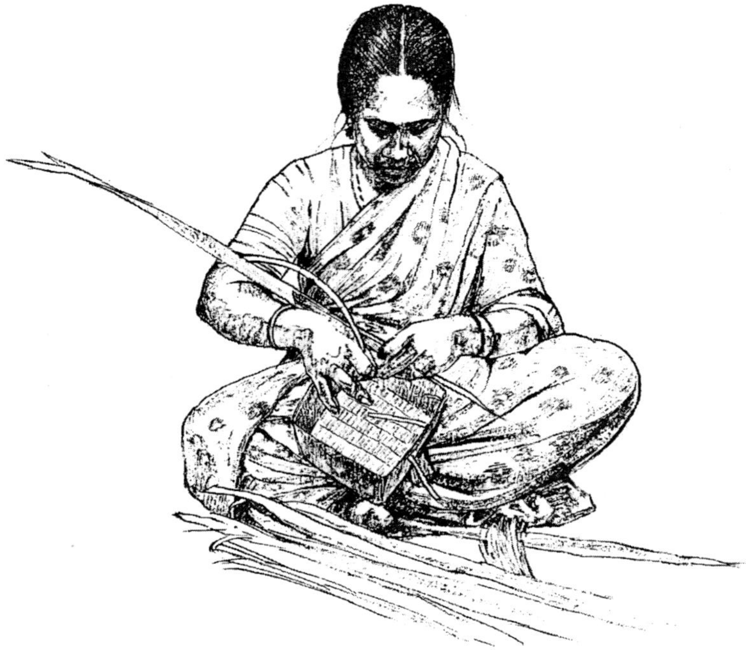

sheeting and labelled the sets. These were then tied in gunny bags and put on top of local buses to be taken to Chennai, where a final rickshaw journey transported them to their destination. If they hired a van at Pulicat to carry a full consignment to Chennai, it cost them as much as Rs 1500. SIPA brings its own van to collect the goods. As their baskets are in themselves a fine example of craft packaging, they have not felt the need for further sophistication in wrapping except to protect them from the rain or to prevent crushing.

The members of the society themselves did not get engaged in product promotional activities, although the Crafts Council had helped them to print a catalogue. Rahila said that they had no names and addresses of any foreign buyers, and thus all marketing efforts were left entirely to the intermediary agencies. Chengalvarayan, who had been working for the society for the last eighteen years was responsible for seeking and following up all orders and met everyone concerned in other towns and cities. With her domestic responsibilities and conservative social attitudes, Rahila could not imagine doing any of these tasks which would bring her in direct contact with formal buyers or officialdom.

In their tiny restricted world of Pulicat, and notwithstanding the long distance contacts with big names like The Body Shop, Rahila and her family have to live with the barest of local facilities, such as a local government dispensary which is the only medical facility available for the townspeople. It remains open from 10.00 am to 1.00 pm, on weekdays only. The doctors come from Chennai everyday to attend to minor health problems like headaches, colds or stomach aches. For the delivery of a child, the local people have to go to Ponneri or Chennai. They even had to buy the saline drip, if it was prescribed. Nothing was free of cost, private doctors who practice in the town charge moderate fees but according to the women they were not good for major emergencies.

"Basket-making keeps us going but it is not enough if we have to conduct a marriage in the family. We need a lakh of rupees for that, so we get loans from local individuals like the transporters.

"We all work, eat and live in the same room. My priority is a home of my own, but I need some land and some help to build my house. The baskets only give us food."

Id was approaching. Rahila was preparing to shop for a small pair of earrings, a petticoat, sari, blouse, and brassiere for herself, a "midi" with *churidar* pyjamas for the girls, and a "pant-shirt" for the boys. A short break for a day's festivities and then it was back to basket-making and the daily routine.

A durrie weaver in the small tourist town of Fatehpur Sikri reflects the situation of Muslim weavers in the northern state of Uttar Pradesh. They work as joint family units in workshed conditions. They are closely linked to wholesale traders who look after marketing. Their production is almost entirely export-oriented and guided by the dictates of large exporters or foreign importers. Here too, the trader necessarily formed a part of the profile, as the craftsperson was not directly involved in marketing and was dependent on the trader for raw materials, designs, and orders.

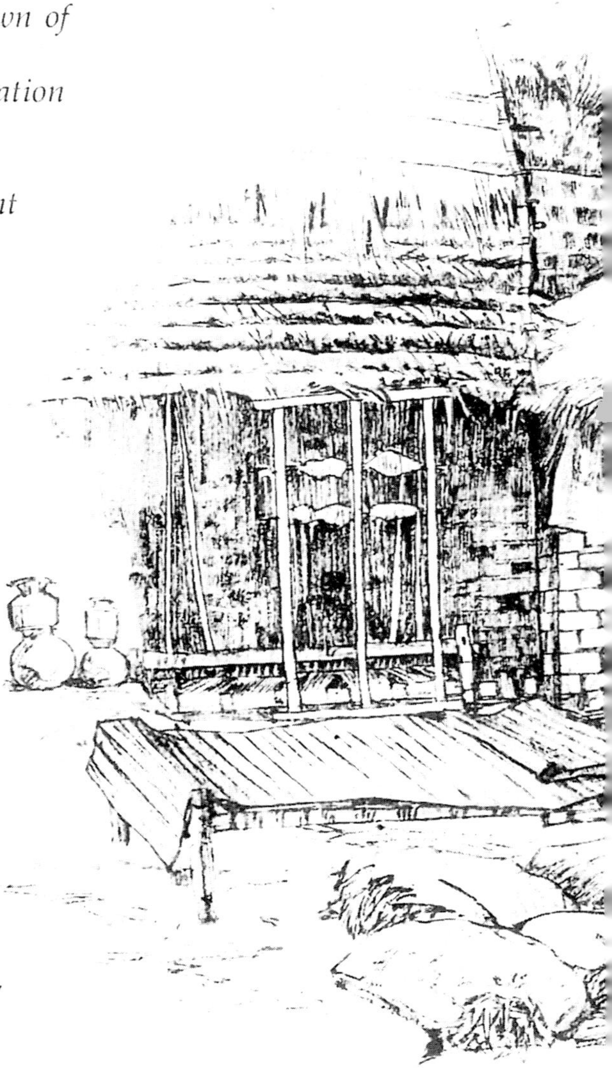

CHAPTER SEVEN

The Durrie Weavers of Fatehpur Sikri

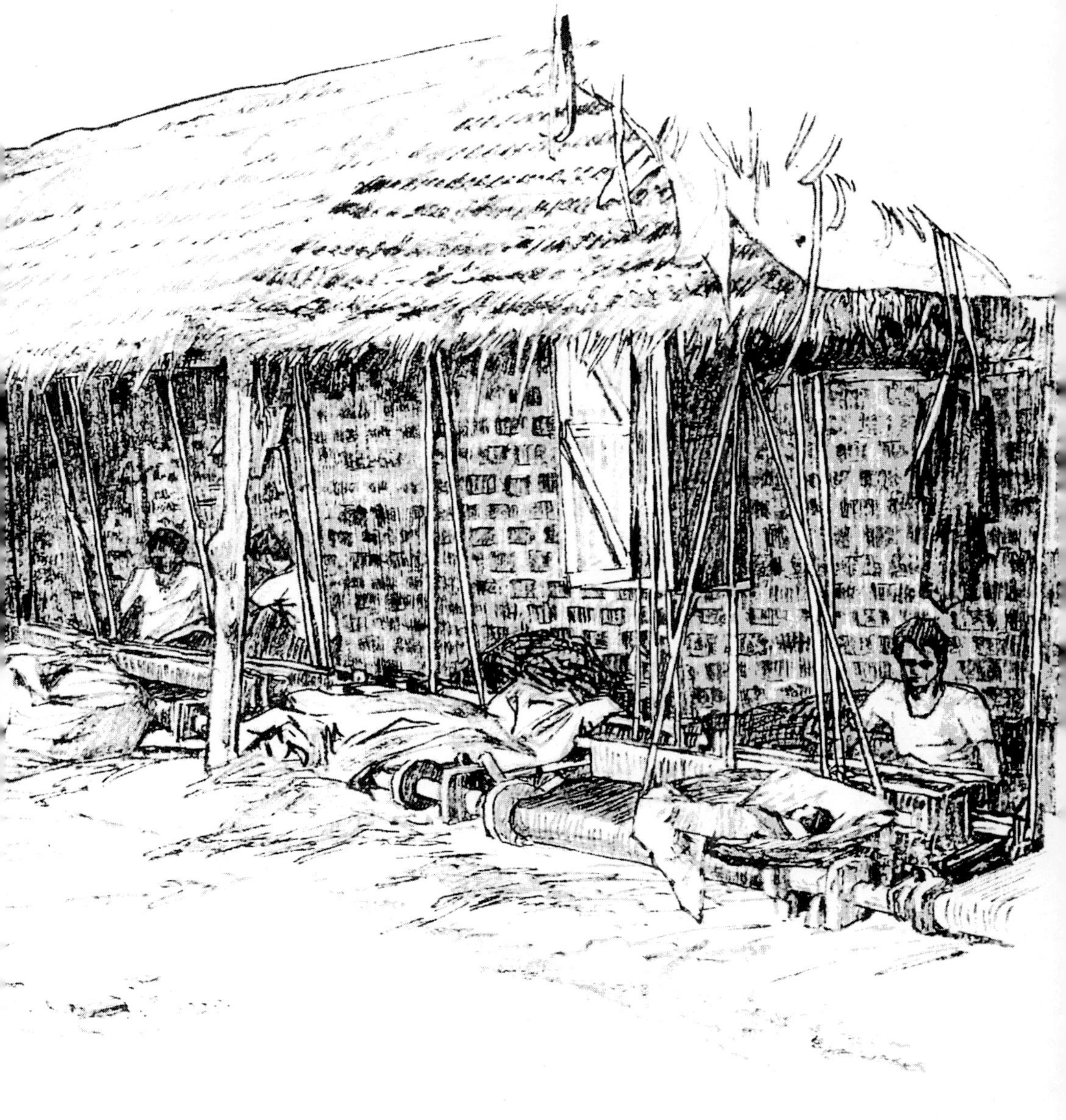

Islamganj lies in the shadow of the Fatehpur Sikri fort in Agra district of Uttar Pradesh. The deep red sandstone of this 16th century Mughal citadel extends into the new settlements surrounding it. Cement blocks are nudging away the older structures but the sandstone quarries still provide enough stone to make deep red the dominant colour of Fatehpur Sikri, standing out against the lush green monsoon foliage. Stone blocks, slabs, pillars and mounds pronounce the sale of this stone as the main activity of Fatehpur Sikri, other than catering to tourists, who come to see the fort after a visit to the Taj Mahal at Agra.

A lesser known but important cottage industry in Fatehpur Sikri is *durrie* weaving. A variety of these floor coverings in cotton, wool and jute, as well as tufted carpets and rag rugs roll off looms set up in small workshops. They are piled on to handcarts to be trundled off to proprietors of small business establishments. From there, they are sent to exporters in Delhi and Bombay who ship them to Finland, Norway, Japan, Germany, and the U.S.A. In the absence of any available statistics, it is left to those engaged in the work to make an estimate of the number of weavers engaged in durrie weaving. "Two hundred?" ventured one. "What are you talking about?" interjected others, "It's twenty thousand at least!"

A durrie weaver in Fatehpur Sikri is not an independent entity who produces and sells his own floor coverings. In fact the actual weaver is not referred to as a craftsperson (*shilpkar*) or artisan (*dastkar*) at all, but rather casually called "labour," since he may have to turn his hand to any task other than durrie weaving when necessity arises.

Shabbir Khan, aged 32, is both a weaver and a contractor. He acts as a centre point linking the local wholesaler with the artisan workforce. Sturdy, yet soft spoken, he looks the quintessential weaver, perspiring in the humidity of a rainless monsoon day, hands working busily at the pit loom while he talks to us about his life and trade. He is the eldest of three brothers, all of whom learnt durrie weaving in the past eight years after leaving their home in Rajoli village, 15 kilometers away. They had two or three *bigha*s of agricultural land in the village on which they cultivated wheat and mustard. It did not yield enough to feed the family, so a skill had to be learnt to supplement the family income. However, when their father died, they had come to an arrangement with some landless tillers in the village to cultivate their land, give them 15 quintals of the produce, and keep the rest as tenants. Even then, the government rate for wheat was Rs 450 per quintal which brought them only Rs 6,750 a year. This was by no means enough for Shabbir Khan's family which consisted of his wife, children, mother, two sisters-in-law, and other relatives in their extended family.

Shabbir Khan learned weaving in Shaifuddin Osman's durrie workshop. His brothers Sirajuddin, 28, and Sharif Khan, 25, learned some techniques from him, and the rest at other workshops. Shabbir's wife Sona, 30, and their year-old baby girl ("write whatever name you wish," laughed Shabbir, as she had not been named yet) live in Islampur at the workshop, while their other daughter Parveen, 15, and son Wafati, 5, live in the village. Parveen has never been to school. When asked why not, Shabbir shrugged with a touch of embarrassment and said, *"reh gaya"* (it was overlooked). Anyway, now they were planning to get her married next year. Wafati was soon going to be sent to school, demonstrating that they did not consider education necessary for girls. The tiny baby lay fast asleep in a round basket hung from the rafters next to one of the looms. Her mother, slim and silent, moved about at work or sat listening to our talk with her head and face fully covered by her purple-coloured polyester sari.

There were four mud pots for storing drinking water, a gas lamp to light the small dark room, a clump of bills and vouchers hanging from a peg hooked to the ceiling, and a broom set handily nearby to sweep up the mounds of rags that are discarded during the weaving process.

The weavers arrive at the workshop at 7.00 am and usually stop work at 4 pm. If there is a large order to be met they work late into the night. While rag rug weaving needs two men to a loom, much of the preparatory and finishing work is done by women who come to work in the godown belonging to the trader. Huge halls are filled to the ceiling with rag strips. Mounds of rags lie scattered along the walkways, courtyard, and verandah. Women of all ages are engaged in tearing, cleaning, sorting, cutting, and dyeing the rags. They are paid Rs 2 per kilogram for each job and thus manage to earn, on an average, about Rs 22 per day. They are aware of the law against the employment of child labour, but still a few young girls about 10 to 12 years old do join the older women at work. Women reach the workplace at 8.30

am and return home only by 6 pm. "They have done a survey here. No one employs a girl child but they may help their mothers with small tasks at home," was how Shabbir chose to explain why eight-year-olds could be seen cutting the excess bits off a rug laid out on the ground outside their home just across the road from Shabbir's workshed.

One of the seven wonders of the world, the Taj Mahal, may be just forty-five minutes away by road, but living conditions in Fatehpur Sikri remain medieval, the water brackish and untreated, and the electricity hardly ever functional. Most worksheds and houses are lit by the natural light that comes in from open courtyards. Their houses have no toilet facilities. They go for their routine functions out into the open grounds; the women go only when it is dark.

Except for a primary health centre, there are no other government health facilities nearby. The state of medical care evoked a discussion that took some time and gave vent to both anger and a lively sense of humour. Some weavers took part in the conversation and the rest would nod and laugh in agreement with whoever was speaking. "All medical care is private because the doctors do not go to the primary health care centre unless someone important is visiting. They see cases quietly in their homes." Medical expenses for a family like Shabbir's amounted to a hefty sum of Rs 6-7000 annually. A private doctor charged a fee of twenty rupees each time, apart from medicines which they were compelled to buy from private shops at high prices. They also spent a lot on *jhola chhaap* (cloth shoulder-bag brand), the colloquial name for quacks, who are a typical phenomenon in rural areas in northern India. As described by Shabbir and his brothers, these are students who have dropped out of the village high school. They pack three common medicines, a syringe, and some saline and glucose intravenous fluid bottles into a cloth shoulder-bag, mount a cycle, and roam the villages in search of patients. For most ailments, they prescribed the administration of the "bottle." The people do not know the value or efficacy of the bottle so they pay Rs 100 for a bottle of glucose, although it costs only about forty rupees. It may not do them any good but they are impressed with the treatment. The big doctors in town charge a hundred rupees just to treat a cold and as for the villagers, the situation is pitiful.

Their main expenses for food are on supplementing their own crop of wheat, and on *dal* and vegetables. Fruit is an occasional luxury, that too only when prices fall during the season. Most families rise by 5.30 or 6 am and have a glass of thick, sweet tea. Lunch follows at 10 am and dinner between 7 and 8 pm. They have *rotis* with *dal* or vegetable, alternately. No one cared for tobaco or alcohol.

New clothing is bought only on festive occasions or a family wedding. These are worn when they go to visit their relatives or if there is some important work like visiting an office. For the rest of the time an old stained cotton vest for the upper part of the body, a checked cotton *lungi* wrapped around the waist and a *gamchha*, the all-purpose handwoven scarf, worn over the shoulder or around the head is the normal clothing of the weavers.

There are no expenses on rent and currently none on education. That would only begin when Wafati went to school.

A question on electricity bills evoked laughter. "They have fitted metres but no one comes to read them. Where's the electricity anyway? They give us an ad hoc bill for our three light bulbs and a television amounting to a hundred rupees for two months. We prefer to use a gas lamp for our home."

The long pilgrimage to the holy shrine of Ajmer Sharif could not be undertaken because of lack of time and finances. However, they did observe all the festivals of both Hindus and Muslims – Diwali, Holi, Makar Sankranti, Id, Bakri-Id – "as all communities live here, we observe all festivals. Only sometimes do we stop work on Fridays to say our prayers. We do not follow any set pattern," Shabbir explained in a very easy going manner, a far cry from the sectarian tensions that occasionally erupt in the state.

Even while Shabbir Khan wove durries for as many hours as the other ten weavers around him, he assumed greater importance because he was the *thekedar*, the contractor who employed other weavers, provided them with a workplace, and conducted dealings with the traders who provided the raw material and wages. He and his brothers had saved one lakh rupees and bought the 200-square-yard plot on which they built the workshed out of red stone and brick along with a single room for his family. The roof was made of dried leaves and the only sign of modern amenities was an electric wire that led to a few bulbs.

This work unit was not registered as they did not find any benefit in doing so. While government statistics largely consist of counting the number of units registered, the advantages of registration are invisible. This results in many "units" functioning informally with no license and thus being missed in the headcount. In any case, a literate person was needed to maintain the records and deal with all the red tape. Shabbir Khan had never been to school but Sirajuddin proudly revealed that he had attended high school at Arera Inter College near his village. Sharif Khan, the youngest of the three, had studied up to high school, but had failed to get a degree. They turned to weaving rag rugs called *chindi* durries because there was a demand for workers in this field. Since the skill was easily learned on the job, it drew many young men from families of small farmers with inadequate land holdings to make both ends meet. Indian durries had caught the imagination of younger, less affluent, cosmopolitan customers abroad. Although hand-knotted carpets faced tough competition from China, Pakistan, and Iran, the promotion of Indian durries spearheaded by Shyam Ahuja, a well known export house, had boosted their demand.

Young men involved in this work had to migrate to Fatehpur Sikri to be closer to the traders. It was impossible to transport the raw material to their villages and bring back the finished goods as the village roads were extremely bad. Proximity was necessary, but

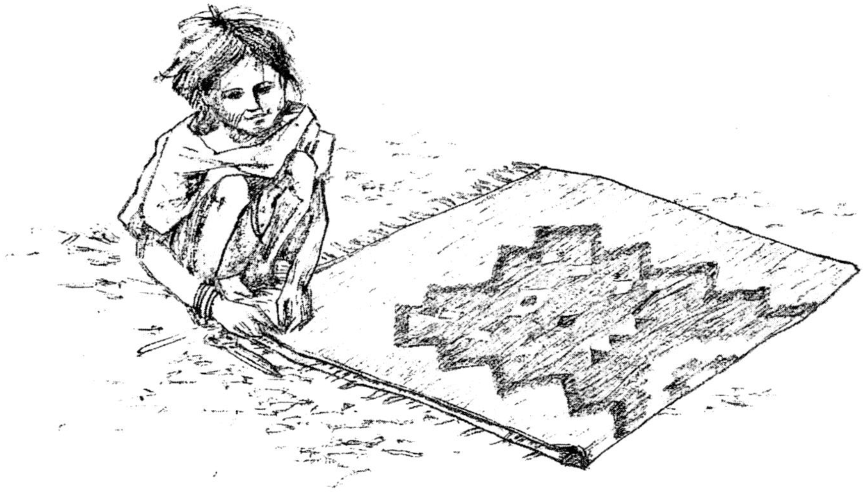

it did mean that the labourers themselves had to invest in building a working and living space there. Sharif Khan usually carried the rags and yarn from the trader, Pavan, to the workshed on a bicycle. He could only carry a load of 70 kg each time, which meant that he needed to go back and forth four to five times a day to bring a full load. Each trip took an hour, but they found this method cheaper than engaging a cycle cart which cost Rs 12 per quintal. Pavan, the proprietor of a wholesale durrie enterprise, in turn brought the rag strips from textile mills in trucks from Pali and Jaipur in Rajasthan, Ahmedabad in Gujarat, and even from as far away as Mumbai in Maharashtra, Coimbatore in Tamil Nadu, and Karnataka. The cost of transportation is about Rs 12,000 for a truck from Mumbai and the rag strips cost Rs 2 to Rs 50 a kg depending on the type of cloth. All transactions are in cash. If "goodwill" is established (they used the English word) they are able to get the raw material on credit at the same rate. "We just telephone the mill and they send the goods on trust. Sometimes up to Rs 1 or 2 lakh of ours lies with the party. There is also a danger that the goods don't reach us, but there's nothing we can do about that.

"Once, a party in Rajasthan owed us Rs 90,000 but the company failed and folded up. We can't go searching for them to get our money back," explained Pavan.

Since the raw material for durries is a waste product, there has been no problem in its supply in the past but now things are changing. Mills in Gujarat and Bombay are closing down creating a shortage of rags. Consequently, prices have gone up in the past two years. Apart from rags, the cotton yarn needed as raw material for the warp has to be obtained from Hathras in Uttar Pradesh. Here, yarn is sold according to the traditional unit of 4 kg bundles called a *paseri*, costing Rs 190-250 each. One hundred grams of this yarn is required for one metre of durrie.

Everything changes with time. Rags which came in cotton are now supplied in polyester and other synthetic materials which create problems in the dyeing process. Earlier, cotton viscose hosiery rags cost Rs 30 per kg, but now this has increased to Rs 55 per kg due to the shortage created by increased exports of hosiery items. "We have no choice of raw materials, we have to make durries with whatever we get," both Pavan and Shabbir concurred. While orders came for dark colours, they could comply only with those that wanted paler colours due to problems of dyeing. Another major problem they faced was the absence of technology in dyeing their products colourfast. Further, Fatehpur Sikri suffered from brackish water which hampered dyeing. All attempts, including the use of the most expensive dyes, have failed and no institution has come forward to help them.

Neither design nor technology has changed radically since the time their work began. The exporter usually provides the designs but occasionally a proprietor who is creative tries out design variations on his own. Very rarely does the weaver provide ideas or his own designs. Since work is linked to specific export orders there is not much opportunity for him to innovate. However, when they find some computer or hand drawn designs are not replicable, they modify them on their own or in consultation with the proprietor who has to satisfy the exporter. "Designers abroad do not always understand the technological primitiveness and problems. A piece with a design covering a space of two metres in a drawing may actually work out to be one metre when woven. In situations like these, we have a problem."

The loom too has been made by the carpenters of Fatehpur Sikri according to their own traditional wisdom. A common six inch pipe is used to roll the warp. The pit loom is two metres wide but can be narrowed or widened as desired. Any number of rugs can be made on one loom, but they usually restrict production to three at a time. The design of the loom has not changed since the early days of its manufacture. Shabbir Khan has to spend a minimum of Rs 125 a year for the maintenance of his looms. With a total of 19 looms to look after, it amounts to a fairly large sum every year.

No one felt the need for advanced technology so they have not even gone in search of it. Apart from in-house training, the outlay for their own survival in terms of infrastructure, training, education, and development is also entirely their own, even when their markets are located in distant lands. All the intermediaries between them and the customers are unknown, unseen, and totally beyond their control except for the likes of Pavan who were their local lifeline.

The raw material is distributed to the weavers by weight. The finished product, the durrie, is weighed again to check for accuracy, providing for a wastage factor of 50 grams per kilogram. If wastage exceeds this limit, the weaver has to compensate the trader, who pays him wages by the metre.

The contractor-weavers get Rs 14 per metre while the labourer-weavers get only Rs 10. The extra payment is for the looms and workplace and the infrastructural facilities provided by the contractor-weaver. Depending on the design, each person can weave one to five metres per day, so the maximum a labourer-weaver can earn in a day is Rs 50 for weaving a plain designless rug. This gives him Rs 1500 per month with which he has to sustain his family. He earns this much provided he works for a full day, every day of the week. Shabbir the contractor, along with his brothers, earn about Rs 5000 to Rs 6000 a month, but they do not necessarily produce to the fullest capacity every month. "If we could get regular work from the government we could even earn Rs 7000 to Rs 8000 per month." To supplement the work given by Pavan, Shabbir and his brothers collect work from other traders as well. They do not have to be exclusively bound to one trader since orders are never regular and looms often remain idle.

To understand a weaver's life it is impossible to ignore the person who provides him with work, since access to the market is through the masterweaver, trader, or shopkeeper, or through whoever gives him the raw material and pays him wages. The discussions have to connect the thread which links the raw material to the weaver and the weaver finally to the market.

Pavan and his family were not benevolent employers but neither were they exploiters. There was a professional matter-of-fact relationship in which each knew the other well, including their problems, limitations, and extent of dependence on each other. Pavan did them no favours nor did they maintain any social links. If they needed an advance for weddings or medical expenses he would extend it against their wages. Just as the cloth mills charged him no interest for a credit delivery he would not expect his loan repaid with interest, but there was no bonus except the customary distribution of gifts and sweets at Diwali.

Pavan too faced problems in getting loans from the bank without paying a bribe, so he too had never applied for one. He invested his own capital into the durrie business, changing from cotton, wool, leather, or jute, to rag durries according to the demands of the exporters. As regards the small business tax scheme, he could pay an annual tax of

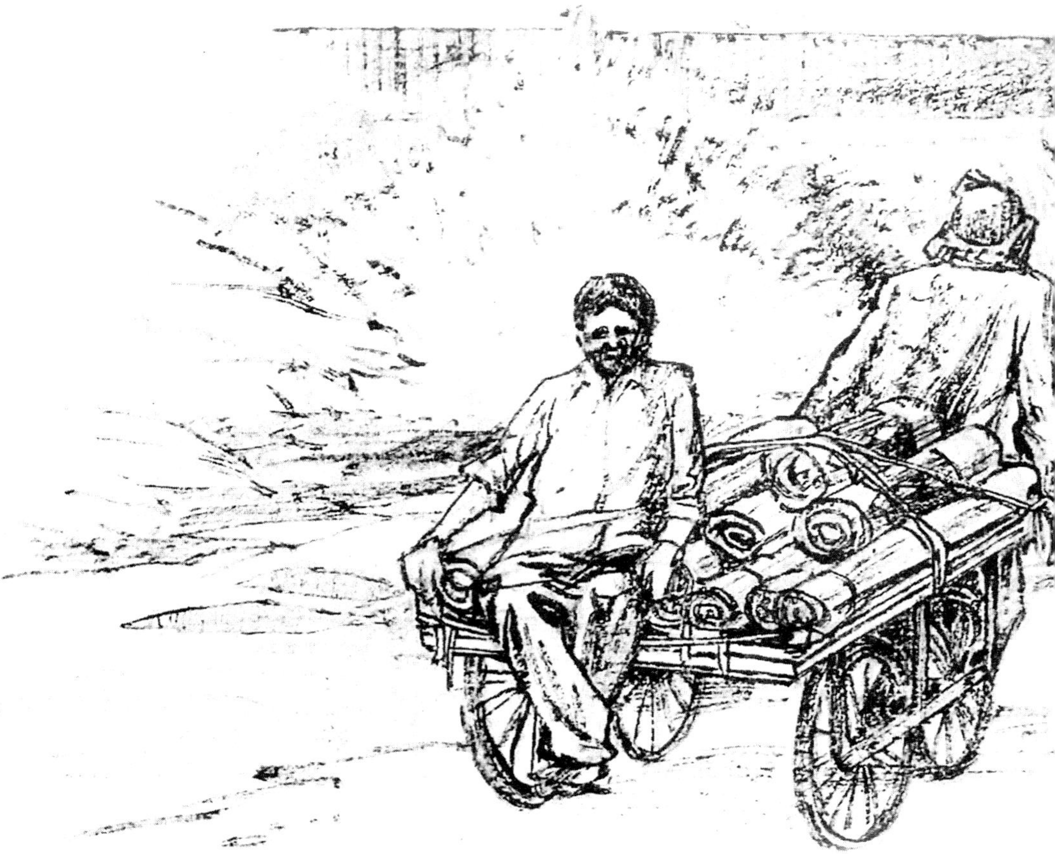

Rs 1400 without having to declare his returns in detail. No sales tax is levied on handloom durries and his payments were received by draft.. What if earnings exceed the amount permissible under the special tax scheme? "You can change the name of the firm to avoid taxes so it never goes beyond the amount stipulated in the scheme," Pavan replied in an off-hand manner, as if it was the most obvious thing to do.

In the durrie trade, the most significant variables involved were raw materials, sizes, and designs. Since Agra was a major centre for shoe manufacture, leather cuttings were available at low cost. Leather floor coverings are coveted items but cannot be supplied at a low cost because the weavers can only produce about a metre length per day. This makes the price of the end product very high.

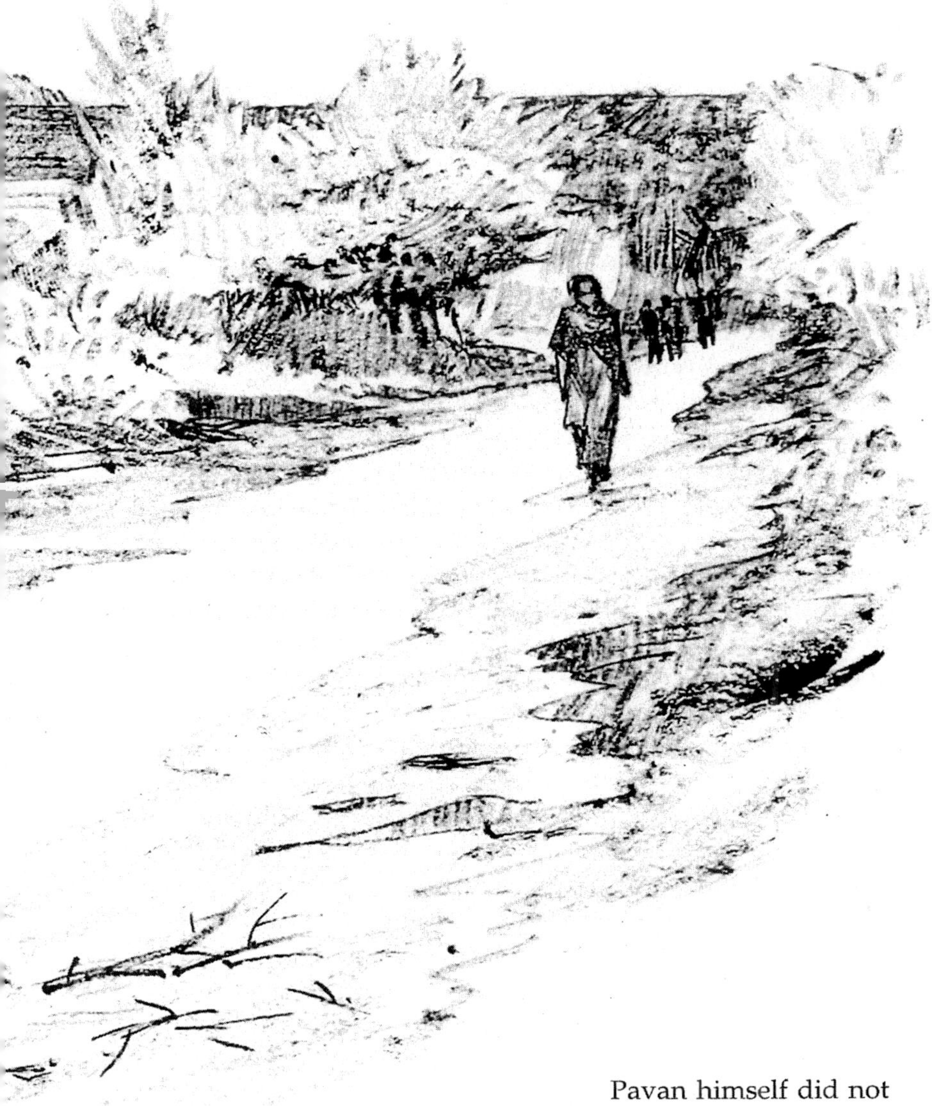

Pavan himself did not supply leather floor rugs because his family did not like the strong smell of leather cuttings. He had about a hundred competitors in Fatehpur Sikri, so he had to be alert and on the mark at all times even though he had a particular number of exporters in Delhi and Bombay who dealt with him regularly. There were no local sales at all.

There is a strange phenomenon in Fatehpur Sikri. Even though the town is full of durrie weavers and traders and the fort is visited by thousands of tourists, no durries are sold in the shops. They should have been as easily available as the red stone, but neither Pavan nor the weavers know of any shop or agency ordering goods for local sales. Sometimes, the truck drivers who deliver the raw material buy a piece for their own use. The government emporium in Agra kept only cotton durries, not rugs. "They say these are for export so we have to believe them, but beyond that we don't know anything. We do not even get the rates we want," said Pavan's father, back at the godown.

Pavan's establishment earns about Rs 36,000 from the sale of durries apart from a small side business of selling raw material (both rags and warp yarn) to other units. Between Pavan and the weavers, they calculated after a lengthy discussion that if they had continuous work, all the durrie traders in Fatehpur Sikri could earn together almost Rs 30 lakhs a month. However, orders were hard to come by and the demand was neither stable nor consistent. Since they did not maintain any stocks other than those on order, there was no scope for reaching out to a domestic market. Because of greater competition, the exporter, according to Pavan, had become more clever and drove a harder bargain. All orders were based on "goodwill" and occasional new contacts came along if one exporter informed another about new sources of supply.

Pavan supplies the finished rug to exporters at about Rs 100 per metre, earning Rs 30 per metre in the process. Both Pavan and Shabbir complained vehemently about the extent of corruption they faced in their attempt to obtain a loan from either the bank or under the block development scheme. "If we want Rs 20,000 to invest in our business, we have to forgo as much as Rs 5000 as a commission. We cannot afford to do that, so we can never improve our own condition."

Neither the weaver nor Pavan had ever participated in any independent domestic marketing experience like attending a local fair or government-organized bazaar. Then how did they expand their business opportunities? "We only maintain our existing contacts. Exporters are not willing to meet or talk to us if we approach them. We wait for them to come to us."

As for promotional material, such as sample catalogues or publicity brochures, Pavan smiled mildly and said it would be too difficult a task for him to handle. He seemed to be content with the plateau-like situation he had achieved. And if durrie exports drop drastically? Pavan was not too concerned. He could always put his capital elsewhere, he explained. For instance, in setting up a cloth shop or going into the stone business. The real problem would be for the "labour," he said, glancing at Shabbir Khan, "what would they do?"

Shabbir Khan looked up and stopped weaving with a wry smile lurking around his mouth. "Manual labour. Roadwork. Digging. We don't worry, we'll see. We only think on a day to day basis. Only if the government thinks about preserving this craft can we think about our future in it."

Outside the workplace, on the dusty lane, children push toys made of wheels and long sticks, and a little wooden platform that carries a brick. These are innovative self-made creations by a generation that may turn to making looms or weaving on them in the next decade. No bright plastic toys for them, only slush, open drains and uncleared garbage amidst the lush green foliage enlivened by monsoon rains which highlight the ancient red of the Fatehpur Sikri fort. The people remember the great past but do not see a bright future. Large Coca-Cola and Pepsi billboards along the roads are the only signs of a new world.

This profile presents the condition of a scheduled caste artisan who works as a single family unit amongst a small group of metal casters in a remote village in the eastern state of Orissa. His traditional occupation and cultural links are much closer to the tribal way of life. In a remote rural setting, he attempts to reach out to urban and international markets through the support of a non-government organization which is itself struggling to survive. Marketing personnel from the organization formed an integral part of the discussions in order to complete the links in the artisan's life.

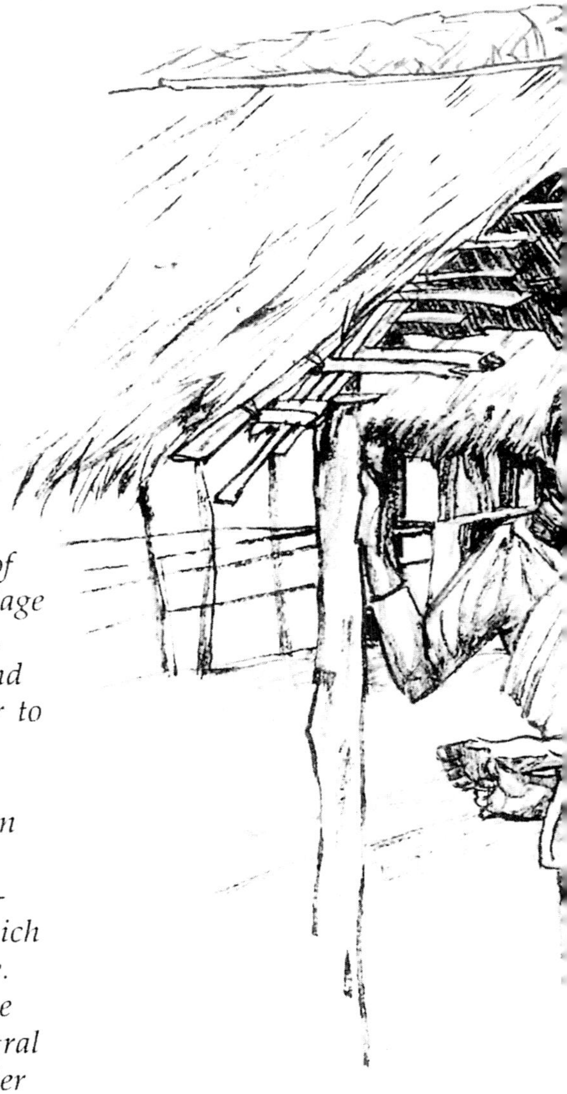

CHAPTER EIGHT

The Dhokra Metal Worker of Jhigdi

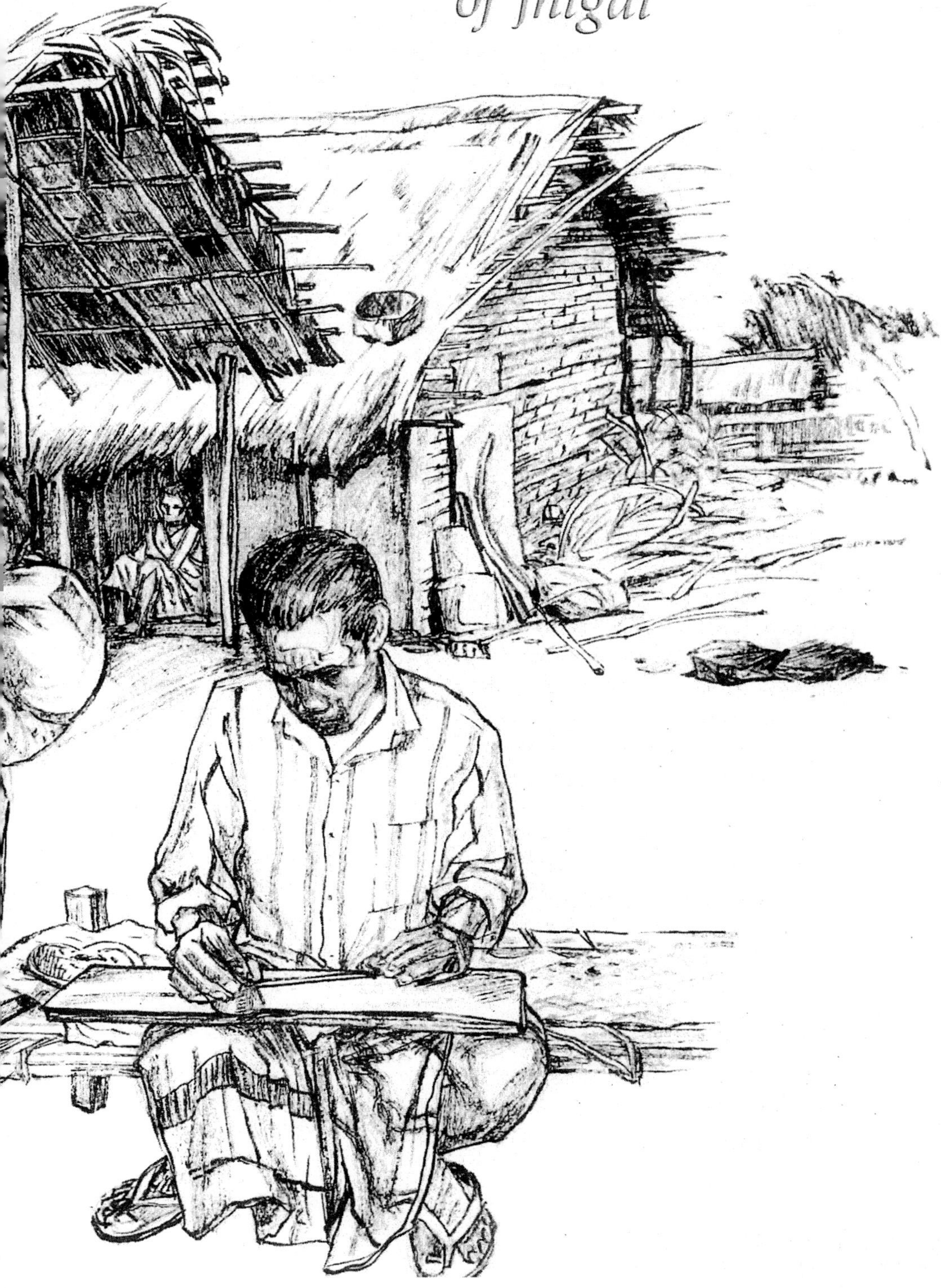

Saheb Mandeka's body begins to ache by four o'clock in the evening, making it difficult for him to continue working at his metalcasting. He wanders about, joining a *kirtan* session or conversing with others in his village. The debilitating effects of six bouts of malaria a year, a spell of jaundice and lack of adequate nutrition limits his output as an artisan and as a part-time tiller of land that belongs to someone else. At thirty-one, he is thin and looks worn out. Most men, young and old alike, look the same in Jhigdi, a tiny village in Bissam Cuttack block of Rayagada district in southwestern Orissa. Well-known as a chronically malaria-infested area, including the deadly cerebral variety, local humour explains that survey operations to lay a railway line between Raipur in Madhya Pradesh and Rayagada in Orissa have not been completed for forty years because the surveyors, one after another, contract malaria and go away. Activists of development organizations fall prey to malaria as well. After working energetically for a few months among the tribals and scheduled castes of this region, they too develop fever, lose weight and after a while hesitate to go beyond Phulbani district into Rayagada.

Jhigdi is a ten-hour drive by taxi through lush, silent forests and vivid green paddy fields from Bhubaneswar via Balliguda in Phulbani district. The road traverses a major part of the tribal area of Orissa, which is home to 62 different tribal communities who still preserve their rich cultural traditions but display an abysmally low level of material development. A narrow red sand road leads off from the main road beyond Bissam Cuttack to Jhigdi. Buffaloes and hand-carts stand still in the middle of the road, compelling anyone wanting to pass to get down and push them out of the way. As we all alight from the taxi near Saheb Mandeka's house, a crowd of children gather around – small girls wearing loincloths carrying their smaller siblings on their hips, some young boys in Hawaiian style shorts in fluorescent colours, and one with a brilliant orange shawl worn around his upper torso which was otherwise bare. For those many hours that we talked about their lives and condition, the children never left, and had to be constantly reminded that they were blocking out the light and air by crowding around us. They readjusted themselves for a few minutes and then forgot our instructions till they were shouted at and shooed away again by irritated elders.

This group of *dhokra* metalcasters belong to the Ghantra community. Although scheduled castes, they not only live in the tribal belt and work to produce goods for the use of tribals but have also adopted all the practices of the ambient tribal culture. Their age-old work and relationship date back to the times of their forefathers and Saheb could not pinpoint when they had begun this form of self-employed artisanry. He migrated to Jhigdi from Gattiguda in Jagdalpur after his brother and his wife died and he did not want to live any longer in a place that had brought him tragedy. In Jhigdi he settled down to work again and married Tulsa Mandeka who is now 27 years old. Four children were born to them – Champa, a girl, now 10, Lakshman, 8, Jayanti, 5 and Chanchali, the youngest girl, aged four. Saheb Mandeka has four brothers, all metalcasters, and four sisters. His parents are no longer alive and as the siblings are scattered in different villages, Saheb has no other financial responsibilities other than that of his own family. He also works as a seasonal agricultural labourer, along with practising his *dhokra* craft and moves around the tribal villages to sell the *dhokra* in the lean season. Neither he nor anyone else in the village group is registered with any government agency, although some including him are members of a Bhubaneswar based voluntary organization called Anwesha Tribal Arts and Crafts Society which promotes and markets the work of tribal artisans spread across Orissa. This society is their only link with the outside world of crafts merchandizing. This non-governmental intervention initiated eight years ago seems to have helped in the transition from selling at weekly markets in tribal villages to reaching out to a wider clientele who were interested in acquiring artefacts of tribal cultures.

Saheb Mandeka was attired in an old handloom *lungi* and striped blue and white shirt. When a Hindi speaking acquaintance joined the group, Saheb asked him to take the chair of honour and speak on his behalf since he could only speak in Oriya. It was only when we insisted that Saheb conduct his own conversation, that he shyly agreed to be the main figure in the discussion. The Hindi speaker was still offered the better chair.

Mandeka's deference towards a Hindi speaker was due to a lack of confidence because of his minimal education. While he could at least write his name, his wife had not even attempted to learn that. It was not the practice in these communities to educate their daughters. Lakshman, the son, was in the 3rd standard at a school in Bissam Cuttack. It was definitely an improvement upon his father's situation. As we sat on charpoys under a thatched projection next to his mud hut, the rain came down heavily from the dark, rumbling sky. Rivulets at our feet and a badly leaking roof did not interrupt our long and intense discussions, even if it meant holding umbrellas while we spoke.

Saheb has his one-roomed hut built ten years ago, with an investment of Rs 3000, on tribal land. He owns a plough, two cows and two bullocks, despite which the family could not drink any milk. The sum total of their assets is one charpoy, a steel chair, some aluminium cooking vessels, and a few steel glasses and plates.

Sahib Mandeka's family members have no land of their own. For two or three months of the year he cultivates paddy nearby for a wage of Rs 500. Apart from the wage, he also gets six quintals of paddy for his consumption but with six family members and a helper, all of whom together needed almost 8 kg of rice in a day, the remaining requirements has to be bought from the bazaar.

Their dietary needs are very basic, as is their daily routine. The entire family sleeps in one small room, unless the male members care to sleep outside. They rise at 5 am and have the previous day's rice gruel – *pokhaal* – mixed with a locally grown red millet, *ragi,* and salt. The slightly fermented preparation is called *mandia.* Brushing his teeth with the neem twig, *datun,* was an occasional activity, he admitted when teased by the bystanders, after which he would have a quick bath under the water pump. There are five tubewells in the village, of which one is shared by the twenty-three artisans. They have some more rice gruel with *ragi* at 9.30 am as breakfast which is followed by school for the children and work for the adults. Saheb's wife Tulsi helps him with the moulding of mud required in *dhokra* metal casting, apart from cooking the midday meal with help from her daughters. Since wristwatches are an unnecessary luxury, the position of the sun heralds noontide, and lunch time. Each person has 200 grams of rice cooked with *ragi.* The low cost of *ragi* (Rs 4 per kg and Rs 2.50 in the peak season) makes it a suitably nutritious constant favourite. Work continues again till 4 pm, when Saheb puts down his tools, except for the occasional periods when a fairly large order motivates him to work till later. At dinner, the family eat rice with a green leafy preparation of spinach plucked from nearby fields. They drink no tea or milk. Children nurse at their mother's breast. When asked what happened if the mother could not feed the child adequately, Saheb explained that the tribals in the forests collect dried droplets of tiger's milk and give them to such mothers in the belief that it would help them produce milk again. At Rs 130 per kg powdered milk from the shops was out of the question.

Major expenses for the family were notebooks and textbooks in June-July when the new session started for young Lakshman, and spices, salt, *ragi* and supplementary rice which they obtained from Bissam Cuttack. Earlier, they used to walk the distance to the shops but with the advent of the "Trekker" taxi which cost two rupees each way, that became their preferred mode of transport. Saheb owned neither a bicycle nor transistor radio, nor did Tulsa own any jewellery except for some brass ornaments made at home. The children wore brass and bead necklaces that are sold at tribal markets.

The major expense was on medicines, because of frequent bouts of malaria affecting almost all the family members. In addition, Saheb Mandeka had suffered from jaundice. Incidence of tuberculosis was also high in the village. The local ANM (public health nurse) visits the village about once a month for family planning care and deliveries of babies, but there have been no health awareness programmes nor have any special measures been taken for malaria control. The side effects of constant malaria result in other ailments as well as lowering of body resistance. They also result in considerable depletion of energy. An average of five to ten days a month were lost because of Saheb's inability to work due to ill health. A Delhi-based voluntary organization called Dastkar had sponsored a five-day health awareness programme with a grant of Rs 13,500 which was implemented through the Anwesha Tribal Arts and Crafts Society and had, according to Saheb, brought about a "twenty-five per cent change" in their lives. Saheb calculated this by saying that some persons gave up the consumption of liquor and the open spaces around their homes were somewhat cleaner. None of their elected representatives, either from the panchayat or from the legislative assembly or their member of parliament have enquired about their health needs, nor has any survey been conducted by any organization to assess the prevailing situation in this area. "If you go to the hospital with any kind of fever, without examining you they will give medication for malaria," said Saheb cynically.

Bipin Sahu, a young marketing activist of Anwesha Tribal Arts and Crafts Society, also participated in the discussions. He related how a young tribal had become seriously ill with tuberculosis. He was taken to the local government hospital in Balliguda and treated. However, he was encouraged by some of his Christian friends to be transferred to the mission hospital in Bissam Cuttack where the same treatment continued. When he recovered, he was told that he should wrap all his traditional ritual objects into a cloth and immerse them in the river and practice a more modern religion. This was seen as an effort to change local cultural practices after conversion. Whatever changes such incidents may have brought about in the lives of the tribals, the makers of these objects ultimately lose their customers. Subtle changes in traditional lifestyles, particularly in religious practices can erode the livelihoods of craftspeople. Saheb listened to this story, looking away sadly, with a furrow on his brow and an occasional nod in agreement.

As Saheb Mandeka could not present the complete picture of the entire production and marketing process on his own. Bipin took over the discussion. It also emerged in the course of the discussion that different methods of assessments and calculations were being followed in arriving at the cost of a product. Many of these differences were resolved only after considerable debate which was largely goodnatured but occasionally turned acrimonious, with Bipin contradicting Saheb's claims and Saheb turning down Bipin's calculations rather contemptuously.

Saheb received all his orders from the Anwesha Society. An advance was received if the order exceeded a value of Rs 2000. According to Saheb, he underwent a loss of about Rs 300 to Rs 500 in each firing. There was a vehement argument about whether his estimate of the loss was accurate or whether skill and careful handling could reduce this loss. Saheb stuck to his guns and after a rather complicated process of calculation arrived at the conclusion that, for an order of Rs 2000, he spent Rs 740 on raw material, lost Rs 500 worth of goods during casting and thus earned only Rs 750. The damage during casting was so great that he could not fulfill an order in one go. Even though Bipin lapsed into sceptical silence, they agreed that Saheb Mandeka or any other skilled metalcaster could earn Rs 3000 a month if orders were good and if he worked diligently. But with the prevailing health and market conditions, they agreed that it was usually not possible to make both ends meet.

Expenses on raw material were quite high. Raw brass was purchased in the local market at Rs 90 per kg, beeswax was obtained from the forest from the Mollar tribe at Rs 120 per kg, mustard oil at Rs 40 per kg came from Bissam Cuttack and firewood at Rs 25 per quintal was bought from the market or collected from the forests. Sand, paddy husk and clay for the outer mould were all collected locally without any cost. While it was possible to walk or take a

Trekker to the market, collection of forest produce meant a walk of at least two or three kilometres. All payments had to be in cash and the tradesman for raw brass had a monopoly, so he gave no credit at all. Over the years, beeswax had become scarce, raising prices considerably, while brass prices had risen by Rs 10 per kg in the past year. Apart from using German silver, locally referred to as 'gitty,' which was available at Rs 150 per kg for what Saheb referred to as 'modern jewellery,' there have been no change in the content of the raw material over the years. Skills have also remained largely constant and rarely varying according to the artisans' innate creative urges.

Saheb Mandeka, like all the other *dhokra* workers, had been creating metal ornaments and artefacts for the large tribal population of Orissa. He had spent his initial years interacting with the tribals in all the village *haats* and moulding designs according to the needs of tribal cultures. The inexorable invasion of modernity in the form of plastic beads and buttons and cheap imitation jewellery in gaudy metallic hues had significantly reduced the demand for traditional jewellery. The conversion of tribals to Christianity over the years had also put an end to the need for ritual objects which were earlier used to celebrate or invoke the various spiritual entities linked with animism and forest cultures.

Saheb's forte was tribal jewellery. He proudly displayed anklets, necklaces, finger rings, earrings, toe rings, lockets, beads for necklaces, hair pins (a special favourite with tribals), armlets, and amulets into which herbal medicines are placed. He also made a range of axes for animal sacrifices, small curved ritual knives, and a slim knife worn by tribal women in their hair knot. It is used for self protection and to cut stalks of grass as they walk through the forest.

After links with voluntary organizations were established, he was introduced to contemporary urban needs such as candlestands, animal and bird figures, and paperweights. He expressed no difficulty in adopting these new designs because he was skilled and ready to learn. However, others around him admitted that there were many whose experience and training were inadequate and they thus found it difficult to easily adapt to modern demands. Saheb had an unusual advantage by having been sponsored to attend design workshops with the National Institute of Fashion Technology in New Delhi for a month and a 15-day workshop organized in Bhubaneshwar by the Sarva Shanti Ayog, a Calcutta based voluntary organization assisting in the marketing of rural crafts. This project concentrated on developing designs for exports as well as for local sales. Costing and marketing were, however, left untouched in the workshop organized by NIFT.

Saheb felt that because a 40 per cent markup was added to the cost of production, the products became too expensive. He had received only one order and no further sales were effected after that. "Who should be held responsible for this?" asked Saheb.

He attributes his ability to produce quality work in a new design range to the vigorous training he received from his father from the age of ten. He had worked along with him until he was fourteen, when his father expired. After that, he worked on his own. "Out of the six *ḍhokṛa* groups in Orissa, Saheb is the jewellery expert of Jhigdi," said one of the onlookers in a matter-of-fact manner, which Saheb acknowledged with matching equanimity.

Even while some aspects of production have changed and some have remained the same, the price factor served as a catalyst for a lengthy and heated debate on how profits had dwindled for the artisan in the past twenty years. Almost everyone joins the discussion which takes place between Saheb and us and between Saheb and his co-artisans, and even amongst those in the crowd of onlookers. Some just look on and laugh, while the children listen wide-eyed although they weren't able to comprehend the conversation. The women listen too but do not join the discussion unless specifically spoken to, and quite often move away after a while to carry out household tasks that brook no waiting. "Earlier, when brass was cheaper, the items were sold for the same price as they are now. Although Anwesha gives us regular work and new design ideas, it would be good if we got more money per piece" says Saheb, launching into the heart of the matter. Bipin Sahu countered: "If you do not work carefully and there is damage during casting, the item suffers in quality and ends up costing more."

They examine a *dhokra* turtle. How much did it cost to produce? Saheb went into a long spell of thoughtful silence. About twenty five rupees. "It costs only thirteen rupees and fifty paise in Mayurbanj district and the quality is better there" remarks Bipin. The debate heats up. If price increases are calculated in rupees and not as a percentage of the inputs it is a loss for the marketing agency and a profit for the producer. "Profit?" shouts Saheb, "Oh, not at all!" How is profit calculated? "Well, we add the cost of raw material, wastage, transport and labour, all per kilogram. If this adds up to Rs 600 a kilogram, we supply it at Rs 750 a kilogram, making a profit of Rs 150 per kilogram".

All this explanation was a result of a lot of heated discussions amongst themselves, but it was still not possible to evaluate the "cost of labour from profit."

Since they worked at will, depending on the seasonal division of time between artisanry and agricultural work, it was even more difficult to calculate the average hourly or daily wage received for their labour. An overall guess which everyone finally agreed upon was Rs 25 a day. All Saheb Mandeka could add to the labyrinthine discussion was that "industrial" earrings with their shiny new metals were much cheaper. Since the local consumer did not care much for the hard work that went into the manufacture of *dhokra* metal jewellery, they bargained a lot and paid low prices. In fact, he had practically stopped producing for the local markets. "If Anwesha paid better prices for the artefacts we would ensure that the quality of the crafts were better." Bipin Sahu laughs in response and suggests that Saheb should examine the problems of marketing before making such demands. Saheb indeed looks and feels as if he is caught in a trap from which he has neither the knowledge nor the power to extricate himself.

The technology and method of making *dhokra* is universally known as the "lost wax process." A wax model of an artefact is covered with a mixture of clay, sand, and paddy husk with a funnel-like opening to pour in the molten brass. If a hundred grams of brass is needed for the finished item, one hundred and fifty grams is used to fill the mould. This is held over a fire and then turned upside down until the brass fills all the empty spaces in the mould. It is allowed to cool, after which the outer mould is broken. Since the brass enters into the space occupied by the beeswax and the wax flows out, the technique is called the "lost wax process". If the temperature is too high the product is damaged. Saheb tests the heat of the fire by hand, examines the colour of the flame, and watches out for the particular aroma that emanates when the brass meets the melting wax. A device for measuring the temperature of the fire had never been proposed in any of the design workshops that he had attended.

His equipment consists of goatskin bellows attached to a bamboo pole to pump air into the fire and a press, rather like the ones used for making vermicelli, for making the threads of beeswax. Eighteen threads can come out at a time. There is a wooden board and a small iron shaped press to flatten and make the beeswax more malleable. Many small strainers with holes of different sizes are used to vary the thickness of the threads depending on the size or design of the final product. They have holes of all shapes, round, triangular and square. A collection of moulds and templates include a ten paise, five paise and one paise coin all tied in a small piece of old red coloured cloth worn by time and use, but as comfortable and reliable as an old shoe. These few wooden and metal tools were all he needed to create his many small works of art. There was no expense in their maintenance except the replacement of an occasionally damaged piece. Saheb and his father before him had used exactly the same tools. Innovative technology has never come his way.

And how could it? The malaria-ridden, tired and somewhat despondent Saheb Mandeka explained that in the past twenty-five years, while tubewells and handpumps, dirt roads and electricity had been provided, there had been no investment in industry in the entire region. The Indira Awas Yojana, a programme for building homes for the poor in the name of the late Prime Minister Indira Gandhi, was abandoned after the construction of a cemented tank which now had nothing but murky and muddy water in it. Many other such abandoned housing schemes are a testimony to the lack of proper planning and the absence of community participation in the decision-making process, resulting in the construction of houses which do not suit the needs of the local inhabitants.

Saheb also speaks of a local workshed, the construction of which was abruptly abandoned midway. The area is littered with such defunct initiatives, perhaps caused by the sapping of energy through malaria or due to cynical politics and bureaucratic apathy. Saheb knew the name of his local panchayat member but not of the member of parliament. "I went to vote. I know my candidate won, but he never came back. I have never been to him to ask for anything". Some people do get things without asking. In a sudden upsurge of emotion, Saheb rose and went inside his hut. He brought out a tattered ration card covered with corrugated cardboard and held it out with anger flashing in his eyes. "Look, I have to pay four rupees a kilogram for ration rice and not two rupees."

"Why?"

"Because I have not been declared BPL." This seemed to be a new kind of definition.

At another village a young artisan who had participated in a month-long demonstration and sale programme at the National Crafts Museum in New Delhi had bought a piece of synthetic material for trousers to wear on "city" occasions, and a BPL. This BPL was, in fact, the ubiquitous "two-in-one," radio and cassette player system, a status symbol purchase. What then, was this BPL that Saheb wanted to be?

The bystanders launched into a discussion on poverty and ration rates. Bipin Sahu untangled the threads of separate experiences and expressions to explain the cause of Saheb's resentment.

"In 1991, a Village Level Worker came here with a surveyor to identify those who would be eligible to receive subsidized rations under the public distribution system. They did not survey anyone's home to identify their living conditions.

Instead, they asked everyone to collect at the local school building and asked the teacher to tell them who was really poor. The teacher did so according to his own whim and fancies. The surveyor noted the names of those mentioned by the teacher and wrote them down in a register as BPL, meaning "Below Poverty Line." No one in the village lived at a different level from the other, yet the teacher's whim and the government's casual approach had denied Saheb Mandeka the opportunity of getting subsidized rice. Some got a loan of Rs 15,000 to "extricate themselves from their present state." The villagers said that no one came back to check what difference a loan of this amount had made in their lives.

How was it possible to increase his income? The discussion again turns to marketing and Saheb sits back, prodding his teeth with a matchstick and watching Bipin Sahu perform. Since he only produces artefacts and has nothing to do anymore with marketing, he appears to use this opportunity to critically assess the efforts of the Anwesha Society to serve the marketing interests of artisans like himself.

The Anwesha Tribal Arts and Crafts society was established in 1989 as a participatory venture between artisan, honorary organizers and activists employed by the society. There were three types of membership, "life, ordinary, and part-time members", and a total of 264 artisans in various skills became members. All the artisans could not be kept fully occupied with regular work. The society maintains a register at the home of each member in which all orders and transactions are noted. Payments are made in cash, occasionally in advance, or by a bearer cheque as few members maintain bank account.

At Anwesha's office in Bhubaneswar, there is a sales outlet through which various tribal products, including painted greeting cards, metal artefacts and ornaments, and some woven textiles are sold. The society sends its activists with all these crafted items to participate in exhibitions, bazaars, haats, and fairs. Exports are routed through Sarva Shanti Ayog. When there are no orders and sales are low, they resort to what Bipin terms as a "pushing sale" to earn enough to cover at least the monthly salaries and expenses of the society. This meant trying to sell items through local shops. Unfortunately, most shops prefer transactions on a consignment basis which does not help in relieving their immediate cash crunch.

Bipin Sahu joined Anwesha in February 1993. Before that he, had worked in All India Radio, the Blue Star Engineering Company, and as a high school teacher. He confesses that he is often disheartened at the dismal condition of the artisans and the marketing of crafts but feels that if he is able to create better markets, he would be satisfied and encouraged to stay on in this field of work. Otherwise, he would yet again have to change his path and Saheb Mandeka would have to painstakingly build a relationship afresh with a new marketing person. Saheb Mandaka was confident of Bipin Sahu's good intentions and efforts. They were friendly enough to carry on a heated argument one minute and then sit down to eat a meal together immediately afterwards.

What were the problems encountered in marketing? Bipin elucidated a personal experience: "Saheb had made a newly designed hair pin which we took for sale to Dilli Haat (a crafts marketplace in New Delhi run by the local government). A brass trader from Moradabad in Uttar Pradesh copied the design in white metal and sold it for ten rupees. Ours costs fifteen rupees. Now there are plenty of such cheap imitations at Sadar Bazar (a vast wholesale market in New Delhi). No one cares for the skill, the process, and the labour. There is always stronger competition from the imitations which have fewer marketing overheads. We wait from exhibition to exhibition. Bastar *dhokra* from Madhya Pradesh is copied in Delhi and sold generally as "*dhokra* tribal crafts."

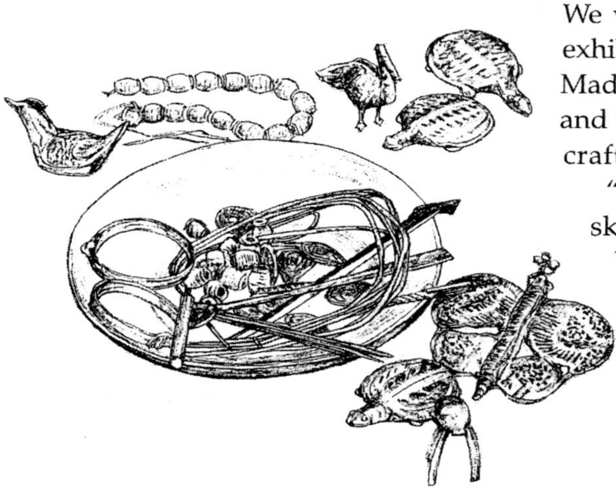

"Where does our identity and skill fit in? They sell these things by the kilogram without examining their quality," said Bipin. Saheb was silent and looked sad again.

What did the future hold for them? Saheb's son is not learning metal-casting because he goes to school. He has not thought about what the child would do after school. There will most certainly be a major problem of employment. Who will give him a job when there is no growth and development around? For Saheb, if Anwesha fails to serve as a useful marketing outlet, he has no choice but to take to agricultural labour as a fulltime occupation. He would earn twenty to twenty-five rupees a day without payment in kind in the form of grain, or he could take grain and fifteen rupees a day.

Just then two men passed by, carrying two vessels supported from a pole on their shoulders. The air was filled with the strong scent of *mahuli*, the local liquor brewed out of the mahua flower and sold at five rupees a bottle. "We only drink at festivals and weddings," Saheb said, as if anticipating a question. The conversation then turned to festivals and weddings. When would his daughters be married and what about the expenses? Although belonging to the scheduled castes, *dhokra* artisans had, over the centuries, adopted nearly all the practices of the tribal culture of their customers. A bride's father can demand cows, goats, barrels of *mahuli* and money as dowry. However, he would have to spend at least Rs 10,000 from his side. Even if it is financially more beneficial to have a girl, she goes away to another village after her marriage. "Only boys can look after their parents in their old age and they are needed to carry the family line forward."

The village has a stereo and public address system which is used during festivals for playing religious and film songs. Musicians and dance-drama troupes, *nachpatis*, live in the village. They perform during festivals or weddings and go to other villages when invited. The main festival of Ghanta Parbo takes place every three years in April. The tribals and scheduled caste artisans collect about Rs 20,000 towards the celebrations which involves buffalo worship and sacrifice on Chaitra Poornima, the full moon in April, at an auspicious time designated by the priest. New clothes are bought for Ghanta Parbo, Dussehra, and Noakhia Parbo when it is the harvest season. Saheb also described the festival of the Earth goddess in June when for three days girls do not cook and do not touch or dig the earth. People from all the surrounding villages gather for this event which lasts for three, five, or seven days. It is a time for making marriage contracts, killing chickens, eating, dancing, talking, and drinking *mahuli*. All work stops, and the world, for at least those few days, seems a better place to live in.

Individuals may or may not eventually represent the average condition. Supplementary data was collected from ten states covering one hundred and fourteen craftspeople. An analysis of the data obtained through the formal questionnaire complements the preceding profiles.

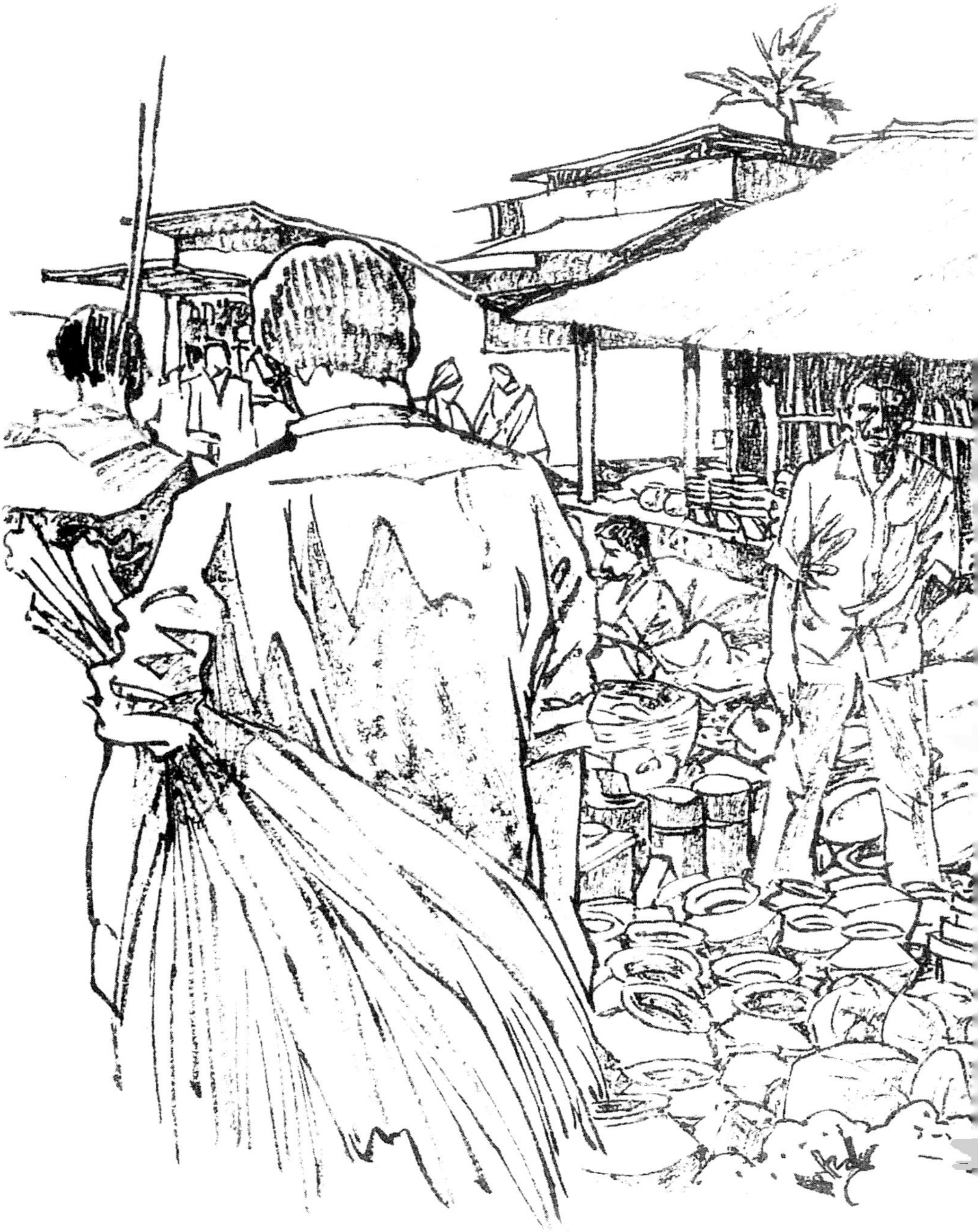

CHAPTER NINE

Explorations Further Afield

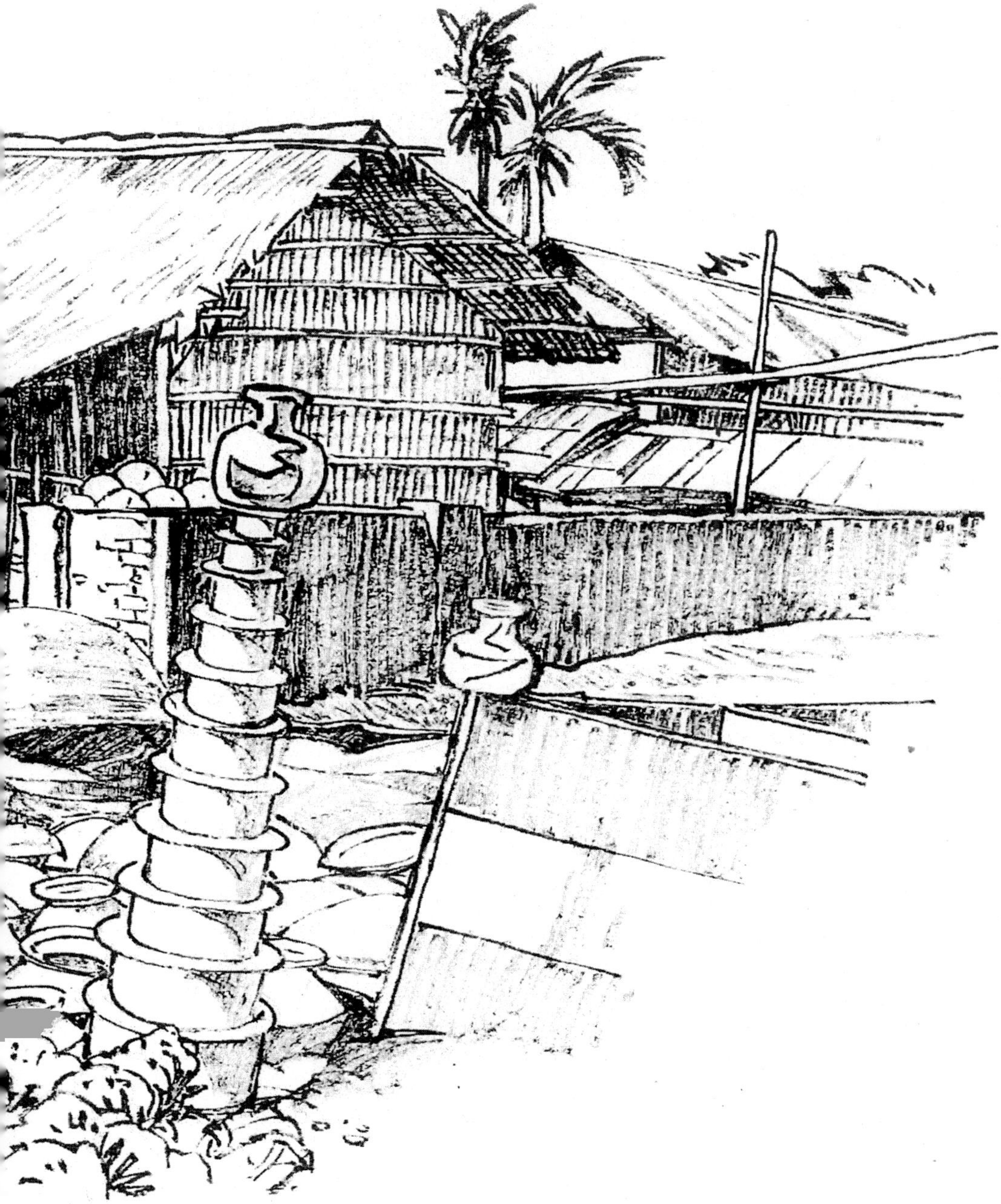

The narratives in the preceding chapters reflect the lives of specific people and the way they deal with their circumstances. They may lead to conclusions that have no validity for a larger group of artisans. On the other hand, when it comes to the essential socio-economic ingredients that place them in a certain position as part of a specific social and economic group, a potter's experiences in West Bengal may not be very different from his peer's in other states. In order to ensure a wider picture that validated, or perhaps, in certain cases, invalidated the stories emerging from the detailed profiles, these were supplemented by a survey of artisans in ten states – Bihar and West Bengal for handloom weaving, Delhi and Gujarat for pottery, Haryana and West Bengal for cane and bamboo work, Andhra Pradesh and Haryana for durrie weaving, Rajasthan for leather, Tamil Nadu for metalcasting, and Uttar Pradesh and Kerala for woodwork. In each state, five to twenty craftpersons' families were interviewed depending on their location and proximity to each other. A greater number of respondents were interviewed in the case of handloom weaving, durrie weaving, and pottery because the craftspeople lived and worked in large clusters, while basketmakers, leatherworkers, metalworkers and woodworkers were living in dispersed settlements or as isolated units in rural or semi-urban communities.

The majority of the respondents (78 per cent) were males. Females constituted a rather small part of the total sample interviewed, reflecting their limited visibility in this profession. Out of the total 114 craftspersons interviewed, 63 per cent were Hindu, 27 per cent were Muslims, and the remaining 10 per cent belonged to other religious groups. The respondents were mostly in the age group of less than 35 years (51 per cent); 44 per cent were in the age group of 36-50 years and 5 per cent were above 50 years.

Members of backward caste communities formed 42 per cent of the artisans interviewed, while 24 per cent belonged to the scheduled castes and the rest to other castes (34 per cent).

The family size of artisans conforms to the national average of five to six members per family. At least 53 per cent of the craftspersons had families ranging between 1 to 5 members, while 44 per cent had 6 to 10 members; 3 per cent of the respondents had more than twenty members in their joint or extended families.

Most rural and urban areas are today provided with some form of basic amenities such as water supply and electricity, even if not regular in their supply. In this respect, 30 per cent of the respondents expressed satisfaction with the level of provision of basic services, a majority (68 per cent) said they had access to some civic facilities while 2 per cent had no access to basic amenities. It is seldom realized that artisans can double their production, avail of technological innovations, and upgrade their own infrastructure only if they have enough electricity and water. Small-scale as well as large-scale industries meet their requirements with major concessions from government and subsidized infrastructure. In contrast, the basic needs of artisans are neglected. If facilitated, they could significantly improve their production levels and the quality of their products.

Few craftspeople work in protected conditions covered by labour laws like the Factory Act. In this study, only 9 per cent of the craftspeople interviewed had some terms of employment formalized, while 27 per cent worked as wage earners under an employer but without any legal protection; 22 per cent had a modicum of such conditions while 42 per cent worked at home where these conditions did not apply. The handloom sector is the largest of all artisan formations in which weavers work as wage earners or in the putting out system with barely any protective terms and conditions. In most other crafts, self-employment is the status of a majority of the artisans.

Our study revealed that whether an artisan was a wage earner or self-employed, the average monthly earning was by and large the same. During the lengthy discussions held for the indepth profiles, it was possible to be fairly accurate in ascertaining the monthly earnings of the respondent, but such a rapport could not be established either in a larger group or by collecting data through a survey. Hence, income levels were not included in the final analysis as the information was likely to be inaccurate. It was possible, however, to assess expenditures on production of various items by the self-employed artisans. Expenses were higher when the raw material or fuel costs were high; they do not signify that the artisan was financially well off. Thirty-nine per cent spent less than Rs 12,000 per year, 14 per cent spent between Rs 12,000 and Rs 23,000, 17 per cent spent between Rs 24,000 and Rs 48,000, and 19 per cent spent above Rs 50,000. It was not possible to ascertain the production expenditures of 11 per cent of the respondents as they were not directly responsible for incurring them.

In craft communities living in rural areas, the assets of a family usually consist of a bicycle, a transistor radio and some cooking vessels, apart from craft tools and equipment. Another category of artisans may possess a small plot of land and a couple of cows. The most fortunate are those who own their homesteads. Given the cost of land, cattle, a house, gold or silver ornaments and metal utensils, the total assets of an artisan family are minimal, in stark contrast to the consumer-driven lifestyles of the urban rich. Twenty per cent of the families owned assets of less than Rs 25,000, 2 per cent had assets valued between Rs 25,000 and Rs 49,000, 10 per cent possessed assets worth Rs 50,000 to Rs 75,000, while 39 per cent had assets valued over Rs 1 lakh. Twenty-nine per cent could not ascertain the value of their family assets. In the case study profiles only two respondents had a reasonable standard of living with assets that define higher status, while the other five were closer to the category which had assets worth less than Rs 25,000.

In artisan communities persons working alone without family help are rare, as has been indicated in the earlier profiles. We found only

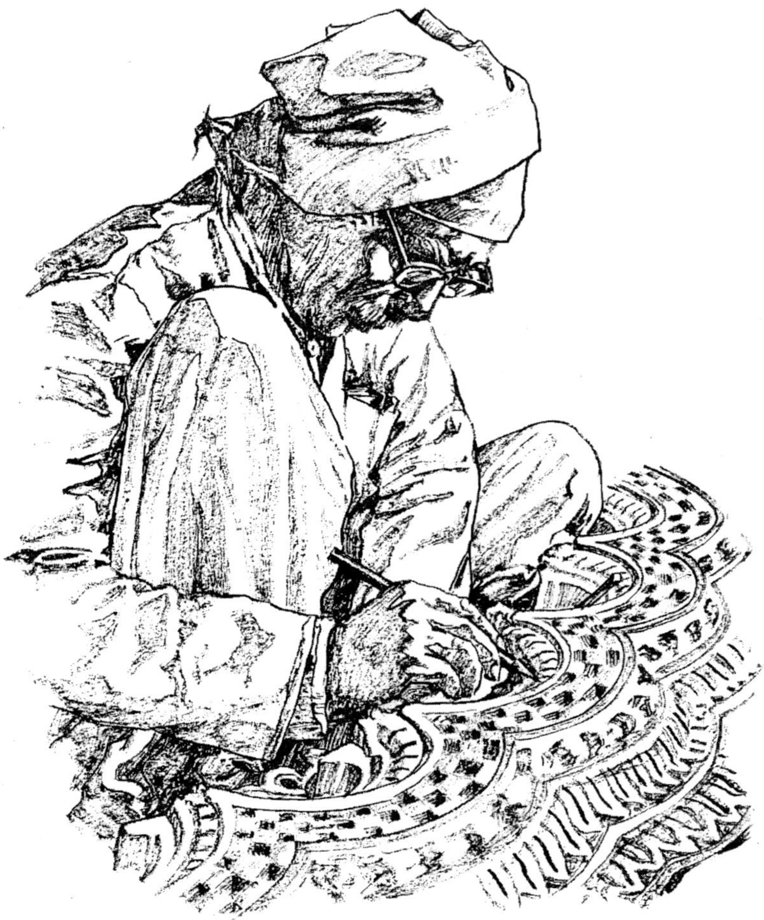

7 per cent working individually without family help. Among the respondents, 71 per cent were working as family units, 8 per cent were a part of a local cottage industry, 7 per cent in a small-scale industry and less than 2 per cent were a part of a co-operative society, while 5 per cent could not be classified in any of these categories. This indicates the inability of artisans for various reasons both within and outside their control, to create and successfully manage a group or co-operative effort, and it also reflects the failure of the existing co-operatives to play the role expected of them. Studies such as Jain and Coelho (1996) have demonstrated that the co-operative movement has largely been undermined by a lack of transparency in management-member relations and by vested interests, particularly in the handloom sector, with some significant exceptions.

Of those surveyed in the supplementary research study, 63 per cent were self-employed, and 37 per cent were wage-earners. In 56 per cent cases the craftwork had been initiated by their forefathers. In some cases (12 per cent) the respondent was a second generation craftsperson, while 25 per cent of the respondents stated that they had taken on crafts as a part of a new income generating activity. Seven per cent gave no clear answer.

Most craftspeople have learned their skills from their fathers or mothers since caste and family affiliation, rather than training or market demand, defines the choice of occupation in rural India. A large majority, over 76 per cent of our respondents, stated that the existence of a family skill was the reason for their taking up craftwork as a means of livelihood. These skills were traditional in nature. A meagre 10 per cent cited the provision of training as the reason for their taking up the making of handicrafts. Market demand as a motivating factor was cited by only 7 per cent as the reason for working. Availability of financial help for taking up of craftwork had encouraged 2 per cent of the respondents interviewed to follow crafts. Other differing reasons were cited by 5 per cent of the respondents.

Despite the need to search for markets, craftspeople are bound by community or family requirements to their home place where the cost of living is considerably cheaper. Forty-one per cent of the craftspeople interviewed were working at their home place, and 10 per cent cited the availability of skilled labour as a reason for selecting their particular workplace. This indicates that the labour, skilled or unskilled, required for the manufacture of their particular products was available either within the family or within the community in which they lived. Better access to raw materials motivated 14 per cent of the artisans to shift the location of their workplace. Better marketing facilities seemed to be limited in terms of access and could attract only 17 per cent to a particular workplace. As many as 19 per cent of the respondents could not point out any specific reason for their choice of a particular workplace. All these factors point to the apathy of the artisan in "chasing" a better market, or the lack of financial ability, incentive or confidence to shift from the secure environment of his or her homestead, however primitive or lacking in infrastructure it may be.

It was in the study of supply of raw materials to artisans that a significant divergence of findings emerged between the survey data and the scenario observed in the case studies. Whereas during the lengthy discussions with artisan families many problems came to the surface, such as non-availability of suitable raw materials and accessibility of support systems, according to the survey, shortage of raw material affected only 15 per cent of the craftspersons, 31 per cent said that the price of raw materials were very high, distances were a hindrance for only 3 per cent, permit difficulties affected 5 per cent, and sundry problems were cited by 7 per cent. While 29 per cent of the respondents said that they had no problems with respect to raw material and its supply, the 10 per cent who were aware of problems connected with raw material could not pinpoint the nature of the problem. In the areas of low quality of materials, diversion to other sectors and depletion of resources, no information was forthcoming.

In most traditional crafts, there has been minimal change in the actual raw material used for production. This can be attributed largely to the lack of provision of education or innovative information to the artisan, lack of mobility to seek alternative materials, and the isolated nature of craft practitioners who follow a traditional craft and thus retain age-old practices, including the raw material used. Sixty-three per cent indicated no change in raw material usage, while 29 per cent had experimented with a change and 8 per cent were left unascertained. Consumer preferences and non-availability of traditional materials were cited as reasons for undergoing changes in raw material. A marginal change in skill was also required because of a change in raw material but usually the consequences of the same were not noteworthy. Only 20 per cent of the craftspersons actually interviewed stated that they had found an improvement in the product after the change in raw material.

About half the craftspeople interviewed had retained production of traditional designs, while the demands of the local market served as a design source for only 7 per cent. New designs were available only to those 24 per cent who were under the guidance of development organizations or, as in the case of weavers, by those involved in the marketing process. Almost 19 per cent of the respondents cited other sources of new designs.

Handwork by its very nature requires minimal investment in machinery. Research and development towards better technology to facilitate the craft sector has been largely neglected. Most artisans work with traditional tools either because they have no knowledge of the alternatives, or cannot afford to seek or invest in either new technology or sophisticated machinery. The artisans were observed to be spending very meagre amounts on acquiring new technology or machinery. Of the artisans interviewed, 96 per cent had spent less than Rs 5000 on technology or machinery. Artisans usually incur some maintenance costs for the machinery. Fifteen per cent of the craftspeople interviewed could afford less than a Rs 1000 annually on such expenses. Those who had changed their tools and equipment in the past twenty years (17 per cent), had found that production had been positively affected by the change. However, a vast majority had nothing substantial to share in the way of new developments in their field. They are restrained primarily due to their weak economic base.

While training has formed an integral part of government programmes, craftspeople largely have no access to modern training facilities. A majority of craftspeople have acquired their skill through the tradition of passing down knowledge from father to son. However, specific training from parents or teachers was obtained by 54 per cent of the craftspersons interviewed, while 24 per cent claimed no formal training apart from household observation and participation. Twenty-two per cent of the respondents could not elucidate any details on their training. In most cases, training was perforce a part of the tradition of continuity of occupations among artisan caste groups, and not a sought after choice based on market needs.

Access to finance has always been a major problem for craftspeople because of the intimidatory nature of banks and government offices and their own illiteracy which denies them direct access to information on how to obtain the benefits of government schemes. Financial viability can only be feasible if there is an assured market. Government sources of finance were made available to those craftspeople who had links with voluntary organizations, who in turn had the capacity to mobilize funds on their behalf. Among the respondents, 29 per cent had availed of government schemes for finances, while only 7 per cent had taken loans from private financiers (more often usurious money-lenders), and 64 per cent had not availed of any financial support at all.

Finally, we come to the influence of the market on the lives of craftspeople. The preceding findings, while linked to the play of market forces and the extent of consumer demand for goods made by traditional craftspeople, have pointed only to their indirect effects. The desperate need for better marketing facilities and other support systems is indicated by the large numbers for whom craft activity is the main source of income. In our study, 83 per cent of the respondents were dependent on craft production alone for their livelihood, while 12 per cent had other sources of income, and 5 per cent could not indicate their exact situation.

A major part of the data collection exercise was devoted to aspects related to the use of their products by themselves or their ability to reach a wider market. Handmade items are largely produced for local and national needs, and many crafts are sustained by rural consumers who use them for subsistence activities, domestic use, and ritual or festival related purposes. Rural craftspersons are integrally linked to the various processes in the agricultural production, from the sowing of seeds to post-harvest celebrations, and their production cycles retain a rhythm dictated by the agricultural cycle. At certain points in history, craftspeople have been promoted by royal patrons and these crafts pursued a trade or export-related path after feudal support systems were dismantled. The famed Kashmiri shawl, carpets, stone inlay work, the brocades of Varanasi, and other such crafts that had been supported by the princely courts moved into the hands of entrepreneurs who set up worksheds, often in the name of co-operatives, even if the system employed were exploitative and iniquitous.

Rural crafts related to an agro-based culture remained largely unaffected by these processes and went along other paths to find customers. While, traditionally, the weekly village markets or *haat*s provided the most easily accessible outlet for handmade products, both mechanization and urbanization have led to rural products finding their way into city markets, where they acquire a certain degree of sophistication, quality upgradation, and metamorphosis of usage to attract the urban customer. There is, however, a qualitative difference between adaptation of skills to a wider range of products and the conversion of one product into another. For instance, *dhokra* metal-casters learned to make soap dishes or hooks to hang clothes, but in many cases the object produced completely changes its traditional or functional use – metal anklets are merely given a base covering and converted into ashtrays, laminated Madhubani paintings became tablemats, and Warli adivasi motifs or *ikat* dyed designs are screen-printed by industrial units onto fabric competing with the handmade sector.

Among the respondents interviewed, 22 per cent sold their products locally at the village or town level, 12 per cent used city outlets, and none dealt directly with foreign markets. About 19 per cent of the respondents sold their goods through private agents who were either mastercraftsmen, wholesale or retail traders, or exporters. Only 7 per cent made use of the mechanism of co-operatives to market their products. Voluntary organizations were used by a minimal 5 per cent of the respondents for marketing their products, and government institutions were used by only 7 per cent of the respondents as channels for marketing. Twenty-nine per cent had no assured marketing channels and depended on whatever support they could gather depending on changing circumstances. An attempt was also made to assess their access to a combination of marketing channels. Less than 10 per cent of the respondents had access to a variety of marketing options and 27 per cent could not enumerate clearly the number of channels to which they had access to for selling their products. While the case studies did not indicate a high level of self-consumption of products, the supplementary research found 54 per cent of the respondents using their own craft products, whereas 15 per cent stated that they did not do so and 30 per cent were non-committal.

The *mela* or fair is an integral part of the social and cultural life of rural India. It is an occasion for commerce, entertainment, and the cementing of social relationships. While traditional fairs connected with the trading of cattle, religious events, and harvest celebrations still continue, nearly all have been flooded with cheap industrial goods that have created strong competition for handicraft products. Simultaneously, tourism and craft development institutions in both private and government sectors have successfully created simulated rural environments to which craftspersons are invited. While these new endeavours may have provided opportunities for marketing, the process for participation becomes bureaucratized and remote, alienating all but those who already know the ropes. A majority of the respondents interviewed had never participated in any mela. This could be attributed to the nature of their product and the unsuitability of a fair as a marketing outlet for their goods. Twenty-nine per cent had participated in traditional melas and only 9 per cent had the experience of having participated in state-organized melas. Very few (3 per cent) of the respondents had participated in both traditional and state-organized melas, while the participation of 17 per cent in such events could not be ascertained. The benefits enumerated by the respondents of participating in melas are: (i) increased sales, (ii) interaction with other manufacturers, and (iii) opportunities for direct sales. However, of the respondents who

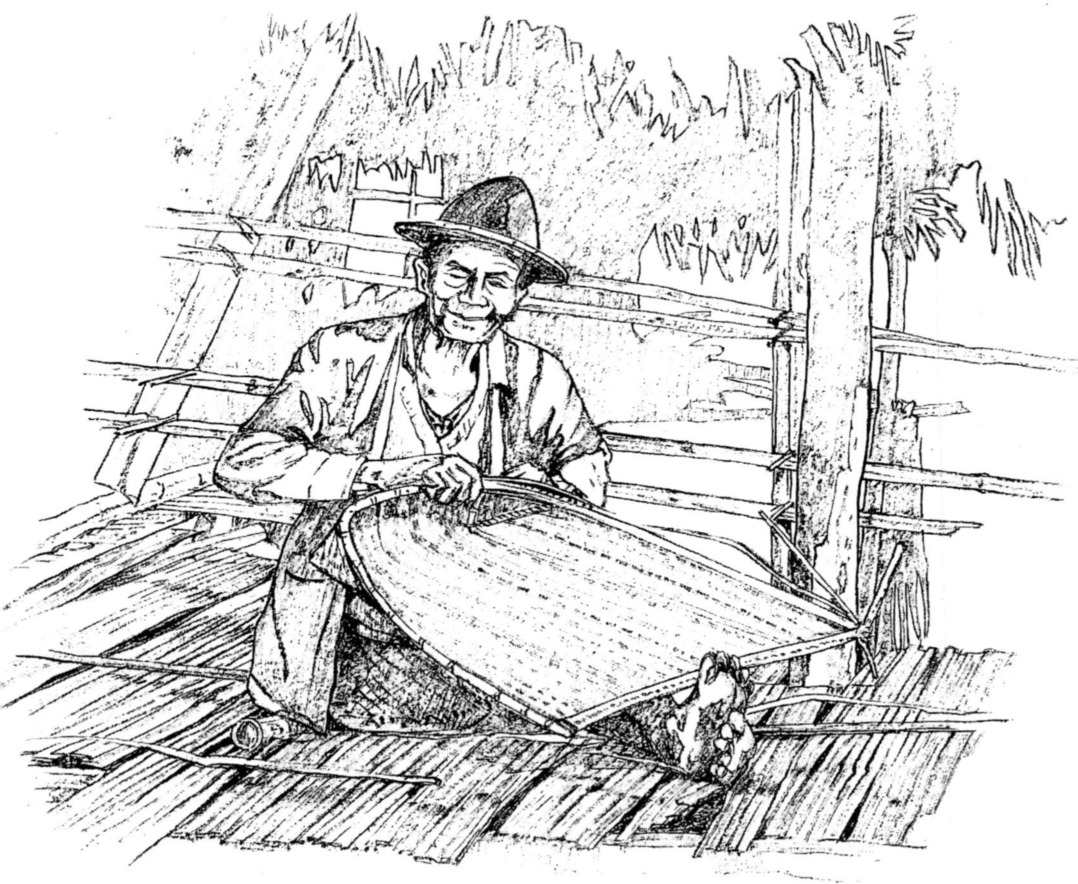

had participated in melas, only 22 per cent stated that this exposure had resulted in increased sales. Contemporary marketing techniques are practically non-existent among craftspeople and there is a sharp contrast between the aggressive confident marketing strategies of modern industry and the more timid, low cost, compulsion-led marketing which is related to the traditional social status of the craftsperson. The packaging of goods, for instance, in the view of a majority of the respondents, had everything to do with protection of the item, and very few (2 per cent) had experimented with new types of packaging to enhance the attractiveness of the item for sale. High costs of sophisticated packaging were a significant disincentive for the craftsperson.

Craftspeople in almost all areas have been primarily concerned with production and not with sales promotion. This is clearly revealed by our findings, with 46 per cent selling their products through contact retailers and being thus unable to understand or influence consumer preferences. Twelve per cent had made no attempt at all to promote their wares, which indicates total dependence on other agencies to undertake marketing of their products, extreme apathy, or the presence of a committed clientele who constantly need their goods. Only 8 per cent used brand names, pamphlets or posters, or other forms of advertising or door to door sales to promote their products. Five per cent of the respondents said that they had at some time made use of more than one of the above mentioned methods. Twenty-eight per cent could not describe their attempts to promote sales.

While craftspersons were compelled to use their only known skills as a part of a continuing social and economic tradition, they were clear in their realization that their sales were by no means commensurate with the desired quantity. Only 12 per cent were satisfied that their supply matched demand, or felt that the demand stimulated a supply that sustained their livelihoods adequately. Forty-seven per cent of the craftspeople interviewed were unhappy about the low quantum of sales of their products, while over 40 per cent felt that they were compelled by fate, personal circumstances, and limited access to alternatives to accept a situation with which they have to be content.

What roles do craftspeople serve and are the present systems that serve them adequate? There can never be definitive answers or conclusive solutions. That is why the story of India's craftspeople remains unconcluded. However fresh attitudes and paths need to be created and explored so that craftspeople can be an integral part of a new and forward looking India.

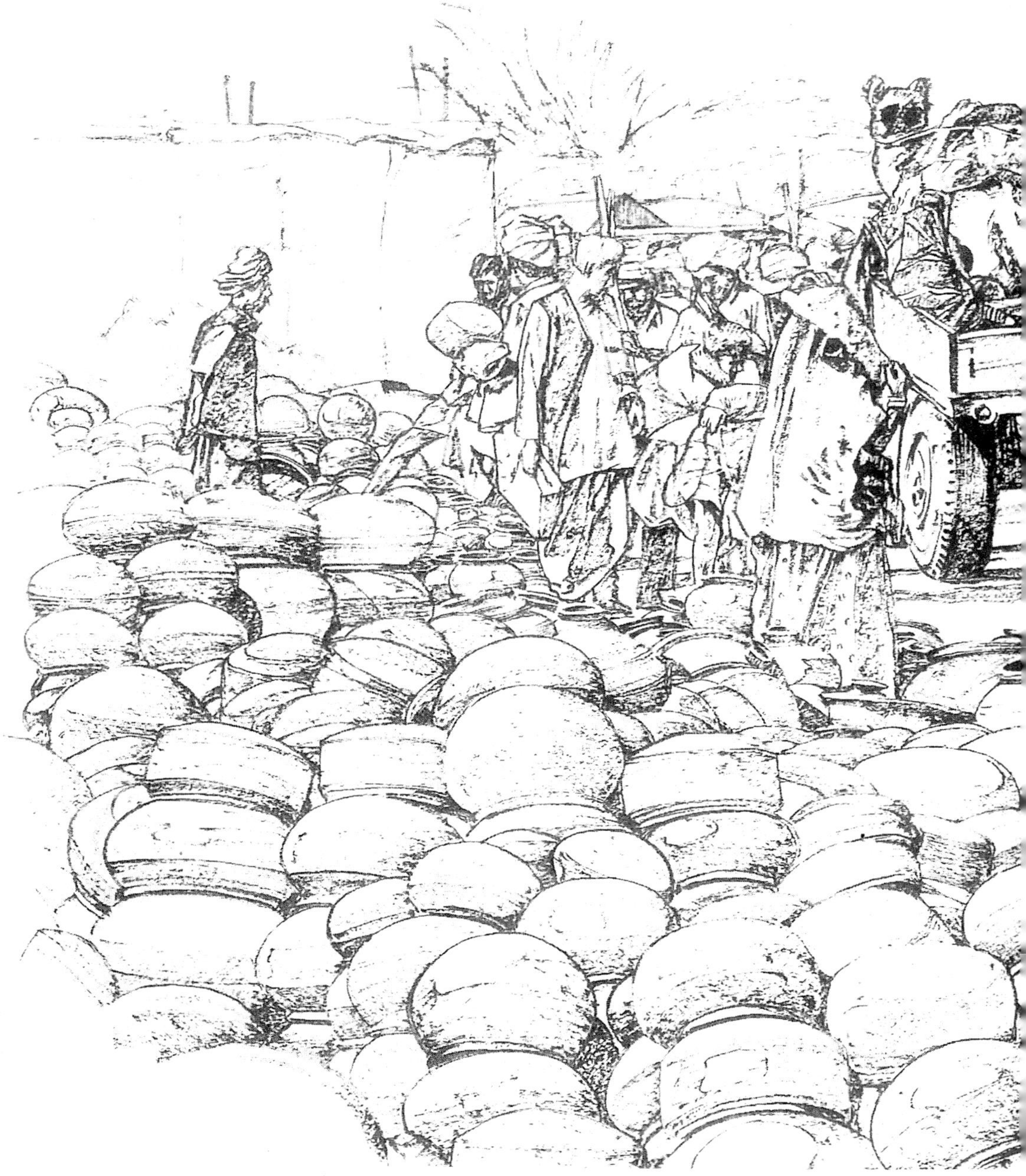

CHAPTER TEN

The Story Unconcluded

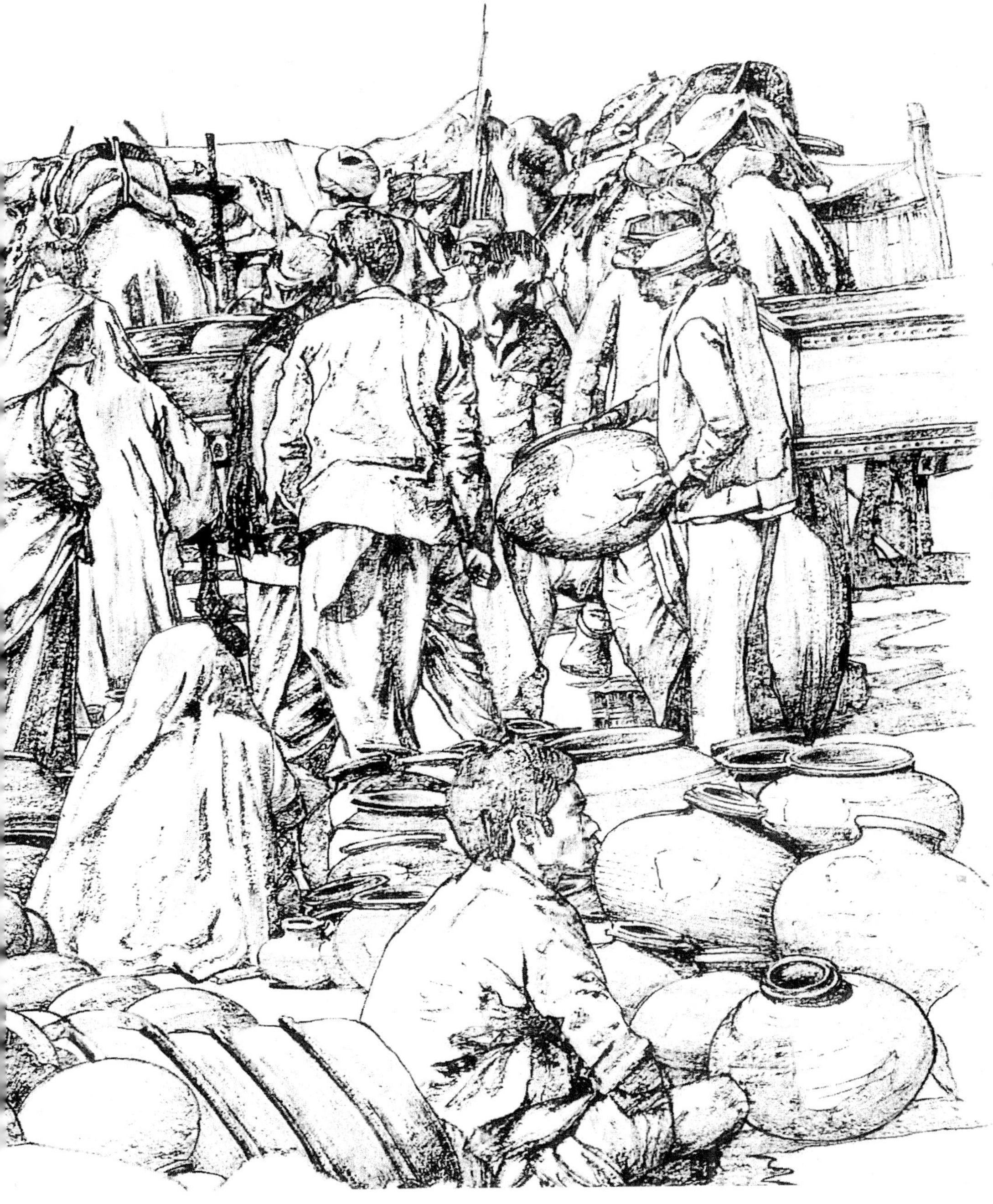

Torchbearers of India's craft traditions, inheritors of ancient technologies and cultural systems, artists and creators living within a binding community ethos, producers in an agro-based economy, and philosophers who accept the link between the spiritual and the material – these are the many roles which craftspeople play. Yet despite their long history and the plethora of plans and schemes evolved for them by various governments since India's Independence, there may be no more than a few thousand craftspeople who are comfortably placed both socially and economically. The rest eke out their livelihoods at bare subsistence level. Even this number is a generous estimate. A census does not reliably ensure coverage of seasonal artisans or those skilled artisans who have been marginalized in rural areas and forced to shift to city slums in search of alternative employment. Handloom weavers in Delhi slums share space with rag-pickers, some produce rag durries or embroider quilts with scraps of cloth obtained from tailoring establishments. Itinerant grass-mat weavers and basketmakers work in empty fields or on crowded city pavements and are seldom enumerated. As part-time or leisure-time craftspeople, they still form a part of a productive economy even if their status remains low and their incomes merely assure one full meal a day for each member of the family.

The average income derived from handwork, as found in our profiles, is Rs 2000 per month for an average family of five members. This amounts to Rs 13.50 (approximately US$ 0.25 dollars) per day per head. It may be pertinent to note here that in a reply to a question in Parliament in 1997, the Ministry of Home Affairs stated that it cost the exchequer Rs 48.60 ($1.13) per day to provide the basic requirements, including food, for a prisoner lodged in Delhi's Tihar jail. When posed with this fact many a craftsman and woman fell into rueful thought and commented, not without a sense of humour, whether a spell in jail were not better than a life of craftwork.

The caste-oriented division of work has remained firmly in place in rural areas, while it is slowly breaking down in urban areas for those who find a sustainable income out of making articles for export or selling to wholesalers. They also occasionally get an opportunity to retail directly to customers at roadside markets.

The privatization of common property resources has serious

implications for the survival of a number of crafts. Being at the lower rung of socio-economic ladder in the village, they increasingly face hardship in obtaining raw materials. The village commons near small towns and larger villages which provided fine clay for potters are colonized to provide for the housing needs of a fast-growing population. Forest produce is usually drawn away by the economically well-positioned, leaving the tribals at their mercy for materials needed to produce crafts. Much of the bamboo in the country is diverted to the production of paper by big mills at very low rates, while the artisan has to pay more than ten times as much for the same bamboo. A vast resource has also been left undeveloped, affecting not just bamboo artisans but those who could benefit from value-added bamboo products even in the industrial and building sectors. Broom-makers, mostly women, in the forest areas of Madhya Pradesh and Orissa face hostile laws and forest officials who do not permit them to cut the local grass to produce their brooms. Sandalwood in Karnataka is diverted to exporters manufacturing perfumed oils, and cotton is exported for foreign exchange leaving the cotton yarn market in a constant state of flux which affects the handloom weaver adversely. In the past ten years, the handloom weavers of Andhra Pradesh have resorted twice to mass suicides after petitions, blockades and various types of peaceful agitations failed to find a sympathetic ear. Even after these incidents, conditions have improved marginally for some only because of emergency measures rather than as the result of a change in long term policies to provide them security and justice. Silk weavers are dependent on policies regarding the import of yarn from China and have also had to resort to agitations to attract attention to their plight.

Organizations of handloom weavers are not of uniform strength while craftspeople in rural areas have hardly any organizational structures at all. Tamil Nadu has the best organized handloom marketing enterprises in the public and co-operative sector and weavers do have some impact on state policies. The north-eastern states have the largest number of household looms, mostly operated by women, but they are not reflected accurately in terms of productivity for the market as most of the articles are still produced for self-use and as symbols of tribal identity. Vast numbers of handlooms have been wiped out by the uncontrolled growth of powerlooms which have taken advantage of glaring loopholes in policies for the textile sector. This took place on a large scale after the announcement of a new textile policy in 1985 which put a Reservation of Items for the handloom sector in place with no monitoring or controlling authority. Powerloom owners challenged the act in court, and in the process powerlooms expanded rapidly, taking over production of many items earlier produced exclusively by handlooms.

The low social status and depressed economic conditions of handloom weavers in the past three centuries preclude any confident action on their own part to improve their position, particularly by influencing government policy. There are, however, those few scores of outstanding weavers, particularly of silk, who are able to continue the quality of work found in earlier times. In Karnataka, Tamil Nadu, and Andhra Pradesh in the south, Gujarat in the west, Orissa in the east, and Uttar Pradesh in central India, masterweavers are able to dazzle the senses of a connoisseur with silk fabric of the kind that cannot be replicated anywhere else in the world. As before, these go into the homes of the aristocracy and the elite – the '*sahib*s' and '*memsahib*s' of the world, while the coarse *gamchha*s, thick saris and wraps made by the simple handloom weaver for a local clientele or for their own use are fast losing their traditional customers. The vast market in between these two varieties have been largely taken over by synthetic blends and cotton fabric made in textile factories or on powerlooms. All efforts at modernizing and improving the textile sector focus on mill and powerloom interests with a few afterthoughts for the benefit of handloom weavers. Even though India's climate requires emphasis on the use of cotton fabrics, a strange logic compels India's policy makers to develop synthetic yarns and fabric for domestic use and cotton for exports. Apart from the difficulties created for handloom weavers, the effect of synthetic fabrics on skin and general health in hot climatic temperatures is an area of study that has been completely neglected.

Brass workers in Moradabad and glass units in Ferozabad, both in Uttar Pradesh, have formed organizations to increase their ability to be heard in the corridors of government. Carpet weavers and bamboo workers are also in the process of linking with national or international organizations to secure policy support. Despite innumerable efforts at creating fora to facilitate the needs of different sections of craftworkers, the results are minimal and usually localized.

With both earnings and social status not showing any signs of significant improvement, most small artisans do not see a bright future in their craft for the next generation. Often, even if the earnings are sustainable, there is a burning desire to escape from the identification of their low status in the social hierarchy. A job as a peon in an office, preferably in government institutions, is the ambition of many craftspeople for their sons, so that they may have job security and official status. The failure to obtain such jobs in a climate where downsizing is the norm dictated by a new global economic order, has resulted in sons staying home and having to help their elders despite this not being the preferred choice. Members of the artisan community do not have the necessary educational qualifications or intellectual environment at home to apply for jobs opening up in the new service or information technology sectors. This necessitates a much greater effort at widening and strengthening policies to sustain livelihoods in which they are already skilled and productive.

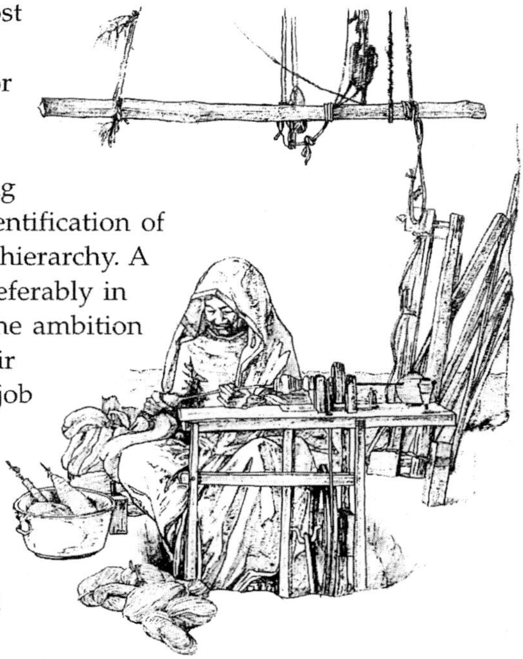

Women in crafts production

Early writings pay little or no attention to the role of women in handwork, whether they were independent producers of goods, or helped the menfolk by collecting raw material or processing the product during certain stages of its manufacture. After the 1970s, as the world became more conscious of gender justice and women's rights at the workplace, some sporadic reports and studies of women artisans highlighted their unequal position. Women weavers who weave at home as part of their traditional cultural practices do not gain any commercial benefit, while women as helpers in the pre- and post-loom processes work largely without any wage, as they are considered to be assisting their menfolk voluntarily as a family exercise. The wage component in the end-cost of handwoven fabric is thus never adequately reflected, since the free labour of women, and often of children, is hidden. Traditional attitudes have slowly changed in areas where persons of one sex operated the loom. In the south of India, women weavers take on men's jobs when family circumstances compel them. In Kashmir, women have taken to embroidering for commercial establishments in what was once exclusively a male domain. Amongst those under the poverty line, women have played the part of providing a supplementary income to the family by artisanal activity. A considerable number of women also head households as the sole earners in both towns and villages. Their enterprise and perseverance as well as inherent skill in handicraft activity have sustained and helped many to achieve a degree of financial security.

An increasing amount of handicraft work practised commercially by women within farming or dairying communities have provided a certain stability of income, particularly in times of drought or other natural calamities. In areas where craft skills such as embroidery, weaving, jewellery-making, and folk styles in wall painting are already a part of community tradition, women have demonstrated considerable enthusiasm in mobilizing themselves for economic benefit.

At the unfortunate end of the scale, women in fishing communities have suffered from the development of export-led aquaculture and multinational trawler fishing by losing the earnings from the crafting of baskets, nets, rope, and leaf mats used for packaging. In potters and stonecutter communities, as far apart as Kerala and Rajasthan, women have been forced to succumb to prostitution because markets for handmade utensils and other locally used artefacts had eroded.

Confused definitions

Handicrafts are officially described as handmade objects of artistic value which may also be utilitarian. This displays the basic attitude towards development policies, which focus on the decorative, ornamental nature of the object, thereby neglecting the technological development of all handmade goods made purely for everyday use, such as simple earthern pots for tea, hand-twisted grass ropes, date palm leaf brooms bamboo baskets for transporting agricultural produce, and other unglamorous but eminently usable items made by hand.

Correct nomenclature, such as referring to utility items as Indian handmade crafts rather than ethnic artefacts, will not only save craftspeople from the vagaries of fickle export markets, but also instill a sense of pride in Indian products which compete with those traded and promoted by the highly industrialized national and transnational corporate sector, as well as the small scale industries sector.

Even though the freedom movement and the adoption of khadi by political workers of all hues meant, at least technically, that *swadeshi*, or self-reliance, was to be our pattern of development, the industrial sector was developed exactly along lines energized by the very same industrial revolution that destroyed many of our village industries in the first instance. The net result of this contradiction was that, while some handmade goods received development inputs at the decorative, higher-income bracket level, village industries became a separate entity, starved and at times obliterated, although they were the basic foundation and the feeder industries for the more elevated, decorative skills of the handicrafts industry. So while a few thousand craftsmen and women are acknowledged and honoured, hundreds of thousands have been divorced from their skills through loss of access to raw material, credit, and, most importantly, markets amongst the masses. The incongruity of having Khadi and Village Industries in the Ministry of Industry under a separate department of small-scale industries, and handlooms and handicrafts placed within the Ministry of Textiles, when they are all part of village industry, needs to be rectified.

The marketing of crafts

The greatest felt need of the craft sector is the creation of wide and well developed marketing facilities. Neither training, nor design and product development, nor easier access to credit and cheaper raw materials can on their own sustain the craftsperson unless marketing avenues with the least number of intermediaries are available simultaneously. Excellence is often demanded from craftspeople who cannot provide it because of the inability to afford the best raw materials or the time required to achieve perfection. Only confidence in a pre-assured market can encourage enterprise in this direction.

In the context of generating employment in the non-farm sector, a major thrust during the Eighth Five Year Plan was to provide marketing opportunities to craftspersons. Apart from organizing short term sales through exhibitions and fairs in all the states, efforts were made to establish permanent marketplaces under the Urban Haat scheme. The marketplace consists of 70-100 stalls and open spaces which are occupied by craftspeople on a fortnightly basis on the payment of a minimal rent. Additional areas are provided for storage, cultural activities, exhibitions, regional food stalls, toilets, and other facilities. The success of the first *haat* in Delhi, established in 1994, and called the Dilli Haat, led to the adoption of this scheme on a larger scale in the Ninth Plan. Over its five year period, twenty more haats are proposed to be established in various state capitals or large towns, opening up a vast informal infrastructure for craftspersons to hone their marketing skills and earn better profits through direct interaction with customers. The call for market-led growth in the early nineties not only meant opening up the country for global players, but assisting to assist rural producers by making urban markets more easily available to them. At the same time the earlier dependence on subsidized marketing programmes were changed to more self-sustaining marketing efforts. The need for providing suitable infrastructure when removing subsidies was the argument behind the concept of Dilli Haat which integrates traditional village marketing systems with contemporary management practices and an aesthetic ambience.

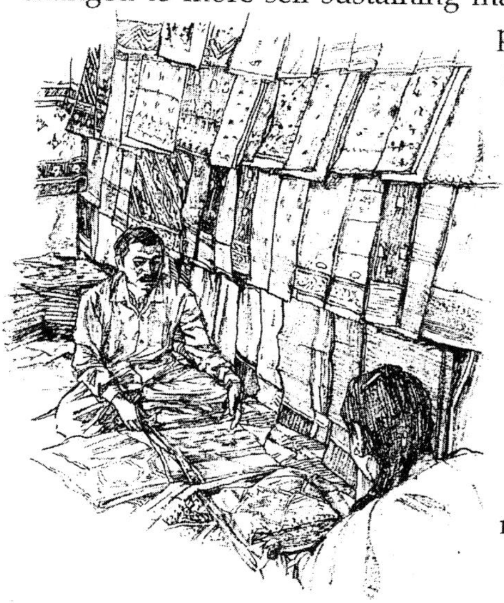

Despite its popularity as a marketplace within a park, the unique experiment of Dilli Haat, still requires better management systems, particularly in the methodologies of identifying and selecting genuine craftspeople to use its facilities. A rotational system of occupation by craftspeople in fortnightly stints needs a co-operative effort from both the bureaucracy running it and the craftspeople who seek space there. This kind of marketplace has attracted a much wider range of customers than the government craft emporia, which often present a picture of bureaucratic apathy, or the private boutiques which cater to an up-market clientele looking for high value exclusivity. It has also provided an interface between designers, exporters, wholesalers, and retailers apart from the casual shopper and the Indian or foreign tourist. The interests of various customers and tourists need to be addressed simultaneously, but the interests of genuine craftspeople seeking a marketplace of their own should remain uppermost in order of priority. The Development Commissioners of Handlooms and Handicrafts in the Ministry of Textiles need to modernize the department's approach towards the administration of the craft sector and set up a better mechanism for implementing innovative marketing strategies such as Dilli Haat. Red tape in the age of liberalization has seemingly become worse with both non-government craft development organizations and craftspeople themselves unable to access funds in a transparent yet speedy manner. Hierarchies and sectionalized structures, corruption, or heavy handed attempts to avoid it, contribute to a slow-moving process in government that kills the vibrancy and dynamism needed to energize individual craftspeople or artisans' societies.

In an era of advertising, where the national and international corporate sector have millions of rupees to spend on pushing their products, the decentralized and largely unorganized sector of handicrafts and handlooms suffer a great disadvantage. Publicity budgets for individual organizations who hold exhibitions are miniscule compared to the high cost of advertizing in newspapers with a wide circulation. Television slots are out of the question also because of prohibitive costs. The "Be Indian – Wear Indian Handlooms" advertisements of the late 1970s to boost the number of big handloom expositions held across the country degenerated into discount sales of products which were often not of handloom fabric at all. Promotional efforts by the central or state governments encompassing the entire craft and handloom sector are sadly lacking and are limited to a few hoardings and advertisements occasionally put out by the state handicrafts emporia. The craftsperson cannot imagine ever being able to advertize his product in the marketplace on his own. In the age of advertiszing and global trade competition, viable support systems in this area are an imperative. The e-commerce outreach is still far from the grappling with basic needs such as electricity. The website offers made by city based agencies are beyond their grasp and active participation.

Information for development

The offices of the Development Commissioners fund many studies on various sectors in crafts and handlooms by NGOs, state governments, and even management consultants in the private sector. Unfortunately, these are not shared with interested development activists, nor is it known whether these reports are studied in depth or acted upon. A user-friendly library and a list of available publications, reports, documentation, monographs, project studies, and status papers on crafts done over the years by various individuals or bodies should be made available to all organizations that stand to benefit from the information. Any useful catalogue, report, or study funded by government must be allowed to be distributed on a commercial basis so that it reaches a wider audience.

The Design Centres and Weavers' Service Centres, set up zonally or statewise by the Ministry of Textiles, could be a major source of design and new products developed with a view to maximize the use of craft skills and lend a contemporary relevance to traditional crafts and textiles. Unfortunately these have been allowed to become white elephants with a desultory output, and have no active links with state or central, or, for that matter, private marketing enterprises. Some of these institutions do remarkably good development work in designs, products, and even technology innovation but this work remains largely within their four walls. Mechanisms for replication of new samples for the market are neither publicized nor facilitated in an effective manner. It is only the most enterprising of craftspeople who would wend their way to these centres to access the results of their work. Again, bureaucratic inertia seems to have rendered moribund any interaction between the institutions and those they are meant to serve. Efforts to put new and good products into the market at regular intervals are thus lost.

Funds for development

Banks such as the Small Industries Development Bank of India (SIDBI) and programmes such as the Rashtriya Mahila Kosh (National Women's Fund) provide small and medium loans to individual craftspeople and for craft development projects. Combining trust, caution, and a fast track approach to reach funds to individual craftspeople, societies, and NGOs is an urgent priority for any task force set up to clear bureaucratic hurdles in this sector. When there have been competent NGOs to facilitate this process results are commendable. Ever since the early 1980s, stress has been laid on NGO involvement. Schemes formulated by institutions like Council for Advancement of People's Action and Rural Technology (CAPART), the Khadi and Village Industries Commission (KVIC), and the Office of the Development Commissioner (Handicrafts) offered government funds to artisans through known, responsible, grassroot development agencies. This gave rise to a large number of "development organizations" mushrooming overnight, some committed and genuine, but many merely fronts for political activism or for siphoning off funds, or a means of employing youth ostensibly for "voluntary" social work. Without expertise or credibility, their efforts at creating "income generation" programmes for rural women or even traditional craftspeople have come to nought, particularly as there were no forward linkages for design, marketing, or self-management. Many of these are now mired in financial problems and have been blacklisted.

Some organizations with a wider vision and agenda, and served by people with considerable experience in the field of development, have converted government funds into worthy longlasting projects benefiting craftspeople. Institutions at Auroville in Pondicherry, Social Work and Research Centre and Urmul in Rajasthan, the South India Producers Association and the Madras Crafts Foundation in Tamil Nadu, the Crafts Society of Manipur, the Xavier Institute of Social Sciences in Bihar, Sarva Shanti Ayog in West Bengal, the Kutch Mahila Vikas Sanghatan and SEWA in Gujarat, and those with a national spread such as the Crafts Council of India, Dastkar, and the Dastkari

Haat Samiti are just a few that have contributed towards building craft related institutions that enhance the self-confidence and earning capacity of craftspeople. Private enterprises such as Fabindia, Anokhi, and Contemporary Arts and Crafts, as well as the state handicrafts and handloom emporia have also contributed to the revival and sustenance of crafts with varying degrees of success for the craftspeople concerned. Many private companies are involved in exporting crafts and selling the less-than-best quality of their stock within the country. Commonly termed "export houses", they keep their designs and production under wraps to avoid imitation from competitors. Much of the "Made in India" handicrafts found in department stores abroad are supplied by private establishments in India.

Integrating efforts for development and marketing

The Khadi and Village Industries Commission set up with ideals of Mahatma Gandhi as its bedrock, conducts a wide range of supportive activity aimed at benefitting rural artisans, but it is hard to understand why this work under the aegis of the Ministry of Industry is not brought together with the work done under the Ministry of Textiles. Old and stultified marketing ideas in the Khadi and Village Industry sector are slowly beginning to give way to a more modern approach. However, its over 15,000 marketing outlets all over the country could be better utilized by coordinating efforts with others who need marketing support, while the old khadi outlets would benefit from a revived and renovated approach both in attitudes and image. Better co-ordination and linkages between them and the craftspeople and crafts organizations who are listed in the files of the Textile Ministry and CAPART (under the Ministry of Rural Development) are required so that development, design, credit and marketing schemes do not either duplicate efforts done by the others or neglect certain sectors of craftspeople because they do not produce up-market goods. Often, new schemes and ideas are put into place without fully clearing away cobwebs of the old ones, rather like putting on new coats of paint without scraping off the damaged undercoat. Excessive compartmentalization of schemes and departments stunts innovative work instead of allowing for free flowing linkages.

Exporting crafts

The arrival of crafts into the chic world of Baba Kharak Singh Marg, the Suraj Kund Mela, and Hauz Khas Village in Delhi, and the Festivals of India abroad made them fashionable and the "in thing." A major thrust in exports has been accepted. Crafts were indeed revived, popularized, and made marketable, but only amongst the fashion conscious. The trouble is that the concept of fashion carries within it the reverse scenario as well. There would be no fashions unless they were "in", which means something else has to go "out". For the rural producers and craftspersons, this can be a matter of life and death, since in their timeless world of skill, tradition, and caste-oriented professions, they have only age-old support systems to keep them going locally. It is an act of cruelty to make them the victims of the "ins" and "outs" of a secure, affluent world, when the profits are uncertain, often temporary, and dependent on systems far beyond their control and understanding.

In most crafts directed towards exports, prosperity is visible only in the persona of the trader and not in that of the producer. Most handcrafted products are produced under primitive conditions and trundled off from dusty villages in wooden carts to find their eventual destinations in New York, Paris, London, Hamburg or Tokyo.

Countries like the Philippines, China, and Taiwan provide sound infrastructural support to low cost crafts such as baskets and paper items, while Japan concentrates on high quality, high value products with sophisticated packaging. Indian products in comparison suffer from low quality promotion and consequent low visibility in the markets of the world. In the free-for-all among private exporters, the 'India look' of special textures, skills, designs and excellence is lost.

Awards for craftspeople

Crafts in India have never been oriented towards putting the spotlight on an individual. The specially advanced and skilled person was always the "master" who would guide and teach others rather than corner benefits for himself. Crafts have instead emerged as products out of community work related to agricultural or household needs, trade objects, ritual and festive artefacts. The idea of creating national and state awards for individual craftspeople was not so much to single out individuals of a superior category, but to highlight examples of the best amongst the production of many hands, or for innovation and excellence within a metier. The recognition of the craftsmanship was to encourage and maintain creativity and skill of a high quality. The effort was to set a standard for others to follow or attempt to achieve. The honouring of the individual was therefore a part of honouring quality craftsmanship, and not a "one-off" artistic effort, as is recognized in the Western approach to art.

One of the reasons for the slow degeneration in the quality of crafts offered or selected for awards is an ubiquitous disease that has infiltrated all aspects of our public and institutional life – corruption. Craftspersons complain of having to pay to have their items accepted, recommended, or forwarded. Many self-styled promoters of crafts gain status by dispensing patronage and recommending awards, selectors are sometimes influenced by political considerations. Craftspeople are adversely affected by such an environment. They offer pieces done not by themselves, but by some unknowing peer in the village community. All this breeds jealousy and sycophancy, and harms quality since artistry is no longer the prime purpose of the exercise. The craftsperson wants a shortcut to recognition, invitations to festivals abroad and fairs at home with all expenses paid, while the promoters, whether private, political or bureaucratic, secure pecuniary inducements or assume a sense of control over the process. There are always exceptions, but the proposition that this sector has remained free of corruption would not find any takers. Even when the situation is ideal, the skilled craftsperson today has to have a fair amount of courage, resilience, enterprise and material security to invest both labour and effort on preparing a high quality piece meant for an award.

In Japan, master craftsperson are designated as "Living National Treasures" and entrusted with the task of selecting and grading other craft works according to the quality and level of skill. They are given approximately Rs 6 lakh (US$14300) per year to pursue their work or train others. In the USA, skilled craftspeople (albeit the few who are viewed as individual, rather than community artists) are designated as National Heritage Fellows and get an endowment of US$5000 to continue their special work, teach, or otherwise develop their art.

India needs to institute such awards to make the contribution of the recipient meaningful. In India, the patronage syndrome has not left us, nor have we considered the possibility that craftspeople, who are highly experienced repositories of skill and culture, should themselves be the best judges of the quality of others' work. To prevent unhealthy competition or jealousy, expert craftspersons could be asked to judge those pieces which are outside their category of products but part of the same metier. They could also be part of a mechanism set up to certify products of varying degrees of quality according to predetermined categories.

Craftspersons with self-respect and dignity have often privately asked why patrons from the privileged classes or government officials should be considered to be all knowling about the history, tradition and technique of all crafts, instead of their own respected peers. It would do well to reconstitute the selection committees for awards by having fewer city experts and officials on them, and more nationally and internationally acknowledged master craftspeople and others from various branches of the artistic community of age and stature.

It would also be worthwhile to constitute a standing body of such craftspersons in each state to interact with their state Handicraft and Handloom Development Corporations so that master craftspeople have a positive and constructive role to play in the selection of quality goods for sale, awards, design development, and price evaluation. Unless such steps are taken, it will always be the self-styled urban patrons who will hold sway and not the craftspeople themselves.

Crafts and education

Modern education has left the practitioners of traditional arts and crafts out of its purview. The urban school has no more than a superficial interest in dabbling with or knowing about such skills and the wisdom behind them. In village schools the situation is worse. Artisan families largely believe that either they must give up old skills and identities and go forth into the mechanized or white collar world to achieve a new status and skill, or they have no use for what is taught in formal institutions since it does not relate to their livelihoods and needs. The agenda for learning must be a two-way process, using the most modern communication methodology to deal with the simplest of dialogues in the most ancient of areas. It would also be worthwhile to examine why this gulf exists between the institutions of modern learning and the practitioners of traditional craftwork. Just as the socially divided hierarchical nature of the caste system keeps craftspeople married to their traditional identities and skills, the motivators and implementers of educational policies have generally taken into their vision the already privileged, thereby in effect denying rural artisans access to the vocations and opportunities available to the upper castes. Schools and colleges have been established across the length and breadth of our land, but craft skills which are indigenous were never incorporated into the curriculum, just as schools in rural areas where craft skills had a high density never had a syllabus that incorporated practical information related to their world. Mahatma Gandhi's Naya Talim contained the essence of the concept of education best suited to create a truly indigenous and relevant educational environment, but these ideas were dropped after the First Five Year Plan. Craft schools or craft colleges are unheard of, and the idea of master craftspeople being accorded the recognition of a teacher with the degree of a Bachelor or Master of Education has only just begun to find acceptance in the rigid educational system.

For urban students a wider appreciation and deeper knowledge of the socio-economic history and status of India's craftspeople is required. This could be followed by some knowledge of their skill and production methods. Finally, problems and prospects in these crafts could be discussed in order to stimulate the students mind towards problem solving and creative thinking. Textiles, pottery, terracota and ceramics, folk and classical paintings, mat and basket weaving, stone work and stone-carving, metal work and woodwork are some of the crafts that could be taken up for study.

The related syllabus should contribute to the development rather than mere conservation of craft traditions, so that production, design, development, packaging, transportation, and marketing can match contemporary requirements, and some appropriate management systems are devised and formalized. In these, a vast need of knowledge and experience lies unexplored, some of which include:

- Organizing cost effective production of crafts through the introduction of appropriate technology to remove drudgery.
- Innovative advertising techniques.
- Identification of products and designs suitable for rural and urban markets, especially with a view to offer competition to industrial products.
- Costing and packaging for local/rural/urban sales and exports.
- Ecological factors related to raw material and quality of crafts.
- Accurate assessments of production and employment potential in major craft areas, linking these to market development.
- New approaches in developing marketing linkages with and through trade unions and women's organizations, public sector corporations, railways and defence establishments, tourism bodies, and other such institutions which have a large outreach.

The important factor to keep in mind is that crafts, while providing the important cultural and aesthetic input required to balance the impulses of the human spirit, today need to contend with the emphasis laid on sciences and information technology in education and the business market. If it is kept in mind that the crafts sector is not a symbol of either a tradition of the past, or of rural backwardness, but is a part of an existing economic resource that has to move with the times, many facets of modern technology, business practice, and resource management can be provided to it.

The kind of syllabus adopted can be patterned to suit university students. Efforts could also be made to reach out to rural literates, both youth and artisans themselves, in regional languages. The thrust of this exercise should be to relate the practical knowledge of artisans with scientific, economic, ecological, marketing and management concepts which can directly enhance the developing of their crafts. The two-way process between scholars and artisans should be maintained at all times so that the relationship is one of give and take, of symbiosis, and poses no danger of possible exploitation.

New attitudes for the future

Certain new strategies are imperative to sustain and develop our traditional village industries and crafts so that our vast heritage is not neglected and obliterated. This requires a broader and more over-arching approach to development.

In place of the largely ceremonial and non-functional boards in existence at present, business development councils could be set up in various sectors such as: forestry (cane, bamboo, grass and palm-related products, honey and medicinal herbs); agriculture (organic fertilizer, oils, processed nutritional foods); fisheries and aquaculture (farming, processing, preserving and packaging methods for traditional fisherfolk); skilled services (yoga, ayurveda, metallurgy, carpentry, masonry); handmade and recycled paper; natural dyestuffs (food and textile colouring); crafts (pottery, metalwork, textiles, stonework, leather, basketry, coir and jute).

In all these areas, the councils could work with trade unions, local and regional governments, tribal communities, non-governmental organizations, university students, polytechnics and vocational training centres to identify the employment potential and link it with research, appropriate technology development, and marketing both nationally and for exports.

The co-operative sector must be entirely revamped, or a parallel system put in place that allows the producers to distribute profits and collectively market their crafts using corporate marketing and management strategies specially designed for the village industry sector.

All craft skills and products identifiable as "ecofriendly" could be designated as such to highlight the need for conservation of the environment and the traditional wisdom that recognizes its importance. The "three Es" of Excellence, Ecology, and Employment could be promoted through national and state awards, exhibitions, publicity, and by facilitating access to natural raw materials, technologies that remove drudgery, and markets that sustain excellence. The replacement of non-biodegradable plastic products by eco-friendly packaging and disposable containers would encourage innovation within the craft sector for this purpose. The sustenance of employment is as important as ecological harmony and must go hand in hand. This concept is best illustrated in the traditions of the handicraft sector.

What have generally been considered the weaknesses of the craft sector can be turned into its strengths and its unique selling points. For instance, standardization is a requirement of the mechanized world, but if all human beings are unique and different, the products made by their hands and minds are and should be different. While the measure to fill a cup is of a specified standard, should the cup itself be the very same as thousands of others? Did the earthern cup not fulfill its purpose even if did not exactly conform to a fixed size or design? Variety can bring about innovation through which comes improvement. Those promoting crafts could thus encourage movement away from the regimen of standardization, and bring about delight in variety instead.

The craft sector is a reflection of India's multicultural ethos, and the vast variety of ways this is manifested in crafts skills and products lends itself to greater adaptability and change to suit different needs. These must be seized upon and confidently presented instead of merely harping upon ancient pasts that have an immovable, immutable quality, rendering them irrelevant in today's world. The craftsperson can and must be an honoured part of a resurgent India.

While crafts best reflect a nation's cultural heritage, the condition of its craftspeople reflects the concern of the people for that heritage. The development of society within a country's unique identity further perpetuates its own cultural expression. Both economic gain and a dignified status in society for craftspeople are necessary and possible if these children of Viśvakarmā are recognized and supported in all the many roles they serve.

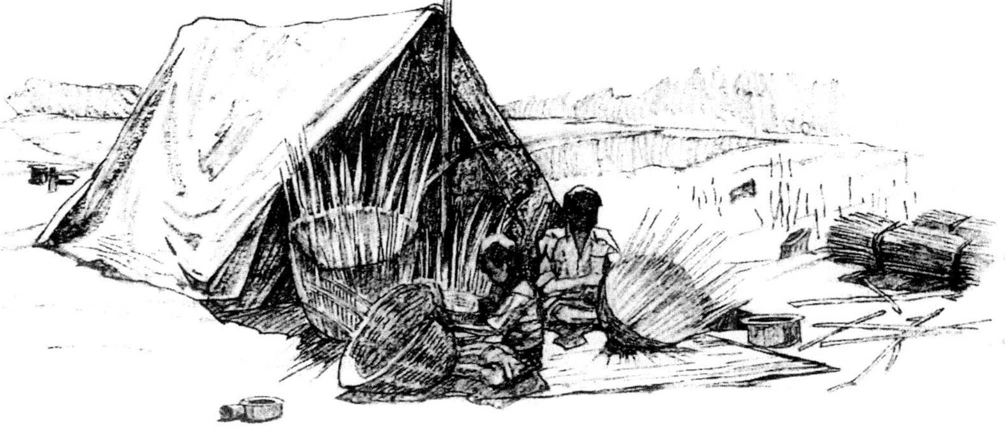

Glossary

andavu copper or brass water container for bathing

asth leather worker's tool

beedi small tobacco cheroot wrapped in tendu leaf

bhakri hand flattened cereal bread

bigha a measure of land, approx 5/8 of an acre, with regional variants

biryani dish of rice and meat cooked together

chapatis flat whole-wheat bread

chappal open sandals or slippers

charpai wooden cot bound with string or rope

churidar tight pyjamas cut on the bias with extra creases at the ankles

dal lentils cooked with water and spices

datun twig toothbrush, usually of neem (*Azadierachta indica*)

Dasara/Dussehra major Hindu festival

dhokra metal alloys moulded by the lost-wax process

dhoti unstitched, draped garment; synonym for sari

Diwali the Hindu festival of lights

dosas ground rice and blackgram pancakes

gamchha all-purpose scarf or coarse towel

gobar cattle dung

haat weekly or bi-weekly shanty market

hisab accounts; calculations

Id major Muslim festival

idlis steamed rice and blackgram dumplings

ikat handloom design where the yarn is tie-dyed before weaving

jajmani system of traditional exchange of services between castes/hereditary occupational groups

jootis from joota, generic word for shoe; Indian style closed shoes

katta a measure of land, approx: 70 to 80 sq. yards, with inter-state variants

khadi handwoven cloth made with handspun yarn.

khedda traditional method of trapping wild elephants in a stockade

kirtan devotional songs

kurta long collarless shirt

ladi instrument for leather-work

lungi rectangular cloth wrapped around the waist and falling to the ankles

mahuli alchohol distilled from the mahua flower

mandia fermented millet gruel

mangalsutra marriage necklace in gold

mela fair, celebration

memsahib woman of high rank; European woman

muri roasted popped rice

nachpatis dancers

ola palm leaves

paan betel leaf with lime and other ingredients

panchayat elected local government body at village, block, or district level

paseri a measure of yarn

patsam a measure of woven fabric

pokhaal lightly fermented parboiled rice

puja worship, ritual, offering

ragi millets

Ramzan/Ramadan ninth month of the Muslim year during which Muslims fast.

rangoli ritual floor decorations with coloured substances

rapi cutting and scraping tool

roti bread of various kinds; *chapati*; a meal

sahib honorific title for person of high rank; official; European

sahukar merchant; moneylender

sal *Shorea robusta*; a type of hardwood

samaj society; association; community

sambar preparation of lentils and vegetables with tamarind

shivalinga phallic emblem of Śiva

shilpi/śilpin craftsperson; artisan; artist; also called *dastkar*

shilpa shastras technical treatises on the arts and sciences

shola *Aeschoynomene aspera*, a plant yielding a white pith

shreni/sreni professional association; class; guild

swadeshi of one's own country; in this context, manufactured in one's own country

thekedar contractor

zari gold and silver coated threads and their synthetic versions

Selected Bibliography

Allchin, Raymond and Bridget 1993. *The Birth of Indian Civilization*, New Delhi: Penguin Books India.

Bhasin, B.B. and K. Kak 1993. 'Towards an Objective for the Handicrafts Sector – An Examination of the Five Year Plans' (unpublished).

Birdwood, G.C.M. 1880, 1998. *The Arts of India*, New Delhi: Rupa & Co.

Blochmann, H. 1927. *The Ain-i-Akbari by Abu'l Fazl Allami*, Calcutta: The Asiatic Society of Bengal.

Chattopadhyay, Kamaladevi 1986. *Inner Recesses Outer Spaces*, New Delhi: Navrang Publications.

Coomaraswamy, Ananda K. 1909, 1989. *The Indian Craftman*, New Delhi: Munshiram Manoharlal.

1909. *Essays in National Idealism.*

1956. *Christian and Oriental Philosophy of Art*, New York: Dover Publications.

Desai, A.R. 1948, 1987. *Social Background of Indian Nationalism*, Bombay: Popular Prakashan.

Gadgil, D.R. 1924, 1972. *The Industrial Evolution of India in Recent Times. 1960-1939*, Delhi: Oxford University Press.

Gandhi, M.K. 1955. *Khadi: Why and How*, Ahmedabad: Navajivan Publishing House.

1960. *Village Industries*, Ahmedabad: Navajivan Publishing House.

Government of India 2000. Annual Report 1999-2000, New Delhi: Ministry of Textiles.

Jain, L.C. and Karen Coelho 1996. *In the Wake of Freedom: India's Tryst with Cooperatives*, New Delhi: Concept Publishing Company.

Jaitly, Jaya (ed.) 1990. *The Crafts of Jammu, Kashmir and Ladakh*, Ahmedabad: Mapin Publishing.

1989. 'Mis-selling the Nation Through Festivals of India', *The Forum Gazette*, 1-15 September.

1989. 'Craft Designs and Development: A Search for Values', *Journal of Design History*, Vol. 2 Nos. 2 & 3. Oxford University.

1990. *The Craft Traditions of India*, New Delhi: Lustre Press.

1992. 'Employment: The Neglected Dimension', *The Economic Times*, 1 September.

1992. 'Handloom Weaver: Victim of Adjustment', *The Economic Times*, 27 April.

1994. 'Village Industry: Struggling to Survive', *Economic and Political Weekly*, 12 July.

1997. 'Organising the Unorganized in Kerala: Case Studies of Aruvacode and Kodungallur', *Economic and Political Weekly*, Vol XXXII, No 28, July 12.

2000. 'Tribal Identity Through Craft', *Verrier Elwin Memorial Lecture*, Baroda: Bhasha Research & Publication Centre.

Kosambi, D.D. 1996. *An Introduction to the Study of Indian History*, Bombay: Popular Prakasham.

Lannoy, Richard 1974. *The Speaking Tree*, New York: Oxford University Press.

Lucie-Smith, Edward 1984. *The Story of Craft: The Craftman's Role in Society*, New York: Van Nostrand Reinhold.

Mendelsohn, Oliver and Marika Vicziany 2000. *The Untouchables*, New Delhi: Cambridge University Press.

Narasimhan, Shakuntala 1999. *Kamladevi Chattopadhyay. The Romantic Rebel*, New Delhi: Sterling Publishers.

NCAER 1991. *Economic Status of Handicraft Artisans*, New Delhi: National Council for Applied Economic Research.

1998. *Census of Handicraft Artisans 1995-96*, New Delhi: National Council for Applied Economic Research.

1999. *Joint Census of Handlooms & Powerlooms 1995-96: Handloom Sector*, New Delhi: National Council for Applied Economic Research.

Pal, M.K. 1978. *Crafts and Craftsmen in Traditional India*, Delhi: Kanak Publications.

Ramaswamy, Vijaya 1985. *Textiles and Weavers in Medieval South India*, Delhi: Oxford University Press.

Rhys Davids, T.W. 1997. *Buddhist India*, Delhi: Motilal Banarassidas.

Roy, Tirthankar 1993. *Artisans and Industrialisation*, Delhi: Oxford University Press.

Sardesai, N.G. and D.G. Padhye (eds) 1940. *Amarakośa: Amara's Namalinganusasanam*, Poona: Oriental Book Agency.

Sastri, K.A. Nilakanta 1988. *Age of the Nandas and Mauryas*, Delhi: Motilal Banarasidass.

Schoff, Wilfred II (tr.) 1912, 1974. *The Periplus of the Erythraean Sea. Travel & Trade in the Indian Ocean by a Merchant of the First Century*, New Delhi: Oriental Books Reprint Corporation.

Shamasastry, R. 1951. *Kautilya's Arthaśāstra*, Mysore: Sri Raghuveer Printing Press.

Shanti Swarup 1996. *Mughal Art: A Study in Handicrafts*, Delhi: Agam Kala Prakashan.

Singh, K.S. 1996. *People of India*, National Series Volume VII, Delhi: Anthropological Survey of India and Oxford University Press.

SRUTI 1995. *India's Artisans: A Status Report*, New Delhi: Society for Rural, Urban & Tribal Initiative.

The Arts of Bengal and Eastern India, Crafts Council of West Bengal (on the occasion of the exhibition at the Commonwealth Institute, 1982, London)

Weber, Max 1958. *The Religions of India*, New York: The Free Press.

Yanagi, Soetsu 1989. *The Unknown Craftsman*, Tokyo: Kodansha International.

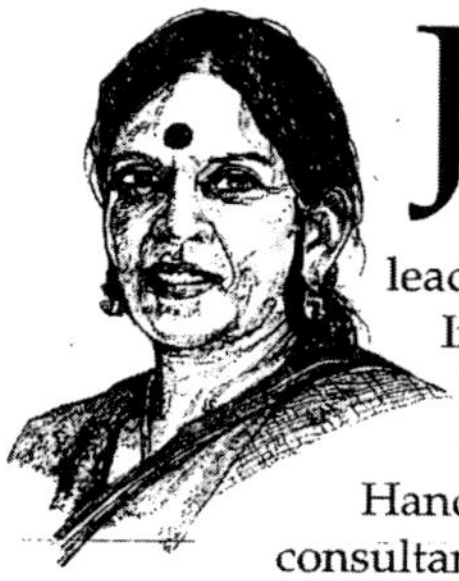

Jaya Jaitly has been involved in the development of the crafts sector since 1965. She worked for many years with craftspeople in Jammu and Kashmir to improve the quality and range of their products, leading to a term as consultant to the Central Cottage Industries Corporation of the Government of India. From 1978 to 1988 she was the design and marketing consultant to the Gurjari Emporia of the Gujarat State Handicrafts and Handloom Corporation. She was also consultant to the Gangotri Emporia of the U.P. State Export Corporation from 1981 to 1983.

From 1982 onwards she began to create organizational structures and linkages for craftspeople, relating the unorganized sector to organized workers through the Hind Mazdoor Kisan Panchayat, a democratic socialist trade union.

In 1985, Jaitly founded the Dastkari Haat Samiti, an association of craftspeople which promotes the better marketing of crafts and handmade textiles through exhibitions and bazaars. It also undertakes training programmes, design workshops, and produces craft maps with artwork contributed by local artists to show craft production and sales areas in the various Indian states.

Jaitly's experiences led her to develop the concept and press for the establishment of the Dilli Haat, now a popular marketplace for crafts and handlooms in New Delhi. The success of this venture has prompted the government to finance twenty crafts marketplaces in the Ninth Five Year Plan.

Jaitly is President of the Dastkari Haat Samiti, Assistant General Secretary of Hind Mazdoor Kisan Panchayat, and is actively involved in Indian politics as a member of the Samata Party.

Her earlier publications include The Crafts of Jammu, Kashmir & Ladakh, and The Craft Traditions of India, apart from numerous articles in national newspapers and journals.

Sitt Nyien Aye graduated in 1973 from the School of Fine Arts in Mandalay, Burma, and later studied under leading Burmese exponents of modern art. Deeply involved in the movement for the restoration of democracy in Burma, he edited and published the dissident newspaper *Red Gallon*. After the army crackdown on the 1988 uprising in Burma, Sitt Nyien Aye fled to India. He has lived in exile in New Delhi since 1992, painting continuously to project the events taking place in his motherland and the aspirations of his people for peace, democracy, and fundamental rights.

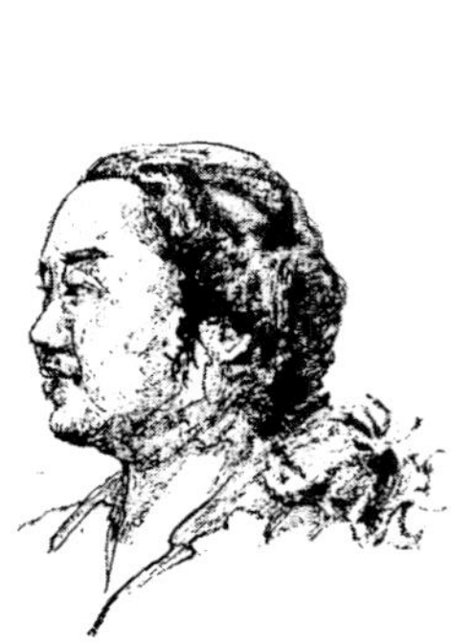